Elie Wiesel

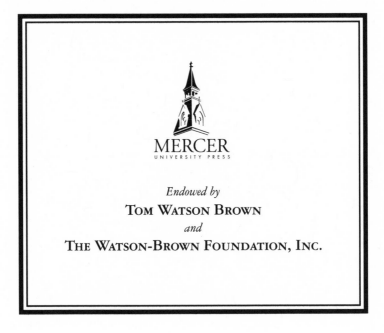

MERCER
UNIVERSITY PRESS

*Endowed by*
TOM WATSON BROWN
*and*
THE WATSON-BROWN FOUNDATION, INC.

# Elie Wiesel

## A Religious Biography

*Frederick L. Downing*

Mercer University Press
Macon, Georgia

MUP/H752


© 2008 Mercer University Press
1400 Coleman Avenue
Macon, Georgia 31207
All rights reserved


First Edition.


Books published by Mercer University Press are printed on acid free paper that meets the
requirements of American National Standard for Information Sciences—Permanence of
Paper for Printed Library Materials.


*Library of Congress Cataloging-in-Publication Data*

Downing, Frederick L.
Elie Wiesel : a religious biography / Frederick L. Downing. -- 1st
edition.
p. cm.
Includes bibliographical references and index.
ISBN-13: 978-0-88146-099-5 (hardback : alk. paper)
ISBN-10: 0-88146-099-0 (hardback : alk. paper)
1. Wiesel, Elie, 1928—Religion. 2. Authors, French—20th century—Biography. 3.
Jewish authors—Biography. 4. Holocaust survivors—Biography.
I. Title.
PQ2683.I32Z656 2008
296.092--dc22
[B]
2008008044

*On April 11, 1945, there was a young Jewish boy in Buchenwald trying to understand whose dream he was dreaming…. I have written many books…and all my books really are my way of speaking to that young boy. I feel his gaze on my face asking me: "what have you done with your life?" And I write and I write and I write trying to tell him what I have done with my life. And I don't know….*

—Elie Wiesel

*To*
*Jonathan and Tiffany*

*who continue to teach me about the intersection of*
*art and the human quest*

# Contents

# Foreword

You hold in your hand a richly researched and compellingly written narrative of the life and passionate work of Elie Wiesel. Its significance as the story of one village's—and one family's—horrendous devastation in the Holocaust is graphic and gripping. Its greater contribution, however, lies in bringing to word the several decades of Wiesel's life as he writes his way through a series of books that recall and retrace the traumas, and the gradual healing, that enabled him to become a compelling witness to a wider and deeper ethic for humanity.

Frederick Downing's writing does not spare his readers the full devastation and horrendous grief of the Holocaust. Nor does he shortcut the process through which Wiesel gradually writes his way from the documentation of the Holocaust's horror to his emergence as one of our most forthright witnesses for a global ethical responsibility and justice.

Downing's tracing of the devastation, and then the gradual rebuilding and growth of Wiesel's journey of faith, is both unique and richly informative. His assessment of Wiesel as an authentic example of Universalizing Faith underscores his importance as a model and challenge to all persons of faith.

The pain and the atrocity of the Nazi holocaust find contemporary expression in Darfur, and in many other sectors of our troubled world. Wiesel's witness and his passion for the dignity, security, and wellbeing of *all* people offer an important claim on us, and on all his readers.

James W. Fowler
C.H. Candler Professor, Emeritus
Emory University

# Preface

On a dark Louisiana morning some years ago, I headed south to New Orleans as I had done many times before. What made this early hour different was that I was scheduled to catch a flight to Boston, where I would study some of the documents and papers Elie Wiesel had just donated to the Special Collections of Boston University. I had heard Wiesel speak in Oxford and in London and later at Vanderbilt University in Nashville. I knew the power of his oratory and the passion with which he approached what seemed to be his vocation. I had read some of the various scholars who had sought to come to terms with the complexity of his life and work. The trip to Boston, I hoped, would help me to understand more. When I arrived at the airport in New Orleans, I picked up the newspaper and read the headlines on the front page. It was the fiftieth anniversary of the bombing of Hiroshima.

The plane ride gave way to daily trips on the subway from Cambridge to Boston University. Yet after reading many documents and hearing Wiesel himself, a question lingered: how can one write about a figure like Wiesel who has endured the kingdom of night and who continues to endure its memories? Surely one who was not there when the ovens were burning cannot begin to fathom such an experience! One who has not known the kingdom of night cannot begin to approach the intellectual or emotional landscape that the word "Auschwitz" now represents. Only the survivors can begin to describe that world. While those who were not there cannot begin to approach the outer perimeter of this realm and cannot begin to fathom what it was like, it seems that today the stakes of the human experiment with civilization are so high and the risks so great that the other side of the issue now seems to be: how can we not be involved with the discussion of such issues, and how can we not listen? To refuse to explore what has happened in the past may make us blind to our present and future circumstances. To refuse to read the works of one like Wiesel and to neglect to write about him is possibly to refuse the challenge to become "true" listeners and readers.

Is it possible that one's study—both reading and writing—of this era and its survivors can be a form of listening, a type of active and sympathetic engagement, an effort to bend the ear and the mind's eye to the text of another's life? In his book on Elie Wiesel, Robert McAfee Brown suggests that the basic rule for writing about survivors is "to provide a place where one survivor can speak for himself."[1] A part of the purpose of this book is to help readers listen closely to the "word" that is the life of Elie Wiesel and to provide a space for that word to be heard in a new way.

When these ideas are put religiously, Elie Wiesel's work is a sustained cry of the human spirit silently asking God for a time when innocent people will no longer be abused and when his own scorched eyes may be given a rest. Elie Wiesel is for some the "poet laureate" of his generation. Not only has he become the author of many books, but his very life is perhaps his most poignant and profound word. To that end, he has written and sought to embody a "poetics of memory and justice" so that the tragedies he has seen and experienced do not happen again. It is Wiesel's praxis orientation—the holding together of idea and action, word and enacted word, as in the symbolic activity of the prophets of old—that allows me to include his enacted word in his poetics and to designate that larger symbolic network of meanings as a metaphor for his own life's pilgrimage.

In this study of Wiesel, I have attempted to create a methodology appropriate to the complexity of his life that will help readers with intense religious and cultural themes. Because of the intense religious aspects of Wiesel's life, I have attempted to develop a strategy that investigates that dimension from several different angles of vision. The nature of Wiesel's life seems to demand such a method of study.

As a part of this interdisciplinary method, I have drawn upon Erik Erikson's theory of religious genius and suggested that this approach shows new aspects of Wiesel's life. Erikson's psychosocial theory is complemented with James Fowler's more cognitive approach that draws upon "spiritual periodicy" or "genetic epistemology." Fowler's approach helps show how Wiesel grew and changed as a person of faith over time, and it demonstrates the nature of Wiesel's universalizing aspirations. Finally, for specific literary and religious aspects, I have drawn upon Walter Brueggemann's work with the "poet/prophet," especially his portrayal of the work of Jeremiah, who influenced Wiesel.[2] This body of work from Brueggemann clearly indicates

---

[1] Robert McAfee Brown, *Elie Wiesel: Messenger to All Humanity* (Notre Dame: University of Notre Dame Press, 1983, 1989) 6.

[2] The basic work is Walter Brueggemann, *The Prophetic Imagination* (Philadelphia: Fortress Press, 2001), but see also "The Book of Jeremiah: Portrait of a Prophet" *Interpretation* 37/2 (April 1983): 130–45 and, most recently, *Like Fire in the*

how Wiesel is indebted to the biblical tradition in his literary and religious themes and helps to identify what Wiesel calls his "code."

As the reader can begin to surmise, the story of Elie Wiesel that I narrate here is not so much a narrative about the Holocaust as about who he is as a human being and religious person. Put another way, the story of Wiesel I tell is about the growth and development of a shy, young, yeshiva student from Eastern Europe who, after being torn from his home in the Carpathian Mountains, endured the hellish regions of Hitler's death camps. Then he wrote his way to prophetic awareness and enacted selfhood that in time began to demonstrate universalizing characteristics. Yet, after having achieved status as a citizen of the world, Elie Wiesel must sometimes wonder when he reads worldwide newspapers if the somber, reflective, and challenging message of his life has been heard and if he has made a difference.

*Bones: Listening for the Prophetic Word in Jeremiah* (Minneapolis: Augsburg Fortress, 2000) 3–17.

# Acknowledgments

My indebtedness for this project is embarrassingly large. I am indebted especially to Professors James Fowler and Walter Brueggemann both for their scholarly work and for their roles as mentors in the development of this project. Their own projects diverge significantly but cohere in this reading of Wiesel's life and work. They have each read sections of this material, Brueggemann more in the early stages and Fowler especially in the later stages. Each encouraged and prodded in unique ways, and surely each would have written a different book. I appreciate greatly the writings of both men and the way that they have allowed me to appropriate parts of their work for this project. They are pioneers and exemplars in their respective fields and, as this book demonstrates, I have learned much from them. Yet neither is responsible for the author's shortcomings. I should also acknowledge that my reading of Erikson and the larger field of psychology and religion owes much—in addition to James Fowler—to another former teacher, Donald Capps, whose own work on religious melancholia also contributed to this volume.

On a hot August day in Saint Louis, I met a gentle Catholic scholar by the name of Harry James Cargas. His various works on Wiesel have extended my understanding. He was also kind enough to arrange a meeting for me with Elie Wiesel. Professor Wiesel was gracious in our conversation and in his invitation for me to join other students in his classroom that day. Alan Berger and I spoke about the larger field of Holocaust studies, and he was both kind and encouraging in his reading of portions of my early work on Wiesel. Conversations with Ellen Fine and Susanah Heschel were also helpful at different times and in different ways. Additionally, Kathleen M. O'Connor's work helped to frame the view of Jeremiah that I present in this volume.

In the second edition of his well-known volume, *The Prophetic Imagination*, Walter Brueggemann writes that professors in the academy can have their energies taken from them, and that no one wants to give "birth to new children for Babylon" or for that matter in the realm of the pharaoh's Egypt. Or, as Wiesel puts it in more poetic terms, the "world has become Jewish." It is difficult to write in a psychic land that approaches "Egypt" or "Babylon." For that reason, I am especially grateful for the community of scholars in Valdosta, Georgia, who share a vision of justice beyond the natural lines of distinction we sometimes draw in the academy, and the gracious ways in which they have welcomed us. That group includes but is not limited to Rich Amesbury, Linda Bennett Elder, Christine James, Ari Santas, Mike Stoltzfus, James LaPlant, and Linda Calendrillo. The spirit of collegiality shared within this group created an atmosphere that encouraged my work. I must also mention a group of individuals at Mercer University Press whose confidence in my work and diligence on my behalf have made this endeavor a work of joy: Marc Jolley, Edd Rowell, Marsha Luttrell, and Nicole Rowe.

Linda P. Downing also read the manuscript in its entirety and was an invaluable conversation partner on the chapters of Wiesel's early childhood, especially the narrative about Eliezer and his mother. Linda also spent hours compiling the index. Wiesel's own literary imagery inspired the artwork on the cover. In his Nobel address and in a speech to the National Press Club in Washington on 11 April 1983, he spoke about the young boy he was years earlier and explained how the boy's gaze is still fixed on his older face, and he is always asking what the older Wiesel has done with his life. This imagery took imaginative form when Jonathan Downing and Tiffany Sewell envisioned possible drawings of it, and in time Tiffany created the image on the book cover. I am extremely grateful for their work, for what they both continue to teach me about the intersection of art and the human quest, and for the many experiences we have shared together—often in the Florida sun or in more remote places in the Middle East.

Frederick L. Downing
Valdosta State University
Passover 2007

# Chapter 1

# Introduction

The testimonies are legion! With a quiet voice, and a crowd seemingly hanging on every word, he gives "speeches which set souls on fire."[1] They are speeches that tell us about ourselves and the tragic dimensions of human history, but also how to transform physical victimization into spiritual selfhood.[2] Such was the affirmation of a disciple writing perhaps for a thousand others. "Who is Elie Wiesel and what has he done?" The follower asked the question rhetorically, and then answered for himself: "A man who has helped change my life." But more importantly, the writer replied, "he has changed the lives of many hundreds, and even thousands of young bewildered Jews."[3]

In similar fashion, Cynthia Ozick wrote about an occasion in the late 1960s when she heard Wiesel speak at the 92nd Street Y in New York City. The auditorium was in "an agony of silence" because a "pack of disciples" filled the hall striving to hear. Wiesel, however, "whispered." Yet Wiesel's whispers "caused us to be a good, even an extraordinary, audience in our silence," Ozick wrote, but being a member of an attentive audience or perhaps being a responsive reader is not enough for Wiesel, for, as Ozick surmised, he is not simply a writer or even a witness. He desires to become a "Rebbe," perhaps a *Tzaddik*—a righteous man or spiritual model[4] who wants to re-create the world.[5] Yet Wiesel also knows, as he later wrote of the Hasidic masters of the past, that "all these great spiritual leaders and guides, who somehow, somewhere, managed to move so many others to joy and ecstasy, often seemed to struggle with melancholy, and at times even with darkest despair."[6]

## Speaking Truth to Power and Accepting a World Stage

On Friday, 19 April 1985, Elie Wiesel, thrown into an international controversy, expanded his audience and in so doing invited the country to witness an extraordinary event on national television. At the beginning of National Jewish Heritage Week, coinciding with the forty-second anniversary of the Warsaw Ghetto Uprising and the national Holocaust Remembrance Day, Elie Wiesel was summoned to the White House to receive one of the nation's most prestigious civilian honors, the Congressional Gold Medal. In the ceremony, President Reagan remembered the central events of contemporary world Jewry: the tragedy of the Holocaust, the birth of the state of Israel, and the continued suffering of the Jews in the Soviet Union. He spoke of how the Europeans had rebuilt "shattered lands," and survivors had rebuilt "shattered lives" despite the "searing pain." Then Reagan said, "We who are their fellow citizens have taken up their memories and tried to learn from them what we must do." In that ongoing enterprise of learning, Reagan said, no one has taught his generation more than Elie Wiesel. He has preserved the story of the six million in his books and has helped to make the memory of that story eternal. "His life stands as a symbol.... Like the Prophets whose words guide us to this day, his words will teach humanity timeless lessons."[7]

When Wiesel began his acceptance speech, he noted that the medal was not his alone, but belonged also to those who remember what the German *Schutzstaffel* (SS) did to their victims. As he continued, Wiesel spoke like one of the prophets to whom Reagan had just referred. Newspapers told the story the next morning. A graphic picture and accompanying article appeared on the front page of the *Los Angeles Times*.[8] The still photograph captured the vivid yet poignant scene. Elie Wiesel stood at the microphone. President Reagan and Vice President Bush looked on with a mixture of puzzlement and reflection. This university professor, invited to the White House to receive a high honor, lectured the president of the United States on the Holocaust and a proposed presidential visit to a Nazi cemetery at a place called Bitburg. Wiesel said, "Following our ancient tradition which commands us to 'speak truth to power,' may I speak to you of the recent events that have caused us much pain and anguish.... Mr. President, in the spirit of this moment that justifies so many others, tell us that you will not go there: *that* place is not your place. Your place is with the *victims* of the S.S."[9] Six weeks later, Vice President George H. W. Bush wrote these words to Elie Wiesel: "You spoke from the heart.... Your life, your message, that innocent men and women will never again be brutalized by savage hatred, offers hope to us all."[10] A year and a half later, Elie Wiesel was given the Nobel Prize for Peace.

## *The Emergence of Reb Eliezer: Wiesel as Myth and Haunted Symbol*

How has a Jewish novelist from an unknown town in the region of Transylvania attained such status in an adopted homeland that he becomes known as the "conscience of contemporary world Jewry," the "high priest of our generation," or a "virtual symbol of those who survived [the] Nazis"?[11] Perhaps James E. Young approaches the truth when he, like Cynthia Ozick also reflecting on Wiesel's annual lectures at the 92nd Street Y, describes how Wiesel has "mesmerized audiences" over the years since the first lecture in 1966, and how in the process both the stories and the storyteller have gained "a near legendary status." Young writes, "It is almost as if, in the eyes of his disciples, the Holocaust had endowed Mr. Wiesel with the kind of wisdom and authority traditionally reserved for Judaism's greatest prophets and rabbinical masters, precisely those whose lives and legends he has narrated at the Y."[12]

Wiesel's journey to symbolic status is the story of an unlikely pilgrimage—a "strange trajectory" whereby a painfully shy young teenager from an obscure village in Eastern Europe descends into the depths of hell, where the memories of tragic loss, seared forever and indelibly etched in his consciousness, eventually propel him to a world stage where he must witness against such atrocities.[13] Elie Wiesel, a survivor of four of Hitler's death camps—Birkenau, Auschwitz, Buna, and Buchenwald—is a small, frail-looking man with a soft voice and a propensity for dark clothes and unruly hair. Wiesel's portrayal of Gavriel, the protagonist in his book, *The Gates of the Forest*, seems to be a self-portrait. Gavriel, like Wiesel's other early protagonists, is a death camp survivor. He has "a sharply defined handsome, tormented face, a pointed chin and a melancholy smile. His eyes, two firebrands, which sear the flesh and pierce the skin of being."[14]

Perhaps Wiesel's appearance is the proper beginning point for understanding his charisma. His face shows pain and anguish and at times appears almost ascetic. The face and the scorched, penetrating eyes not only mediate suffering but give a clue to his credibility and authority. There is congruence between what he has seen with those eyes and what he writes and speaks. This congruence is understood by most as "authenticity," or as Ezrahi puts it, his "personal validation of events."[15] That is, Wiesel "has managed to blend his person and his ideas into a single, charismatic presence."[16] Yet despite the quiet and solemn nature of his voice and the ascetic look, his words communicate a reserve of power and inner strength that contrasts with his demeanor and appearance. The strength of the voice almost belies the image of physical being.[17] The dark suits, deeply lined face, and disheveled hair not only give Wiesel a rather haggard and "perpetually distracted" look, but in combination with his soft voice they provide an atmosphere of "controlled theatricality" for his public speeches.[18] The result is that these occasions become, for many listeners, spiritual events of a lifetime. As one Jewish writer put it, "In both appearance and expression, Wiesel seems to embody and summarize the 20th century 'Jewish condition,'" or as another author says, he seems to have "...absorbed the spirit of a people."[19]

What does the audience see when Wiesel takes the podium? He is a living reminder of the camps—the atrocities. His face mediates the wrenching pain. His authentic presence penetrates the numbness with which people live from day to day. Listening to Wiesel, thereby, becomes an encounter with irrefutable memory of unspeakable evil. For some older adults, such a confrontation may stir a feeling of guilt for either surviving the Holocaust while others died, or perhaps for not doing enough to stop the evil. Wiesel reminds Jews of their past and their heritage, but also of the future and the way toward it. He reaches out especially to the young and attempts to give them some sense of their past, and also to help them understand their heritage. He reminds Jews, whether they are devout or assimilated, who they are and why, but he appeals also to Christians, helping them to take responsibility for the world around them, to understand that Christianity had a role in the Holocaust, and to realize that questions of faith are universal. But for all gathered and listening to Wiesel, the power of his presentation seems to come not only from his sense of authenticity—that he looks like the "poet-survivor"—but also from the "spiritual urgency" with which he speaks, infused by his own overactive conscience that sears the hearts of all who hear. After one of Wiesel's speeches in St. Louis, the audience broke into spontaneous Jewish folk dances. And at the conclusion of one of Wiesel's speeches at a Holocaust Commission ceremony in Washington, President Reagan, incredibly moved by the speech, put down his prepared text and spoke extemporaneously of how he would never again support dictators.[20]

## Memoirs: Reading the Life of a Spiritual Pilgrim

Haunted by the horrors of Auschwitz, Wiesel spent the early years of his career writing books in which the characters struggled with the immense suffering that he himself had witnessed firsthand. Those characters were like Abraham on their own Moriah or Isaac shuddering under the "slaughtering knife," while in the background God refuses to intervene as the execution takes place.[21] Wiesel's writing, therefore, portrays ultimate confrontations, a breaking point in human civilization, a chasm between heaven and earth with corresponding tensions between God and the human. Wiesel's stories describe the emergence of a new pilgrim-protagonist, the survivor who is forever alienated from "home" and consequently propelled on an unending journey. Wiesel's fictional characters, often guilt-ridden, live out tortuous relationships with women and sometimes go without sleep for days. Here again, Wiesel's own life mirrors his art. For as his wife Marion testifies, in the sixties when the couple first met, Wiesel would often frighten women with his emotional distance, but even in later years, Wiesel continued to work compulsively, sometimes driving himself for days on end without sleeping or even eating.[22]

Wiesel, so described, also has much in common with Edward Lewis Wallant's fictional character, Sol Nazerman, albeit with a different outcome. In Wallant's story of suffering and redemption called *The Pawnbroker*, protagonist Sol Nazerman embodies the basic characteristics of the survivor experience: the indelible imprint of death upon the soul, an overwhelming sense of guilt for one's survival, the numbness of the psyche, and an ongoing struggle for meaning.[23]

Nazerman, a survivor of the Holocaust whose family died in the camps, lives after the war devoid of human emotion and is described by Becker with a series of death images such as "something exhumed" or a "walking corpse."[24] Just as the Nazi medical experiments have left him physically disfigured, so has the trauma of the Holocaust left him psychically deformed. Nazerman hates everyone. All people—red, yellow, black, and white—receive equally his disdain. His inner sense of meaning has been taken from him. Everything that gave his life meaning has gone up in the smoke of the crematories. Thus Wallant's fictional portrayal of Nazerman is, as Becker puts it, the account of "a silent auto-maton" who, "already dead," must now "arm himself against the living, against life."[25]

Though in reality Elie Wiesel shares a common background with Wallant's fictional character—and all of Wiesel's early protagonists experience the same struggle of the survivor—the stunning direction of Wiesel's journey has been in stark contrast to Nazerman's nihilistic pilgrimage. Wiesel's life evolved over the years "from the abyss of the death camps" to the point that he became "a messenger to mankind—not with a message of hate and revenge, but with one of brotherhood and atonement."[26] How does one understand such an unlikely pilgrimage? Wiesel's has been a pilgrimage from the ashes and despair of the death camps to his emergence "as one of the most important spiritual leaders and guides in an age when violence, repression and racism continue to characterize the world."[27]

One reads a memoir for such distillation and clues to the driving force for a lifetime of action. Wiesel recently published the first volume of his memoirs, titled *All Rivers Run to the Sea*.[28] This book is a natural beginning point for reading the life of Elie Wiesel. Despite autobiographical pieces across the years, this is the first of Wiesel's volumes that seeks to place the events of his life in a comprehensive perspective. It covers the events of his life from his childhood years in the village of Sighet in the Carpathian Mountains beginning in 1928 to his wedding in Jerusalem in 1969. His childhood stories paint a warm portrayal of this traditional Hasidic kingdom. The stories abound with portraits of his home, his profound love for his mother and father, the mystical and bearded rabbis, his own appropriation of the Hasidic ideal of friendship, and his affection for and devotion to his devout grandfather, Reb Dodye Feig. Wiesel tells a stunning story of his adolescent and dangerous fascination with the mysticism of the Kabala, and the near fatal rituals in which he engaged, hoping all the while to hasten the coming of the Messiah and thereby halt the onslaught of the Nazi machine. He writes poignantly of the Holocaust—the loss of his parents and beloved little sister, and of how he himself should not have survived because of his sickly and fearful nature, of the creation of a kingdom within Creation, a new universe contrary to all the laws of God. Wiesel describes the years immediately after the war, being taken to Paris, eventually going back to school, and the ensuing time of crisis that brought him close to suicide. Yet his vocation as a writer led him in a different direction. In the early years after the war, a job as a journalist allowed him to travel the world: to Israel, to India, and finally to the United States.

In the mid-fifties, Wiesel met Mauriac in Paris. This encounter led Wiesel to write his first and best-known work, *Night*. After an accident in New York that hospitalized him for an extended time, Wiesel became an American citizen and continued his work as a journalist. The memoir clearly indicates Wiesel's involvement on the political front. He narrates the major events in Jewish life after the Holocaust: the birth of Israel, the Eichmann trial, the emigration of Soviet Jews, the Six Day War in 1967. Though one may sense that profound mood of sadness that grips his life, especially as he describes the memory of deceased loved ones who still haunt his memory, one does not find an articulation of the driving force of his life. As one reviewer put it, "*All Rivers Run to the Sea* doesn't tell us...what made Wiesel run."[29]

In 1999, Wiesel published the second volume of his memoirs titled *And The Sea Is Never Full*. He begins this volume by describing his 1969 wedding to Marion in Jerusalem. Written from the perspective of one who is already famous, this volume is filled with stories about his relationships with other well-known people like Golda Meir, Teddy Kollek, and leaders of government in the United States, France, and the Soviet Union. One reads about his human rights activities for various groups around the world, about his teaching career at three American institutions, and the birth of his son. While Wiesel portrays himself as a shy, yeshiva boy from Sighet, one gets the sense from reading this volume that history, fate, or some larger will keeps pulling him into compelling causes. As one reviewer wrote, "you become persuaded that something about his combination of seeming innocence and moral honesty has the power to move if not mountains then those who have the most power."[30] This second volume charts Wiesel's emergence as a "world-renowned figure," who in time becomes a symbol of both suffering and survival, as well as a "champion of the oppressed."[31]

In a review of Wiesel's memoir, Bill Marx raises the question of the author's identity. After listing Wiesel's many accomplishments and awards including the Nobel Prize, the Congressional Medal, and the French Legion of Honor, Marx asks, "But who is behind these achievements?" The answer, according to Marx, is that the memoir gives one only the "bare facts" and "reveals little behind the public face."[32] Thus Wiesel's memoir raises the question of the nature of his long pilgrimage. James E. Young poses other important questions: "How did Elie Wiesel, of all the thousands of Holocaust survivors, become a living icon of that catastrophe, and why? How deliberate was his ascension, how accidental?"[33]

## The Current Context: A Critique of the Journey

For many years, Elie Wiesel was the one Jewish figure who was beyond public criticism. But even in those years, controversy often loomed behind the scenes. His totalism—such as when he denounced the television series *Holocaust* as a "trivialization"—tended to alienate groups of people. Yet criticism of Wiesel seldom became public. People talked behind the scenes. Critics would decline offers to review his newest book instead of writing negative opinions about him.[34] The hesitation to criticize Wiesel seems to have diminished somewhat now. In a recent essay, labeled by one writer as "explosive," Naomi Seidman argues that Wiesel catapulted himself into the limelight when he purged and sanitized his reflections of the Holocaust in *Night*. He did so, Seidman argues, in order to rid the manuscript of appropriate Jewish rage so as to please Mauriac and a European audience, and thereby to position himself in the existentialist tradition and not as a Yiddish memorialist.[35] According to Seidman, when Wiesel reworked the Yiddish version for publication in France, he created an image of the survivor that would appeal to Mauriac. Wiesel, Seidman claims, "replaced an angry survivor desperate to get his story out, eager to get revenge and who sees life, writing, testimony as a refutation of what the Nazis did to the Jews, with a survivor haunted by death, whose primary complaint is directed against God, not the world, the Nazis." In so doing, Wiesel, according to the argument, "turned the story of the fate of the Jews of Sighet into a more archetypal drama, taking it out of the context of the Yiddish memorial books and making it a story of all shtetls." The effect of such writing was to sacrifice the particularity of the Jewish story of the Holocaust for a more universal one.[36] By sublimating Jewish rage and redirecting his complaints to the Jewish God, Wiesel created something of a rapprochement, Seidman argues. With Mauriac and Christianity unscathed, Wiesel opened avenues of communication between Jews and Christians. In return, Mauriac gave Wiesel his full literary support, found him a publisher, and wrote "glowing reviews." This, according to Seidman, was the beginning of Wiesel's emblematic status.[37] The vengeful survivor of Wiesel's Yiddish testimony is now replaced by what becomes Wiesel's public persona described by Seidman as "a spiritualized, passive, victimized, silent, sad, still somehow dead Jew."[38] The editor of the journal *Jewish Social Studies*, Steven Zipperstein, indicated that though Wiesel is a prominent and influential figure, "the making of his reputation remains obscure." He went on to praise Seidman's essay as "the first article...that begins to point in the direction of the man behind the emblem" and "explains why Wiesel emerged as the quintessential voice of the Holocaust" and not some other.[39]

In her book, *Worlds of Hurt: Reading the Literature of Trauma*, Kali Tal also raises the question of the nature of Wiesel's public life and the growth of his symbolic status. In giving the "Elie Wiesel Remembrance Award" to Henry Kissinger—who is connected with the Nixon strategy in Southeast Asia that, Tal argues, led to the bombing of Cambodia and the eventual rise of the Khmer Rouge—Wiesel "has chosen to engage in morally questionable behavior...[and] has, finally, completely ungrounded himself."[40] Tal concludes that Wiesel has lost the moral high ground and is now a "professional Holocaust survivor."[41]

Like Seidman and others, Tal is interested in knowing more about the man behind the public image. She raises the question "How does one learn 'who' Wiesel is...?" Then she asks, "By what process was Wiesel selected from ten thousand others? How did Wiesel become the 'who' he is, the voice of 'the' survivor?"[42]

In part, this recent criticism suggests a growing interest in the complexity of Wiesel, the man, as well as the beginning of an effort to understand the way he recapitulates in himself the Jewish story. That is, there seems to be an awareness of the central and symbolic role Wiesel plays in this post-Holocaust generation as well as an understanding that the man and the symbol are not one and the same. Critics of Wiesel are asking questions of motivation. Some who know his life story and work seem to want to know the nature of the driving force of this figure who has come to epitomize morality and conscience. He has now been called a "professional Holocaust survivor" who has lost the moral high ground, accused of opportunistic and utilitarian behavior and as willing to betray his own convictions in order to gain popularity. The various critiques merge in their severe questioning of Wiesel's moral character. The composite portrayal, created by this collective critique, is an image of Wiesel as a weak and silent figure who gives up his "integrity" and seeks to profit from his misfortune and the tragedy of others.

Indeed, there is an abiding sadness, a melancholy spirit about Wiesel that may be an important clue to the person behind the mask. Silence is one of his themes, though more accurately, a silence between the words. For after all, he has written more than forty books and maintained a heavy load of speaking engagements. And no one could deny that Wiesel has seen more of death than the average reader could comprehend, or that the "death immersion" somehow continues to abide in his spirit, making him, at least on some level of his being, still the "victim." Yet the critique misses important elements on another level.

In attempting to appraise the life of Martin Luther, Erikson wrote that one comes to know such a figure "by the inner logic of his way of life, by the logic of his working gifts, and by the logic of his effect on society."[43] When this approach is applied to

Wiesel, one could argue that Erikson demonstrates that this recent appraisal simply does not go far enough in attempting to understand Wiesel and the logic of his life. For someone as complex as Wiesel, it is not enough to critique the way he published his first book, or to criticize him because an award is given to a public figure like Henry Kissinger. Erikson's challenge is for the student of Wiesel to look for an "inner logic," for "working gifts," and for the "effect on society."[44] Perhaps then one will begin to come closer to understanding the man behind the emblem, and to have some understanding of why he, out of all the others, became the voice of his generation.

## Life as Commentary: Elie Wiesel and a New Genre of Religious Biography

The life and work of Elie Wiesel calls out for a method and an interpretation that takes his radical faith seriously. One might assume that an author's literary project is appropriate commentary on the author's life. With Wiesel, such is not the case. He declares that "my life is a commentary on my books, not the other way around."[45] Perhaps this means that for Wiesel the pilgrimage lived out in view of the world is also an important statement, one that must also be understood along with the project. For Wiesel, like the writers of the Hebrew Scriptures, life has a praxis orientation: action and belief cannot be separated. Hence, the author and the text are, to some extent, one single story.

A "lived word"? Wiesel is considered not only an important spiritual guide in the contemporary world, but also a voice of conscience, a *Tzaddik*—one who has learned to live out beliefs established and lessons learned. Having lived beyond the breaking point of civilization that was the Holocaust, Wiesel assumed the burden of becoming an architect of a new world. In the process, he has come to recapitulate in himself the story of a people. How can one study such a life in a manner that takes that life seriously? As David Lyman puts it, when the biography of Elie Wiesel is concerned, one needs "an examination as fierce and probing as his passion for life."[46]

The thesis of this book is that Wiesel's religious faith is the driving force of his life and the core of the personality that stands behind his emblematic status. That is, Wiesel is essentially a generative religious personality—a poet/prophet—who by deepening his own particular Jewish vision becomes a "link" with humanity, a stance of "Universalizing" faith by which over time he begins to identify with the oppressed the world over, and whereby he, like many writers and dominant personalities of the Bible, can be seen as *homo religiosus*. As a religious genius and spiritual innovator, this conflicted individual joins his own personal and existential struggle for meaning and identity with the quest of the group. His struggle is totalistic. It is "something like Jacob's struggle with the angel, a wrestling for a benediction" and the right to a new name.[47] Therefore, in trying to resolve his own struggle, this figure projects his own solution onto the group and attempts not only a new sense of identity for his fragmented life but for the entire generation as well.[48] This leader attempts also to restate in positive terms what has been experienced as a negative overstatement. Hence, Wiesel's own reaction to Hitler's dehumanization of the Jews finds focus in his life as a vigorous defense of the humanity of all Jews, eventually projected outward to include all oppressed persons.

Contrary to the popular view, the spiritual innovator lives a life of extraordinary conflict that begins in childhood or youth and becomes an existential debt that remains unsettled for a lifetime. As a part of his effort to find a cure for his own dilemma, he is likely to attempt a new ideological synthesis that brings together old and new patterns from religion, politics, or economics. As a cultural worker, this pilgrim-protagonist in the current drama creates a new identity for the young people of his age by his own answer to the central and basic conflicts of the age. Put another way, the religious genius is that individual whose personal identity conflicts merge with those of the group and who eventually seeks to establish a new and more humane sense of personhood for himself and for his generation.[49] Could not this be the way—and the most profound sense—in which Elie Wiesel begins to recapitulate in himself the story of a people?

It is this theme in Wiesel's life—the story of a young man whose identity conflicts begin to merge with a generation—that answers some of the major questions now being raised concerning his life and work. The theory of Wiesel as *homo religiosus* counters the accusation of Wiesel as a "professional Holocaust survivor" who has lost the moral high ground, and begins to explain how Wiesel's life joins with the lives of an entire people.

## A Poet/Prophet in the Post-Holocaust Era: Moses, Jeremiah ben Hilkiah, and a New Exile

In the stories of the Hebrew Bible that nurtured Elie Wiesel from his earliest years, the prophets of Israel are a breed apart. As poets who write and proclaim words from God, they are generative religious personalities who reshape the religious world of the day. In this sense, they are *homines religiosi*, spiritual innovators of the highest order.[50] Often sleepless and grave, and in communion with the divine consciousness, the prophets feel fiercely and take the burden of that relationship to a place deep within their souls. In the worldview of the Bible that Elie Wiesel first learned on his mother's knee, the words of the prophets become the voice that God loans to the silent agony of the oppressed. This voice expresses the divine pathos as God rages in the words of the prophets. What gave the prophets the courage and strength to demythologize the certain realities of the present, to shatter the shared conventions of the day? They themselves must have been shattered by some excruciating experience in order to so challenge others.[51] The traditional view of Judaism, however, is that prophecy ceased with the Babylonian Exile. God, therefore, no longer speaks in this direct fashion with humankind. The religious messenger must now discover new forms of address.

In this view of an innovator searching for a new approach and synthesis, Irving Greenberg writes about Elie Wiesel. Citing the work of Thomas Kuhn, *The Structure of Scientific Revolution*, Greenberg notes that a "dominant paradigm" underlies every worldview. That is, human beings do not live objectively but within the appropriated view of shared assumptions that make up a paradigmatic way of life. Elie Wiesel grew up in a village dominated by the classical paradigm of ancient Judaism—a paradigm shattered with blitzkrieg-like force by the Holocaust. Consequently, Wiesel, who wanted to locate himself within the Jewish tradition of messianism and redemption, had to find a new model and a new method for articulating his message.[52]

Wiesel went back to his Jewish tradition to search for other models and methods for telling this story that cannot ever be completely told. The paradigmatic model for the prophet in the Hebrew Bible is Moses, and the core narrative of the Hebrew people is the Exodus tradition. Because of the need of the people for continuing interpretation, Moses eventually becomes more than the mouthpiece of God at Sinai. He becomes the primal figure in the Hebrew Bible and the key interpretative voice for Israel and her experience. That is, in the book of Deuteronomy, Moses addresses the people at the border—at the point of crossing over into a new land and new experience. Moses becomes an interpretative voice and principle for the crossing point between wilderness and land. At Mt. Nebo, Moses takes the memories of Sinai and interprets them for the people in a new context. In this manner, the old ways and memories of former times are made appropriate for the new situation. The assumption of Moses seems to be that the faith of Israel must be continually recast and reformulated. Moses, as primal voice at the border crossing in Deuteronomy, is pressing Israel to ask how she may be obedient in the context of changing times.[53]

For Wiesel, there are two central realities, Sinai and the anti-Sinai—the Holocaust. Wiesel's dilemma is how to be faithful to the old traditions in the midst of the horrific confrontation with Hitler's genocidal mentality, which could be only described as an anti-Sinai. This, in the mind of Wiesel, was the most extreme form of border crossing—ontological exile. Like Moses in Deuteronomy, Wiesel asks how one lives in light of the new reality when the old ways no longer seem relevant. Moses as primal voice and interpretative principle is a major influence upon Wiesel, who eventually finds it necessary to rework the core narrative and provide a new Torah.[54]

Moses is a paradigmatic figure for the later prophets, and echoes of his voice can be heard in theirs. Consequently the voice of Moses merges with the prophet Jeremiah, who is perhaps the major biblical figure for Wiesel and clearly the most influential on his work. Jeremiah ben Hilkiah, one of the greatest of the Hebrew prophets, had the unfortunate function of presiding over the cataclysmic event of the Babylonian Exile. From Jeremiah, Wiesel takes his literary code and the need to shape the moral character of the community after the disaster. Like Jeremiah, Wiesel responds to the exile in terms of "shattering," "evoking," and "enacting."[55] As the prophet did before him, Wiesel also takes on the model of the "ideal survivor." Through the publication of *Night*, Wiesel's name becomes synonymous with the Holocaust and his life story the image of *the* survivor. And Wiesel, like Jeremiah, attempts to shape the moral character of society through speaking and writing. Wiesel's portrayal of the disaster, like the portrayal in the book of Jeremiah, is relentless but lacks coherence and structure, creating "an ending that does not end." Like his biblical predecessor, Wiesel writes a story in which "the text stutters toward a meaning that is never found." Thus Wiesel's strategies for writing seem, like those of Jeremiah, to push his audience toward reflection and consideration of how to confront the realities of a post-Holocaust world. Since language after the Holocaust cannot be trusted and since art for art's sake cannot be done when applied to the Holocaust, Wiesel places his literary art in the service of testimony. Yet Wiesel is aware that the age of the prophets is over. This in part means that while his work was shaped by Jeremiah ben Hilkiah and even though he can be understood as something of a poet/prophet writing parabolic fiction, other models influence his work, such as later Jewish writers who stand in the tradition of the prophets—the poets and scribes who see their task as keeping memory alive through stories, songs, and laments.[56]

Such innovation is not new in Judaism. When the prophets of Israel went into a period of decline during the exile, the rabbis eventually replaced the prophets as tellers of the tale and interpreters of the tradition. At that point, the rabbis no longer attempted to bring messages directly from God. Instead, the rabbinic stories and teachings became more secular and their messages more hidden. Likewise Rabbi Yohanan ben Zakkai, who lived during the destruction of the Second Temple, understood the threat to Judaism during the time of Vespasian. He fled an occupied Jerusalem and founded the Academy of Yavneh where he became one of the key figures in the elaboration of the Talmud. What Rabbi Yohanan ben Zakkai gave to Judaism was a "poetic temple" that became a "kind of haven in words."[57] If the Jewish teacher could no longer work in the prophetic mode during the age of the rabbis, then after the Holocaust a far more secular guise becomes necessary—the literary figure, the teller of the tale, but also a spiritual model whose life is a commentary on that story.[58]

For Elie Wiesel, the Holocaust inaugurated a new era—a major paradigm shift that altered civilized life forever. The death and destruction of the six million that Wiesel first described with the word "Holocaust" is ironically also a *bereshit*, resulting in a new beginning, a type of anti-Sinai with its own mysterious dark revelation. Such paradigmatic historical change requires new thoughts and new writings in religion. Wiesel describes the theological nature of this change in a legend he places as an epilogue to his novel *The Town Beyond the Wall*. Man speaks to God and says, "Let us change about. You be man, and I will be God. For only one second." After the change, neither was ever the same, and the liberation of the one was tied to the other.[59]

Just as Yohanan ben Zakkai gave a poetic Jerusalem to his age, Wiesel suggests that the traditional texts of the current age must also be rewritten in light of the tragic events of the Holocaust. Wiesel's portrayal of the anti-Sinai in *Night* becomes a type of new Torah for the era after the Holocaust. In as much as Wiesel's later works are built on *Night*, they become the beginning of a new Talmud—a poetic structure necessary for life after the anti-Sinai. These works not only provide a sense of identity for Wiesel himself, but also an avenue for him to project his understanding of the nature of societal identity necessary for justice and peace in a post-Holocaust world. With these rewritten texts, therefore, come new images of God, humanity, and society—a type of poetics of memory and justice. In a time of the silence and solitude of God, Wiesel seeks primarily to restate the overstatements of human beings who have gone too far. Hitler's negative overstatement of the Jew as victim eventually reduced the Jewish people to a Nazi-imposed status of "life unworthy of life," and thereby set the stage for genocidal madness. Wiesel's project as *homo religiosus* is to restate this negative overstatement.

Consequently, in all of his volumes he searches for a way to re-create the world so that justice reigns, and no human being will ever again be so victimized.

## Stages From and Toward Faith: Faith as Fiction and Fiction as Faith

If Wiesel is a generative religious figure—a *homo religiosus*, seeking a new name for himself and a new way of being for all Israel, a poet/prophet in a post-Holocaust age—then what is the nature and direction of his journey? In an early article, Robert Alter argued that Wiesel's books are "the stages of his way both from and toward faith...."[60] That is, Wiesel's moral journey can be found in his works and described in terms of different styles or periods of a larger spiritual journey. But more importantly, his life as a "lived word" becomes the most important statement, and it too can be seen from the perspective of pilgrimage with a focus on how Wiesel envisions the world around him at each particular juncture or stage of the journey.

How does one chart the spiritual periods or the stages of Wiesel's life? One begins with the understanding that "faith" is a human universal; that is, all persons have some form of faith. Then, "faith" is essentially a way of composing meaning. The human being is like a cosmologist; he or she creates a cosmos, and this picture of the world is an inherently human construction dependent upon the individual for its unique shape and configuration. Ernst Cassirer put it this way in his book *An Essay on Man*: "In language, in religion, in art, in science man can do no more than to build up his own universe—a symbolic universe that enables him to understand and interpret, to articulate and organize, to synthesize and universalize his human experience."[61] Albert Einstein wrote something similar in his book *Ideas and Opinions*. He noted that the human tries to make for himself or herself "a simplified and intelligible picture of the world" that is then substituted for his or her present world of experience. In this way, says Einstein, one tries to "overcome" the chaos of one's world and, by making this new cosmos the center of one's emotional life, seeks "to find...the peace and security which he cannot find in the narrow whirlpool of personal experience."[62] Put in more religious terms, "faith" is trust or devotion that becomes a basic stance of the person or self. That is, religious faith presupposes a type of theological world construction. The way one "pictures" or "constructs" the world is directly related to one's faith as a basic stance toward existence. Therefore, books like Wiesel's memoirs reveal a series of "basic stances" or "styles" of faith across a lifetime that then comprise the religious or spiritual pilgrimage.[63]

## Reading the Life of Elie Wiesel: Autobiography and a Typology of the Life of Faith

The broad outline of Wiesel's pilgrimage is evident from the descriptions given in his memoirs and in other places. What is clear about Wiesel's autobiographical narrative is that he tells his story according to a certain literary pattern that he may have inherited from the Bible—perhaps from Jeremiah and the Psalms. When Wiesel tells his story, it is typically that of an idealized portrayal of the past that provides a stark contrast with the horrors of the Holocaust, which, in turn, demands a new understanding of the meaning of life and the human. The literary pattern seems to suggest a movement of orientation, disorientation, and reorientation.[64] More specifically, he has written about his childhood and adolescent faith within the traditional confines of his beloved Sighet; the crisis brought on by the Holocaust faced in late adolescence and early adulthood; the quest for new meaning after the war; and the career/public life with its many dimensions. One knows that after the war, Wiesel's faith took a reflective and iconoclastic turn, that he made an important "return" toward his old faith based—in part—on his encounter with the Jews of the Soviet Union when he traveled there, and that at a later time Wiesel became involved in issues of justice in countries around the world. This brief sketch is only the broad outline, but it yields an initial framework that guides the reader into the deeper levels of the story, the end result of which is the portrayal of enacted selfhood—a life lived for all the world to see—where Wiesel eventually rejects solitude and indifference for solidarity with others and a life in search of a place where justice and peace can be found for all persons everywhere.

Our task is to begin at the beginning—in the early years of Wiesel's story—long before he was *the* survivor. There in Wiesel's little European Jerusalem, we will begin to look for clues to the more complete story of this unlikely moral journey, clues to the "inner logic" of his life, his gifts, and eventually to ask how his life became interwoven with that of his generation. In so doing we will on occasion have to follow a "disciplined subjectivity" as we search for ways especially to find glimpses of Eliezer the child and, later, the young man prior to his having reached the status of a world-renowned figure. Those privileged glimpses may yield an enlarged construction of the figure behind the public face.[65]

# I

# Orientation/Shattering

*The Prophets must have been shattered by some cataclysmic experience in order to shatter others.*
—Abraham Joshua Heschel

# Chapter 2

# Sighet:

# A Small European Jerusalem

The wheels of the coach clattered against the pavement in the town of Sighet. From a distance a young Jewish man peered into the coach at a young woman and her father, Reb Dodye Feig, a celebrated figure in the Hasidic kingdom of Wizhnitz whose Hasidic fervor was legendary in the small hamlet of Bitskev 7 kilometers away. There, he owned a small farm and ran a grocery store. Reb Dodye Feig's youngest daughter, Sarah, was an accomplished and exceptional young woman who shared her father's fervor, but also attended a secular high school and could quote Goethe and Schiller from memory. Consequently, she held within her being an unusual tension for a young Jewish woman of that era—the faith of a Hasid with an openness to secular culture. On this fateful day, Sarah accompanied her father into Sighet. As she and Dodye Feig rode through the streets of Sighet, Shlomo Wiesel caught only a glimpse of her, yet he was so struck by her beauty that he began to chase after the carriage to find out who she was. The coachman told him, and Shlomo Wiesel went to the village to speak to her father. Shlomo won the hand of the young lady in the carriage.[66]

This is an exceptional story for those days and times, the early part of the twentieth century in Eastern Europe. Wiesel does not tell us most "precisely" when his parents met. It was likely shortly after the end of World War I. Young people were not supposed to marry for romantic love. Good Jews were obliged by tradition to call for the "matchmaker."[67] Consequently, Sarah and Shlomo caused some gossip in the community when they wed the year after they met. Two daughters were born: Hilda and Beatrice. Then a son, Eliezer, was born in Sighet on 30 September 1928—Tishre 23 in the Jewish calendar and an important holy day, Simchat Torah. Eliezer was the third child but the only son for Shlomo and Sarah Wiesel.

## The Child as Father of the Man

The dictum "the child is father of the man" actually comes from the poet William Wordsworth. But the truth of his poetry has gained a psychological currency that in some fundamental way the life of the child is more than a precursor to the later adult. Elie Wiesel ponders this relationship in the second volume of his memoirs, writing, "Could it be that an individual's fate is sealed from the moment he takes his first step?"[68] One of the tasks of this volume will be to ask if there are clues to Wiesel's adulthood in his childhood. Is Eliezer the child the father of Elie Wiesel, the world-renowned writer and activist? What in Eliezer's life as a child could help us to understand Elie Wiesel the adult?

The difficulties of such an endeavor are obvious. Those early childhood years are never well documented, though we are now fortunate to have Wiesel's memoirs, which give important clues. Yet, where there is documentation as with Wiesel's memoirs, one must always ask if this record has been shrouded with the aura of later heroic status. Has Eliezer the child been obscured by Wiesel the icon of suffering and survival? While difficult to appreciate because of the factors listed and more, the pilgrimage of faith actually begins in infancy where the small child lives through a crucial yet vulnerable period and seeks to resolve the first dilemma of young life, the dialectic of trust over against the tendency to mistrust and doubt. This first of life's crises is played out in the context of the emerging mutuality established between the infant and caregivers resulting in a form of "primal faith" established in the earliest era that becomes foundational for all that comes later.[69] Our immediate task is to survey Eliezer's childhood looking for images and clues as to what that period was like, asking all the while how this informs our understanding of Wiesel the man.

## Sighet as a Promised Land:
### The Myth of an Earthly Paradise

Sighet was a special place, one that Elie Wiesel later called "a small European Jerusalem." It is written large in Wiesel's work. He writes with a picture of his home on the wall in front of his desk. His writing and speaking strategy seems to be the intentional juxtaposition of his childhood in Sighet with the unspeakable tragedy of the death camps. When writing or speaking of Sighet, Wiesel's words remind one of what James Olney calls the "myth of an earthly paradise." Such a re-creation of the universe is the elaboration of one's own vision and portrayal of individual selfhood. Olney puts it this way: "The myth of an earthly paradise...tells in all ways more about us than about a material universe: it expresses us in our selfhood as it creates us, and it gives us a reason for living as it suggests to us how to live."[70]

This town of 25,000 was nestled in the Romanian region of Transylvania near the Ukranian border. Tucked away in the Carpathian Mountains, Sighet provided a richly traditional environment of eastern European Orthodox Judaism and gave young Eliezer a secure and ordered world where he could grow up as a God-intoxicated child and a devoted Hasid. Eliezer grew up knowing who and where he was, and the purpose of his existence. That purpose was to do good, and to defeat evil, to accomplish the will of heaven by fitting actions, dreams, and prayers into the

27

design of God. By consulting the calendar, one learned all that was necessary. And in so doing, one knew when to rejoice and when to lament.[71] Yet, Wiesel's memories of his childhood portray a darker, more foreboding side to this environment, one that would be a precursor to fear, doubt, and struggle in a precocious mind and sensitive spirit.

As the only boy in his family, Eliezer grew up privileged. The principal figures of Eliezer's first world were his father and mother, his sisters, his grandparents, and later school friends, teachers, and religious leaders. Eliezer's father, Shlomo, was a merchant who owned a store near their home. He was a hard-working and practical parent, seen by his son to be something of an "absent" father. Shlomo worked from morning until night in the store, often to the point of exhaustion. When not busy in the store, Shlomo was usually involved in community issues. As a progressive leader of Sighet's Jewish community, he was often contacted when anyone was sick or in jail and in need of funds. He was involved in "resistance" activities that saved the lives of many Polish Jews from the Nazis, and on one occasion was jailed for two months or more for such activities.[72]

Though busy with work and community activities, Shlomo enjoyed simple pleasures like treating his children to fruit and candy in the evenings. He was a man with an open mind and progressive temperament who brought his son books on Freud, astronomy, and modern Hebrew literature. Wiesel confesses, " I really discovered him only later, in the camps, because I was closer to him there than before."[73] Shlomo was an emancipated Jew—a *maskil*. Though he did not wear the beard typical of the orthodox, he was religious. Yet, he seldom spoke to Eliezer about the Torah, or the laws governing divine-human relationships.

That task was reserved for Eliezer's mother. Sarah Feig Wiesel seemed to care more for the world of the spirit and the ways of the past than did her husband. In fact, Dodye Feig's fervor lived on in the life of his daughter, Sarah. It was Sarah who took young Eliezer to *heder* to teach him to be a good Jew, and it was Sarah who took him as often as possible to see the Rebbe of Wizhnitz to seek his blessing. Sarah was, of course, Eliezer's first teacher, and naturally some of the child's first memories are of the mother. As Sarah rocked little Eliezer to sleep at night, she would sing a lullaby of the "aleph-bet," or she would sing of the coming of the Messiah and her deep conviction that his coming would protect her child. "Fear not my child," she sang, "there will be no more armies." Sarah taught Eliezer to await the coming of the Messiah with fervor and in love and anticipation.[74]

In his first volume of memoirs, Wiesel includes pictures of his family and his home. There are four pictures of his mother, Sarah. In three of these pictures, she has her children with her. In an early photograph, Sarah appears alone with her cousin Golda. Sarah is an attractive person with a sweet, caring face. She has something of an aristocratic look, but there is some element of reserve about her that may belie a tendency to be overly firm, perhaps even stern. She has a look of self-confidence on her face, the same "air" of distinction found on the face of her celebrated father Dodye Feig. One could describe that element of confidence as an air of "somebodiness." Sarah's children appear at ease in the photographs with her, indicating through body language that they are close to her and glad to be in her presence. Elie appears in two of the four pictures. In the earliest of the pictures, he is sitting in his mother's lap and leaning against her. In another picture when he is older, Elie still leans slightly toward his mother and has a smile on his face as if to say, I am still comfortable and happy to be here.

Eliezer grew up with two grandparents: his paternal grandmother and his maternal grandfather. His grandmother lived just a few steps from his home. Grandma Nissel had a thin, pale face framed by a black scarf that she seemingly never took off.

With her bluish-gray eyes, she gave Eliezer her full attention when he came in for his regular Friday afternoon visits, just before the beginning of Shabbat. She was a "saintly" woman—humble, quiet, and respectful—who would always have fresh-baked bread for him. Before he left, she would want to know what he had learned at school that week. Her husband, from whom Eliezer received his name, was killed in World War I in a battle near Sighet. He was a "stretcher-bearer" who died trying to help a wounded man. In life, he too had been immersed in the study of the Scriptures, in love with God and the Torah. Grandma Nissel often helped in the store on days when business was greater than usual.[75]

Grandma Nissel had a special place in Eliezer's life. But it is Dodye Feig who dominates the portrayal of Wiesel's childhood landscape. Eliezer and his grandfather were especially close. He was "my best friend," Wiesel remembers. As *the* Hasid in his family, he was an influential and captivating presence for a little boy in a Jewish kingdom. He had ruddy cheeks, a wrinkled face, and a beard so white it looked like snow. He was an active and robust man, seemingly always on the go. His voice was warm, and his love for stories and tradition inspires his grandson to this day. Dodye Feig's gentle strength and passion for life radiate from the pages of Wiesel's writings.[76]

Dodye Feig lived on a farm about 7 kilometers from Sighet. There, he had horses, cows, goats, and fruit trees. The farm was a self-contained world where Dodye Feig did everything by himself. The trip to the farm to see grandfather was always special. The family went by horse and buggy. Seven kilometers was, therefore, a long trip. But the joy of seeing grandfather made the trip worthwhile. And when Dodye Feig came to Sighet for Sabbath services, the time was "doubly holy." Dressed in his Sabbath clothes, Dodye Feig would linger on Eliezer's doorstep to beckon the angels in song and to invoke their protection for the children and for the joys of Israel. Dodye Feig would sing with so much fervor that Eliezer could hear the "rustling of wings" above his head. As Eliezer joined his grandfather in song, gently moving back and forth, he knew the peace and serenity of Shabbat. Grandfather and grandson "radiated happiness," the kind of warmth that comes only from the depth of unconditional love.[77]

When Wiesel later called Sighet "a small European Jerusalem," he gave recognition to the quality of life that he knew there from his earliest days. It was a virtual "promised land" in terms of its nurturing context—a place where he could identify with his primary caregivers and their values because of the quality of care he himself received from them, but Sighet was a little Jerusalem in other ways as well. One of the most important treasures of this town for Eliezer was its Jewishness, especially Hasidism—a Jewish reform movement that began in the eighteenth century and spread throughout Eastern Europe and into the Ukraine. Just as in Jerusalem, so in Sighet is one especially aware of the presence of the divine, for Hasidism taught that the divine presence is everywhere, and that the faithful should be alert to recognize the holy in all things. In such a way, Hasidism taught faithful Jews to lead a life of total dedication to God.[78] It was in this milieu that Eliezer spent his formative years. He was "profoundly religious" in those days.[79]

In Sighet, the Hasidim gave a prominent place to the religious education of the young. The primary aim of such teaching was to learn to sanctify one's action as a part of proper devotion to God. To achieve this high purpose, religious education began within the first two years of life. When a young child awakened in the morning, the mother brought water to the child to perform the first ritual of the day. After pouring the water on the child's hands, the mother led the child in a prayer. By age two or three, a glass of water was kept in the child's room and he said the prayers himself. As soon as a child like Eliezer began to speak, he was taught to say blessings over the food he ate and to include all of his daily activities in the realm of the sacred.[80]

At the age of three, religious training became more intense for boys. Prior to this age, a young boy's hair was long and uncut. Now the child's hair was then clipped with only the side curls or *peyees* left. He was given a special undershirt with fringes that he blessed every day as a reminder to keep the commandments. A young boy also began to attend *heder*, or the all-day elementary Hebrew school, known for its rote memorization and strict atmosphere. By the age of four, the child was expected to read Hebrew letters with the class, and a short time later, he was reading individual words. The young boy's education continued at home where he practiced his vocabulary and learned to translate the Hebrew words into Yiddish, the mother tongue. He learned other things at home as well. Special deference was to the father, who sat at the head of the table and was not to be contradicted on any matter. The father typically commanded by his presence. He was usually reserved but very involved with the child.[81]

## Childhood Faith: Nurture and
### the Growth of Conscience

Eliezer grew up in this richly traditional realm of faith, and as with other young children, the rudiments of his religious life are traceable to this first basic world—the context of nurturing that takes place between the child and his primary caregivers. Through the process of identification with the nurturer, the child learns imitative behavior and, in due course, to take on a sense of conscience. The type of faith characteristic of this period in a child's life is intuitive and imitative. That is, based on the actions, examples, stories, and images presented by significant adults, the child learns to understand intuitively and thereby to feel the ultimate conditions of his universe.

Furthermore, the quality of that earliest set of relationships continues to be a factor in living in as much as all human beings live with a powerful compulsion to return continually to that first life-setting by attempting to do unto others as was first done with them. The earliest years of life, then, are typically the most important in determining a direction in faith and morality. With imitative and intuitive skill, the child envisions the world through his caregivers, who take on larger-than-life qualities. The child's first image of God is a simple blending of the perceived character of these parental figures.[82]

These early years comprise a magical and heroic age for a child like Eliezer. As a little human being, one is introduced daily to the mysteries of life, which become impressionable memories that affect one for a lifetime. The drama of life takes on a mythic proportion and the actors on the daily scene become heroes and godlike figures who in fact prefigure how a child builds images of the divine. The mysteries include such mundane things as noises in the dark and the brightness of daylight, bodily functions like eating, the process of food disappearing in the body, the reappearance of food as body waste, the discovery of one's sexuality, the origin of life both human and cosmological. In the midst of such discoveries, the child begins to contemplate an image of God. Ana-Maria Rizzuto puts it this way: "From that point on, the child, like a little Dante, has to go through his own Divine Comedy until he and his God make peace with each other...."[83]

## Eliezer's First Memory: Solitude, Abandonment, and the Parental Matrix

What clues for understanding Wiesel the man can be found in the years of Eliezer the child? A first reading of Elie Wiesel's work might lead one to conclude that he was a typically religious child who, after the crisis brought on by Auschwitz, gave up on

God and faith. In fact, some have read his life in this way. But Wiesel's reflections on his childhood suggest a more complex interpretation. Indeed, the narrative he tells concerning his earliest years reveals a stunning story with themes traceable throughout his life. The initial clue to understanding his first stage of life and the theme he carries with him for a lifetime, influencing all other perspectives on living, is that of a sense of separation and abandonment.

An individual life may be oriented around one particular psychosocial theme, especially when this experience has an enduring influence on one's personality.[84] The theme of separation and abandonment is for Wiesel a central life theme traceable from his earliest years through his teenage years and the Holocaust to his later years when his attempted resolution to the crisis becomes that of solidarity with oppressed Jews in Russia, but eventually with all oppressed persons everywhere.

The issue of separation and abandonment actually presents itself to the human being in the first year of life. The child gains a foundational sense of trust through the quality of interaction with the mother. Erikson theorizes that the foundational trust learned by the child from the daily and ritualized experience with the mother caring for the child's every need is the basis on which the child begins to create an image of God and a sense of faith. The quality of the child's exchange with the mother is experienced as a dialectic of "trust versus mistrust." One's sense of the world as trustworthy depends to some extent on the reliable and predictable quality generated by the nurture and care of the mother. By the same token, a lack of reliability generates some element of mistrust in the life of the child. Yet in the process of relationship with the mother, the helpless and completely dependent child begins to experience the numinous. That is, this ritualization of experience—in which the mother greets the child with a special name in her unique tone, and lifts the child to her face—is much like the encounter with the divine (the numinous experience) in the religious life. Such experiences help one to overcome the threat of separation and abandonment, which is the overwhelming fear in a child's first year of life.[85]

Wiesel begins his recent memoir with the statement "I never really knew my father." As a child, Eliezer felt "rejected" and "abandoned" by a busy and often absent father. Likewise, he was "attached" to his mother, perhaps "too attached." She was his only ally, his only support, the only one who truly understood him. As a little child, Eliezer could not understand why his mother could not spend all of her time with him and him alone. As a child, his one dream was to be with her. Wiesel tells about his sickly nature when he was young. "I was hardly a model child," he said. "I complained easily."[86] Since he did not eat well and was so thin and pale and afflicted by migraines, his parents tended to worry a great deal. The solution, the parents thought, was to take him to doctor after doctor looking for a cure. But Wiesel confesses that it was not illness that kept him in bed as a child. He stayed in bed and feigned illness, the adult confesses, because it facilitated the fulfillment of his childhood dream. So Wiesel's earliest memory is about "a little boy sitting on his bed, calling for his mother."[87]

Already at the age of three, like the other young Jewish boys of Sighet, he was sent off to *heder*. He felt rejected by his mother and "harassed" by his schoolmates. Eliezer did not understand why he could not stay home with his mother. His first dream: never to leave his mother. He would cling to her skirts even when she went to the ritual baths. He wanted to go in with her to the baths, but it was forbidden. "Why?" the child cried out. The answer: It is forbidden in the Torah.[88] When away from his mother, Eliezer felt "lost" as if "surrounded by enemies." In his mind's eye, his teacher during that first year away from his mother looked upon him "with scorn," and another had a "cold and indifferent air."[89]

A story with the same dynamics and themes is Wiesel's narrative titled "The Orphan," published in *Legends of Our Time*. It is also a story about his experiences at *heder*. Wiesel tells us that he is now five years old. But he is still like some other five-year-olds, reluctant and hesitant to go to school. He continues to make excuses. "I made up countless illnesses," he writes, "so that I could stay home with my mother for just one more day, to hear her say she still loved me, that she was not going to turn me over to strangers."[90] Eliezer wanted to remain a child like his other schoolmates. This incident made him feel like "the victim" of parental injustice. But there was one who was different in his class—the orphan. He acted differently because he was different. His mother had died in childbirth. "Secretly, I began to envy him," Wiesel writes. "My mother was alive and that seemed to me unjust," he says. "When I was with the orphan, I felt at fault: I possessed a wealth denied to him.... I would have given everything to restore the balance. To redeem myself, I was ready to become not only his debtor but his admirer as well, his benefactor."[91]

A third parallel story is found in an essay titled "The Solitude of God." Here, Wiesel reflects on his childhood and writes, "As a child...I dreaded solitude. Left alone, I felt abandoned.... Above all, I did not want to find myself alone, cut off, excluded from whatever was happening to them...." Wiesel goes on to juxtapose the condition of abandonment with the themes of solidarity and friendship found within Hasidism. Later in the essay, Wiesel extends the theme of abandonment to the Jewish circumstance during the days of the Holocaust. "Our loneliness in those years denied all precedent. Abandoned by men, forgotten by God, the Jew felt discarded by Creation."[92]

What are the themes of these stories, and how are the themes related? The first two stories have in common, of course, the abiding love for the mother—the desire to be with her forever. The second story, however, adds to this theme the emergence of conscience—the sense of being "at fault." But the last essay demonstrates that, for Wiesel, this theme of abandonment seems to be the Jewish problem in the kingdom of night. In other words, he traces these themes from his childhood to adulthood where they remain central to his experience. They are now not just the unique experiences of a young boy growing up in a remote village in Eastern Europe. They are rather the unique experiences of an entire people.

To be sure, these themes—of the extreme love for a parent and the development of conscience—in the life of a young child are not unique. What makes them so in the moral journey of Elie Wiesel? The clue is the extreme nature of the conscience. How does a child of five get such a precocious sense of guilt that he feels "at fault" in the presence of an orphan? How does a young child gain the capacity to judge the merits of his parents' action, to judge the decision to send him to school an injustice, and to connect this with the same narrative about the orphan and the root of his feeling of being "at fault"? To answer these questions, one must look for additional clues in Eliezer's first world—his first images of faith, the beginning of his moral journey.

Most would agree that the earliest years of life are foundational for the nature and direction of the moral journey. Further, it is the child's identification with the parents or other caregivers that in some way helps the child to take on a sense of conscience. Eliezer's moral journey begins, however, with an overactive conscience that suggests a precocious sense of guilt. Where does a child of five acquire such a sense of guilt? Is not the answer to be found in the process that is normal at this age—the process of identifying with the father?

## *An Absent Father: Feeling Like an Abandoned Child*

When one reads the stories of little Eliezer, one finds him especially tormented at this point. He wants desperately to be with his mother, but he is beginning to realize that is no longer possible. His father is portrayed as an "absent" figure who works every day except the Sabbath either in the store or for the community. In his recent memoir, Wiesel begins with reflections on his father: "...It hurts to admit that, but it would hurt him even more if I deluded myself. The truth is I knew little of the man I loved most in the world, the man whose merest glance could stir me."[93] Further in the narrative he writes, "As a child and adolescent I saw him rarely."[94] It was only on Shabbat that Eliezer saw his father with any sense of regularity. Wiesel describes how he and his father would walk to services, how sometimes his father would take him by the hand, how much he liked that then, and how he likes to remember that now. His father's presence brought reassurance and contentment. "Bound to me, he belonged to me," Wiesel writes. "But if a fellow worshiper joined us, my suddenly useless hand was returned to me. Did my father have any idea how much that hurt? I felt abandoned, even rejected, and after that it was never the same."[95]

At about the age of three or four, a young child like Eliezer begins to find the courage to make the first tentative steps toward autonomous existence—that is, autonomous from the maternal matrix. Beginning at this point, the father has the opportunity to become the guardian of the child's autonomy. Assumable only by the father, this role of sponsorship allows something to pass from the father's bodily presence to the emerging selfhood of the child.[96] But what if the father is not there?

Precisely at this point, Eliezer remembers that he felt abandoned and rejected by both mother and father. From one angle of vision, one could argue that Eliezer's story does not appear unique. That is, all children experience the fear of abandonment. Such fears begin in children as young as six months old. For the child, the realization of this fear of abandonment is tantamount to the fear of death. Being helpless and virtually dependent on the parent, the child realizes that he or she is at the mercy of the parent for survival itself. So this fear of abandonment that dates to the first year of life, if not offset in the mind and psyche of the child with the care that leads to a deep and pervading sense of security, can lead to a primal element of fear and insecurity.[97]

Elie Wiesel's writing about his childhood demonstrates that he suffered a strong fear of abandonment and that, in actuality, in his mid teenage years he was abandoned through death by both of his parents, which leads to the vision of his own death recorded in *Night*. In the later course of his writing, one reads his portrayal of God's abandonment of the Jewish people and how they were abandoned by the nations of the world. This feeling of abandonment that emerges in Eliezer's childhood is not only a foundational image of childhood faith; it is also the central issue of his life—described in later writings about the Holocaust and the post-Holocaust era. The theme of solidarity with the victim, which emerges in Wiesel's later years as in the case of the Jews of silence in the Soviet Union or the Cambodians who suffered under Pol Pot, is an adult way to answer a central problem that emerges in its most personal form in his earliest childhood days.

## Eliezer's First Crisis: Childhood Despair and Melancholia

Eliezer feels like an abandoned child. He cannot stay with his mother, and his father is absent. How can he resolve this predicament? The answer is, of course, not easily. Yet, in his beloved grandfather, Dodye Feig, the little boy finds a "refuge." A superficial reading of Wiesel's story implies that Eliezer appears to resolve the dilemma by identifying with his grandfather, who becomes a father figure. But this transaction, however, comes with a great price—a precocious conscience. That is, the child compensates for moving beyond parental authority at this young age by internalizing an extraordinary sense of guilt that encourages him to absolve himself internally by assuming responsibility for the pain of those around them. In this way, Eliezer begins to feel "at fault" in the presence of his schoolmate, "the orphan."

There is, however, another more complicated aspect to Eliezer's moral journey. The complexity of his own life will not be seen until the melancholy spirit of his earliest days is shown to be what it is—the foundation and impetus for his religious vision and journey. The reader may tend to dismiss an author like Wiesel when he writes about childhood. But a sensitive reading of his texts about childhood shows that Eliezer is a child in despair. The emerging "I" of his childhood autobiographical texts is a "melancholic I." Eliezer's childhood melancholia is traced by Wiesel himself in a number of sources to his relationship with his mother and his growing realization that he could not stay with her. Put another way, his childhood despair has an object, and it is his mother. This first relationship becomes Wiesel's childhood "prehistoric core" and is, therefore, both the starting place and the impetus for his long moral journey. Put differently, religion in the life of the child becomes a substitute for the mother or the relationship with the mother, and when the child like Eliezer grows to maturity, this experience will continue to exist as a foundation for his composition of the world, or the way he looks at life. Consequently, for some young men, the journey of faith becomes a quest for the lost object and that primal environment—the natural mother and the way she was known and understood in early childhood. This experience of separation from the mother propels the child in search of religious answers.[98]

While it is generally true that young boys typically "separate" from the mother and all seem to experience a "sense of loss," there are some for whom it appears to be more deeply felt and therefore more complicated. Eliezer seems to be in this group for whom the natural process of separation from the mother is experienced as traumatic, perhaps, in part, because he sees his father as "absent" and therefore unable to sponsor his emerging autonomous existence—autonomous from the maternal matrix. This trauma—in turn—tends to push him in the direction of melancholia and ultimately toward a greater propensity for faith and the religious journey.

## Sighet as Ultimate Environment: Eliezer and Early Childhood Faith

In Elie Wiesel's literary landscape, his hometown of Sighet is a metaphor for the Promised Land. His town is a small European Jerusalem. The foundational cultural component in that "promised-land" existence is the family, and the maternal matrix was the milk and honey of his young existence. Eliezer's earliest memory and later stories imply that there was a time early in his life when his first ecological metaphor—his first way of making meaning intuitively sensed from the network of maternal mutuality—was nothing less than the sweetness and nurture of life. But Eliezer's stories also indicate an emerging ambivalence so that his first map of life includes feelings of absence, separation, and a feeling of abandonment. In his naturally egocentric view of the world, Eliezer could not comprehend the loss that came his way. This infantile curse visible already in his first ultimate environment will be projected forward in later stories and quests and will seek eventual transformation in adult deeds.[99] Is this, at least in part, the seed bed for the adult's later efforts to understand his then larger history, the circumstances of the Jewish people, and to bring comfort and liberation to oppressed and abandoned people everywhere?

Wiesel's stories of his childhood landscape show a young child experiencing a personal trauma of losing his mother. Even though his mother continues to be present to him, the stories show that Eliezer is becoming aware that the two of them must relate to one another in different ways now. Wiesel's stories—about Eliezer going to *heder* for the first time, about waiting for his mother at the ritual baths—imply that he has lost the mother who initially held him close and was always present. Because of this awareness, young Eliezer soon realizes that he too is changing—he has to give up the image of the little boy loved unconditionally by the mother. Now, he realizes, that love must also be earned. These two losses—the loss of the mother and the first childhood image of himself as the mother's beloved—push Eliezer in the direction of melancholia, which in turn propels him toward religious faith. Wiesel's stories about experiences at school and with his grandfather indicate his gradual turn from this first matrix. Feeling abandoned and alone, young Eliezer struggles with feelings of loneliness and anxiety. Wiesel, the writer, gives a sensitive portrayal of a child's first crisis and Eliezer's attempt to negotiate the chasm. Typically, young men revisit these crises moments in young adulthood. Little Eliezer could not begin to fathom how difficult his next crisis would be.

In summary, as seen from the later reflections of the adult, young Eliezer is a child with a consuming love for his mother that is frustrated by an abiding fear of abandonment that may actually date to his first year of life. This ongoing fear, however, is intensified by the experience of *heder*, where the manner and modality of his teachers stand in contrast to the unconditional love of his mother. When combined with what appears to the child as the loss of his mother's unconditional love, the absence of his father compels the child to look for other sources to provide identity and affirmation. These factors also seem to propel young Eliezer ultimately toward a propensity for the religious journey. When he discovers that his grandfather can provide both a refuge of unconditional love and a model of the religious life, Eliezer enters one of the most joyous periods of his life. But his view of the world would be forever marked by this first period, which would become the foundation for his composition of the world. From this period comes what appears to be the central dialectic of his life: abandonment over against solidarity. This central theme, coming from his first years, informs his writing and speaking, as well as his activism in causes for justice.[100]

# Chapter 3

# A Refuge:

# Grandfather and His Stories

In 1933, when Franklin Delano Roosevelt became president of the United States and Adolf Hitler became chancellor of Germany, there were nine million Jews throughout Europe. During that year, the world population continued to suffer under a severe economic depression. In Germany, many hoped Hitler and his Nazi party could bring an end to the political chaos. Instead, Hitler seized the reins of government and instituted dictatorial power. Racism, the central tenet of Nazi ideology, became the ruling idea. Based on racist premises, the Nazis set out to re-create the world: the Germans were to be the "master race," while Slavs, Gypsies, Blacks, and Jews were ordained to be inferior—in fact, "subhuman."

As a five-year-old child, Eliezer did not know these realities. There were other struggles serious enough for a child his age, but Eliezer found refuge in his grandfather and his stories. At this point in his life, he is making his first tentative and reluctant steps in his moral journey. The first stage of that journey, as described in the previous chapter, is an "intuitive" effort to incorporate and project meaning primarily from his parents and grandparents.[101] To put it another way, the first stage of life for Eliezer is focused on the ability of the child to identify with his primary caregivers. The religious journey of a young pilgrim-protagonist like Eliezer begins as a journey into culture with the family being the basic and foundational unit of culture.[102] This first era, as Wiesel later testifies, is clearly foundational for him. The perspectives internalized with intuitive and imaginative skills provide a basis for his later growth. The second era of his journey will involve learning the stories of the Jewish people and those of the wider culture. But before he enters that world, he must negotiate an important turn from the family context to the larger world of school, religion, and culture beyond the family. In order to make that transition, Eliezer must deal with the struggle Freud calls the "Oedipal Crisis." How would Eliezer deal with his attachment to his mother?

## The Generational Complex: Eliezer and the Burden of Greatness

As Eliezer wrestled with this first crisis, he found himself entering different worlds at school. Reading tended to isolate him, sent him into many different kingdoms, and he left his classmates behind. Caught up by the world of words and stories, Eliezer realized that his mother was also left behind. This troubled him. His solution—which shows how religion, for him at an early age, began to take on the quest for the mother as a lost object—was to take her with him through the use of imagination.[103] So when he entered the world of Adam at the beginning of time, Eve took on the face of his mother. When he followed Moses and Israel into the wilderness, it was Miriam who took on his mother's characteristics.[104]

As was her custom, Sarah Wiesel continued to take young Eliezer to see the rabbi to seek his blessing. On one such occasion when when Eliezer was eight years old, Sarah took him to see Rabbi Israel of Wizhnitz when he came to Sighet. The blessing she sought included health for the family, success for her husband, a good marriage for her daughters, and the "fear of God" for her son. Mother and son approached the rabbi hand in hand.

Eliezer was attracted to the radiant face of the rabbi whose love for Israel and its people was legendary. The rabbi put Eliezer on his lap and began to ask him about his studies. After a few minutes, he asked to be alone with the boy. Sarah left the room, and the conversation continued. After a time, Eliezer went out and Sarah came back in. When Sarah came out, she was crying. He had said to her, "Sarah, daughter of David...I want you to know that someday your son will grow up to be a great man in Israel but neither you nor I will be alive to see it."[105]

What does such a story mean in the life of one so young? A child so devoted to his mother that he confesses he does not know his father until he is fifteen or sixteen years old. A mother who tells stories about her son's greatness when the child is only eight years old. In writing about Gandhi, Erikson noted that the Oedipal crisis is actually part of a larger crisis, the "generational complex," for such conflicts are inherent in the way humans experience the larger issues of life in the "turnover of generations." Then Erikson theorized that it is likely that uncommon young men experience these conflicts because they sense in themselves some aspect of "originality" that early in life seems to point them beyond the competition with their individual fathers. Thus, the precocious and demanding conscience makes these young men—at a young age—both feel and appear older than their peers and perhaps their parents, who may reciprocate by regarding the child as a redeemer. So these young men grow up with a sense of obligation, grounded in a profound sense of guilt, to succeed and to create whatever the cost. Such a dynamic prolongs the identity confusion in adolescence and may later lead the young man to accept a whole body of people, perhaps humankind itself, as the object of his rescue.[106] Could this, in part, be the reason the rabbi recognized that eight-year-old Eliezer had the potential to be a great man in Israel?

## Grandfather as Refuge

In retrospect, it seems clear that the rabbi was right! But in Eliezer's case, is there a connection between the child and the man, between his childhood melancholia, his overactive conscience, and his later greatness in the adult world? To answer this question, one must turn to Eliezer's special relationship with his grandfather. In short, Dodye Feig helps Eliezer negotiate the turn from his first image of the child loved unconditionally by the mother to the pursuit of the lost object through the religious quest. Dodye Feig is " *the* Hasid" in the family, and with Sarah Wiesel he continues to look over Wiesel's shoulder as he writes even now. Dodye Feig is the one figure in Eliezer's family from whom—outside of his mother—he might hope to receive unconditional love. And, indeed, in him Eliezer found a "refuge."

Wiesel uses the word "refuge" with guarded economy. The Sabbath was a refuge for Jews in Sighet. Later, after the war, Wiesel's childhood and his memories of it become a refuge. And in those early years, his grandfather provides this hallowed place for the child. Given the emotional change levied upon little Eliezer at the age of three, four, and five of having to attend *heder*, and the child's realization that he can no longer stay with his mother, it is clear that Dodye Feig provides a model of love and stability the child can find nowhere else. Perhaps he later becomes what Erikson once called "one of the last representatives of a more homogeneous world."[107] As such a representative, the grandfather serves as a "provider of identity" for Eliezer, who is an especially sensitive and responsive young boy.[108] By identifying with his grandfather and taking up the religious life epitomized by him, Eliezer unconsciously absorbs the deep commitment to Dodye Feig's world of faith.

When Eliezer was a child, his grandfather would come to Sighet for Shabbat and for the Holy Days. Eliezer would spend the entire time with his grandfather. Wherever the grandfather went, the grandson went: to the ritual bath, to religious services, to visit with the Rebbe. Whenever grandfather sang with fervor, the grandson joined in with him. When grandfather spoke to his grandson, Eliezer the child thrilled to every word, but Eliezer was not the only one who listened to Reb Dodye Feig. In the House of Study, all the others demonstrated respectful silence when he was there, for he knew how to captivate an audience with his storytelling art. Eliezer first heard the Hasidic tales from him.[109]

The one story, above all stories, that demonstrates Eliezer's identification with his grandfather, and the profound nature of the relationship as seen through the perspective of a child, is found in Wiesel's portrait of his grandfather in *A Jew Today*. One day, Eliezer as a young boy missed his grandfather so much that, without thinking it through or receiving permission to do so, he simply began walking the 7-kilometer journey to his grandfather's farm. When he arrived, he was worn out. He sat in a chair as his grandfather inquired about the trip. Dodye Feig asked why he had come. The child replied, "I missed you, Grandfather." That was the only reason, the real reason. His grandfather quizzed him more. Was there an argument, perhaps with his father? Did someone offend him? Was there a problem at school? To each of the questions little Eliezer answered in the negative, and simply repeated his need to see his grandfather. After sending a message to Eliezer's parents by the next coachman, Dodye Feig spent the rest of the evening telling the child stories of his own childhood. He told Eliezer that he used to run away also, except he went to visit the rabbi. That particular evening Dodye Feig told Eliezer about his great-grandfather, who at the age of seventy had taken up the violin, and how he would gather the children together on Saturday nights and play gypsy and Hasidic tunes.[110]

## *The Grandfather, Reversal of the Generations, and Emergence of the Religious Self*

How does a young boy like Eliezer attain such a sense of identification with a grandfather, and what does this have to do with Eliezer's moral journey? In brief, this propensity to identify with the grandparent can bring on what Ernest Jones called the "reversal of the generations"—the ability of the child to substitute a grandparent for a parent, and in the process to become—in a child's eyes—the parent of a parent. Likewise, this ability, in Eliezer's case, to reverse the generations further serves his moral quest in two important ways: (1) in his mind, Eliezer wins the competition with his father—who is the first major obstacle of authority in the child's life—by the identification with the grandfather, which in turn reduces the father to the level of a sibling; (2) Eliezer adds the capacity to envision a "spiritual father" based on this veneration of the grandfather as "the Hasid" of the family.

Eliezer's attachment to his grandfather and his ensuing identification with the Hasidic world of Dodye Feig parallels in important ways the story of Martin Buber's early life. Both Buber and Wiesel were greatly influenced by Hasidism and the Bible, and both came to understand theology in terms of human relationships. In addition, both were influenced in profound ways by grandparents. Buber's parents were separated when he was three years old. At that point, he went to live with his paternal grandparents until he was fourteen years old. Greatly influenced by his grandfather's love for the Scriptures, he seems to have been affected even more by the piety of his grandmother, who had a "love for the genuine word." By this Buber meant her love was self-evident in human relationships: "To the glance of the child it was already unmistakable that when she at times addressed someone, she really addressed him."[111] In marked contrast, Buber's relationship with his own mother was characterized by what he called "mismeeting," which he later used to illustrate the failure of meeting between individuals. The central theme in Buber's most important book, *I and Thou*, is that all real living is meeting between individuals.[112]

## *Eliezer, Torah, and Expanding Faith:*
### *Learning the Story of a People*

Wiesel's writing about his childhood indicates how he, like Buber, was freed from the first major crisis to the extent that he was able to begin the pursuit of the mysteries of life in religious terms and thereby enter into a more expansive view of the world. In *Legends of Our Time*, he describes himself in the terms of a young child exploring religion and the sacred ways of one's group. He sees himself in childhood as an "unsophisticated little boy, in love with religion and with the absolute." Typical of young school-age children, Eliezer becomes interested in the stories of his people. That is, young children around the age of seven or eight begin to take on for themselves the stories and beliefs that symbolize belonging to the community. Usually a child attempts to clarify what is real and what only appears to be real. Stories and beliefs are appropriated with literal interpretations as are moral rules and attitudes.[113]

Through the exploration of biblical narratives, Eliezer was oriented to the mysteries of time and existence and integrated into a larger family of faith with its stories about God, humankind, and society. In school, the stories were learned by rote memory and understood in literal and concrete terms. "All things seemed simple and miraculous: life and death, love and hatred." The righteous were on one side and the wicked on the other. And God kept the account in his book—a book where "the Jewish people had the most beautiful page of all."[114]

Eliezer also grew up with a "veritable obsession" to know what it meant to be Jewish. He came to understand the requirement to obey the Law—to learn and remember it; to love God and all in his creation that bears his seal. Having done so, he was taught to believe, to expect that "His will would be done." So Eliezer drank in the tradition: the covenant with Abraham, the *Akedah* (binding of Isaac), the Sinai revelation, the wilderness march, the blessings of Moses, the conquest of Canaan, the pilgrimages to Zion, the "beautiful but harsh words" of Isaiah and Habakkuk, the lamentations of Jeremiah, and the legends of the Talmud. "My head was abuzz," Wiesel writes, "with ancient memories and debates, with tales teeming with kings and prophets, tragedies and miracles."[115]

Growing up in the *shetl*, Eliezer became immersed in the rich traditions of his Hasidic past. He learned to venerate the Torah. In time, the Scriptures provided Eliezer with a compelling language world in which the mysteries of life are mapped out. The ancient rehearsals found in the Bible and as practiced by the community through the centuries imposed archetypes and paradigms on the chaos felt near by all. For a young boy like Eliezer studying for the bar mitzvah, the "overarching plot" of the Torah created a "graph of destiny." Sighet became for him a "well-lighted" place providing orientation and coherence as he searched to know the ways of God and the Jewish people. Sighet took on the significance of an Eden before the loss of innocence and a Jerusalem away from Jerusalem.[116]

As Eliezer learned to read the Hebrew Scriptures, he was immersed in a "world story" that secured human life against death, meaning against the irrational. The overarching story itself gave testimony to these realities. The stories of creation and covenant guaranteed the stability of the cosmos. Life was secured against death—meaning against chaos—by the very power of word and story. The first long narrative of the Scriptures—the story of creation, the patriarchs, exodus, and the journey to the Promised Land—looks toward the goal that through the fulfillment of her vocation Israel could bless all the nations of the earth.[117] Eliezer sought for a way to be a part of that fulfillment and to hasten the coming of the Messiah.

A central tenet in the faith of Sighet's Hasidic Jews was the belief that God permeates and sustains all things. In response to the presence of God, Eliezer as a young Hasid was taught to give total dedication to God as appropriate worship of the divine. In so doing, Eliezer learned to infuse holiness into all aspects of life—in work, in eating, and in social life. He was taught that dancing should be seen as a form of prayer and service to God. Thus, when the Hasidim danced joyfully on Shabbat as a token of their devotion and as a symbol of their passionate faith in God, Eliezer was taught to join in and to share their passion.[118]

## Eliezer and Stories of the Culture: The School Years and Anti-Semitism

Eliezer learned other stories at this time in his life. Unfortunately, he also learned firsthand about the vicious nature of hatred directed against Jews. An anti-Semitic group known as the Iron Guard sometimes wrote messages on the walls of the Jewish community, messages like "Jews to Palestine!" They were thugs who occasionally roamed the streets assaulting Jews and tearing at their beards and side curls. Then there were the Kuzists—a Romanian version of the Nazis. They roamed the streets looking for a confrontation and Jewish blood. During such times, Eliezer and his sisters would stay home from school. The store was closed and the door bolted. If the danger seemed imminent, the family would go to the cellar. Eliezer remembers his mother singing a mournful song about a Hungarian village in which a Jew responds to the centuries-old anti-Semitic charge of blood libel. When the Jew is accused of murdering a child for ceremonial rites, he exclaims, "Cursed be our enemies who claim the Jews need blood to practice their religion!"[119]

# A Refuge

Some of Eliezer's classmates at the secular elementary school participated in the anti-Semitic ways. At Christmas, some would wear masks and carry whips and take their places in the hunt for Jews. When Eliezer walked down the street past a church, he would cross over to the other side. The Christian churches inspired nothing but fear. In times of the worst outbreaks of hatred, Eliezer would ask himself and his teachers why the persecution. His teachers responded by asking Eliezer and his classmates to read and reread the Bible and the stories of other Jewish martyrs. There, Eliezer found models of faith and a paradigm. Faithfulness to the covenant made Abraham, Isaac, and Daniel immortal. Eliezer responded strongly to these stories and the chronicles of Jewish affliction such as the children of Jerusalem massacred by Nebuzaradan. The biblical stories told Eliezer of a "permanent conflict" between Jews and the other side. Haunted by the ordeal of the faithful, Eliezer was, nonetheless, encouraged by their fidelity. His question was a personal one: could he remain Jewish if persecuted?[120]

Troubled by the questions, Eliezer sought answers in the stories he was learning. He did not play sports. He found relaxation in playing chess and cards. Sometimes he spent evenings with Hasidic friends. In spring, he occasionally walked in the park or by the river. His mother took him to the cinema a few times. Once he saw a Yiddish film about Jewish settlements, but he did not see the secular Hungarian films. When he noticed the posters with the attractive girls, Eliezer was troubled. Satan was tempting him, Eliezer thought.[121]

Other things troubled Eliezer during his elementary school years. He continued to be plagued by guilt. He thought his family was rich. Other children seemed to have so little. His conscience continued to be active and overly zealous. The truth was that Eliezer's family had to work hard to make ends meet every month. Nevertheless, Eliezer still felt compelled to give his snacks away. He thought his classmates "detested" him, so he tried to win them over with bribery. Until his bar mitzvah, any present he received he gave away to his classmates. He also thought his teachers were "cold and indifferent." So he tried hard to win them over by doing a good job in the classroom. His grades were good in elementary school, though secular subjects did not interest him. Eliezer was deeply sensitive to his friends. The slightest argument would cause him to lay awake at night searching for an answer to the breach in relationships. Eliezer began to sense a change in his life around the age of twelve. He noticed that the bonds of friendship grew stronger. He no longer felt a need to bribe his friends. A new era loomed on the horizon.[122]

## Mythos and Childhood Faith: Story and Ultimate Environment

Eliezer's spiritual landscape expanded during his school years. His propensity for the religious life found a joyous grounding in his beloved grandfather, who helped him win the competition with his own father at an extremely early age but left him with a precocious conscience and an abiding sense of guilt. Like Buber, Wiesel was one day able to understand theology in terms of relationships. Because of his grandfather, Eliezer was later able to envision a spiritual father and to take up the religious quest. During these years, Eliezer adopted a rich heritage as he immersed himself in the world story of the Bible and Judaism. The child knew who he was, but remnants of his earlier struggles continued to mark his life. His overactive conscience and abiding sense of guilt continued to plague Eliezer.

Eliezer's childhood years indicate that he likely grew to maturity in an environment where he was "called," like Jeremiah, at an early age. That is, he lived with a sense of obligation, grounded in a severe and profound sense of guilt, to succeed, to create, and to redeem. This burden would manifest itself in extreme ways in Eliezer's adolescence, and would mean a protracted struggle for identity and intimacy in his adult years. This call is the foundation for his later emblematic status and the basis for understanding how he became *the* survivor. That is, this dynamic of obligation grounded in guilt pushed a budding innovator to envision an entire people as the object of his rescue. It appears that Eliezer did indeed shoulder the burden of greatness at a young age. This view is born out by the extreme nature of his adolescent faith—a faith that, if only in the immature dreams of a teenager, sought to redeem Israel.

Yet Eliezer as child and later as adult was sustained and nurtured by the stories he learned from his beloved grandfather. For a time, Eliezer's spiritual geography was linked directly to the narratives that he heard in Sighet and that helped him to define a larger world. As a child, Eliezer learned from these stories who he was and what he was commanded to do. They illuminated his world, gave him models by which to live, and became a guide for the pathways that unfolded before him. When Eliezer grew to be an adult, these same stories provided a link to tradition and a vocabulary when language had died. The stories were rewritten after the war to give new meaning for an entire generation. The stories and the storytellers were a foundational aspect in Eliezer's growing and developing faith. Both would live on in Eliezer's spiritual geography and provide a wellspring for later nurture and inspiration. Originally encountered in the realm of the first naiveté, these stories came to live again in Wiesel's reappropriation characterized by the world of a second naiveté.[123]

# Chapter 4

# Bar Mitzvah and

# Approaching Tyranny

The year 1941 marked an important turning point in the life of young Eliezer and in Hitler's genocidal policies. In a similar manner, the word "tyranny" would soon unfold as a double entendre for Eliezer. This was the year of his bar mitzvah, the time when he became a full member of the house of Israel, which carried a new sense of status for a growing young teenager. Germany's invasion of the Soviet Union also marked 1941. Here, mass murder of the Jews became standard operational policy. Small units of the SS and Police called Special Action Squads traveled with the German Army and were tasked with orders to kill any Jews that were found. That same year, more than a thousand "foreign"-born Jews were deported from Sighet and sent to Galacia in Poland. Still, the Jews of Sighet were not greatly troubled. Though Moshe the Beadle came back to tell about the slaughter of the foreign-born Jews, the Jews of Sighet did not believe him. In large measure, it was because of their uncritical acceptance of the cultural story of inevitable progress attached to the humanistic vision of modernity, and because of the naive confidence Eliezer's neighbors had in the German soldiers who had been kind to them in WWI. The Jews of Sighet fell into a trap set in part by the history of the region. And Eliezer entered a new era of faith characterized by a naive, uncritical, and dangerous allegiance to a compact formed among his peers—a genuine "tyranny of the they"—to track down God as known through the mystical traditions of the Kabala.[124]

During World War I, Sighet had been overrun and occupied by the Russian army. Jewish citizens were beaten and oppressed by anti-Semitic Cossacks. When the German army came in, they treated the population with courtesy. During the early years of WWII, the Jews of Sighet could not believe the Germans would be any different now. After all, German culture represented a pinnacle of achievement in literature, music, architecture, and science. How could the sons of these people do evil things? Therefore, when Moshe the Beadle came back from Galacia and attempted to tell the Jewish citizens of Sighet a story of genocide, he was laughed at and mocked. Moshe, they said, had gone "mad."[125]

## *Bar Mitzvah as Turning Point:*
### *The Emergence of Adolescent Faith*

Meanwhile, Eliezer celebrated his bar mitzvah in the synagogue across the street from his house. The Rebbe of Borsha led the service. Rebbe Haim-Meir'l helped Eliezer strap on the phylacteries. Eliezer read from the Bible and recited prayers. Following the service, the synagogue faithful came to a *Kiddush*—the evening prayer on holidays or Shabbat. The bar mitzvah service was a turning point for Eliezer. This event inaugurated his life as a "responsible adult" in the community. But in truth, Eliezer, like all thirteen-year-olds, remained an adolescent, and his faith was that typical of teenagers—unreflective, naive, and based upon group opinion. When Eliezer joined the synagogue youth group, the *Tiferet Bachurim*, he was elected president. In the privacy of their own room, the group met to celebrate the holy days, study, and pray.[126]

With his youth group, Eliezer sought effective ways to pray, meditate, and unlock the mysteries. Since the time of Moses, who first requested to see God's glory, the more mystical Jews had sought a symbolic as well as a literal meaning of the Torah. The faithful within Hasidism looked especially to the Lurianic Kabala of the sixteenth century for mystical understanding. The sixteenth-century mystics had intended such esoteric learning only for the select few, but for the Hasidim, learning by necessity involved mystical revelation. Through mysticism, it was thought, one could penetrate deeper in the text than with a literal reading. In contrast to the sixteenth-century mystics, the Hasidim opened up the mysteries to the many. In the minds of the Jewish population in Eastern Europe by the early twentieth century, the quest for mystical revelation of the absolute involved the encounter with a realm of supernatural forces and sympathetic magic.[127]

Hasidism also transformed the tradition of the isolated mystic into a new role, that of a community leader. A young mystic might live in isolation for a time, but he would emerge to fulfill the role of a *rebbe*, a leader in his community. In the Hasidic realm of Sighet, Eliezer, as a God-intoxicated young man, wanted to prove his status in the community of adults—to show that he was faithful and to experience as much divine reality as possible. He was attracted to the Kabala and what seemed to be beyond present reality. What could be more romantic to an adolescent than finding answers the adults did not have? What could be more alluring than the mystical teachings? Eliezer began to read about astrology, magic, parapsychology, and the beyond. He grew fascinated with mysticism and the possibility that Satan could be stopped by some mixture or formula, that the forces of evil could be halted in their tracks. Eliezer involved himself in countless prayers and formulas to make his savings grow, to liberate the Lord from his imprisonment, and to stop Hitler.[128]

## Eliezer and the Mystical Quest:
### The Trio and the "Tyranny of the They"

Eliezer and two of his friends felt a special attraction to the mystical quest. They began meeting with Kalman, the Kabalist, to penetrate further into mystical truth, to go into the Pardes—that "orchard of forbidden knowledge." Fasting was the first part of the journey. This they did on Mondays and Thursdays. Captivated by this quest and what he was learning, Eliezer would stay at the House of Study until midnight. The group would sit together on the floor and repeat the litanies and incantations. Kalman guided the group to the moment when, by pronouncing the appropriate occult formulas, they might expect to promote the coming of the Messiah. They knew the dangers. Others before them had failed in such attempts, and some had lost memory. It happened to the founder of Hasidism, the Baal Shem Tov. But they were his disciples and would not abandon the quest for enlightenment and salvation.[129]

News of their experiment spread all over town. Shlomo Wiesel heard about it and confronted his son. When Shlomo spoke to Eliezer, he asked him if he were not too young to be exploring and practicing the Kabala. Eliezer's typically adolescent response was no. After all, he had become a "bar mitzvah," had he not? Shlomo inquired further about Eliezer's activities. But Eliezer had taken a vow of silence with his two friends. Shlomo became angry. He ordered his son to answer, which Eliezer did. Then Shlomo made a deal with his son. Eliezer could study the Kabala all he wanted if he would continue to study the Talmud and modern Hebrew. It was a deal.[130]

Shlomo was not the only one in town worried about the trio. Parents told their children to stay away from the three boys. The consensus was that this was a forbidden domain—a virtual religious minefield. One could not enter the orchard of forbidden knowledge with impunity. The risks involved madness or heresy or, in extreme cases, death. After all, one must remember the limits. The human being cannot absorb too much light or emotion. Kalman responded by saying that there are obvious risks, but the potential for reward makes it worth the risk and the effort.[131]

After six months, the first defeat came. The oldest of the three boys, Yiddele, became seriously ill. He lost his ability to speak and the will to live. Rabbis came to say prayers. Doctors were brought to see him. Yiddele remained the same. Finally, a psychiatrist from Budapest came over and spent several days. The doctor stayed an entire day with Yiddele and then visited the schools and interviewed friends of the patient. Eliezer had entered into a pact of secrecy and would not give any information that would endanger the sacred mission. A week or so later, Shlomo spoke to his son, suggesting it was time to "stop this senseless business." Once again, Eliezer refused. He had to promise to be careful.[132]

Eliezer and Sruli, the two remaining members of the trio, picked up their work again under the guidance of Kalman, the Kabalist. With a mixture of asceticism, incantations, and litanies, they descended once more into the abyss. Could they come close to redemption and usher in the coming of the Messiah? Perhaps. Eliezer and Sruli wanted to defeat the enemy of the Jewish people and bring redemption to Israel. But the evil one won again. This time, Sruli fell sick with the same symptoms as Yiddele. Once more the doctors came. As before they left without bringing healing or finding answers to the dilemma of the tyrannical attack on these adolescents.[133]

Eliezer's faith, at this point, was conformist in nature. That is, what seemed true and real was mediated to him through the authority of his friends and Kalman, his teacher. Eliezer did not have the ability yet to think through issues and reflect on them critically. In part, the "tyranny" that controlled him during this period was the shared naiveté that formulas, incantations, and prayers could stop evil and change the destiny of the universe. What seemed so dangerous to the citizens of Sighet was the willingness of these adolescents to risk so much based on such little understanding.[134]

After Sruli fell ill, Eliezer was alone with Kalman. But the master was undaunted. "It's enough for a single being to want it, to want it sincerely and completely, and the universe will be saved." That night, master and disciple began again, this time only the two of them. In 1943, on the evening of Tisha b'Av when the Lamentations of Jeremiah were read at the synagogue, Eliezer went to Kalman's house. That night, Eliezer had an experience that could have brought him to the same place as Yiddele and Sruli. Master and student stayed awake all night repeating mystical texts and phrases. Eliezer felt a force dragging him down from one level to the next. It was about four o'clock in the early morning when he apparently had a vision of a figure chained to a huge dead tree. The face of the figure was hidden, yet motionless while he appeared to hold up the heavens with his head. A thousand dogs were barking, and flames of fire were leaping. Eliezer called to Kalman and told him what he saw. Kalman encouraged calm and care. But Eliezer awoke in a sweat, delirious and unable to tell what was dream and what was reality. At that moment, madness stalked both master and disciple. Eliezer was determined to carry on the quest, and he would have likely suffered the same fate as Yiddele and Sruli, who fell ill unable to speak, except for another fire and another form of madness.[135]

## Eliezer's Dangerous Quest and the Religious Self: Homo Religiosus and the Covenant Sealed with God

Eliezer's quest took on extraordinary dimensions during his adolescent years, and these years tell us much about the nature and dimension of his spiritual pilgrimage. Though his adolescent quest was, in part, a journey shared and sealed in covenant with two teenage friends, it reveals a totalistic and zealous commitment to God. These stories about Eliezer's adolescence reflect a young but naive religious personality "stirred by a yearning after the unattainable." He was one who wanted "to make the distant near, the abstract concrete, to transform the soul into a vessel for the transcendent, to grasp with the senses what is hidden from the mind...." He attempted to have a heart that was open to the inner life of God, and he sought to live his life in dynamic response to this Divine pathos.[136]

The extent to which Eliezer pursued God with a disregard for his own well-being indicates his religious personality is that of *homo religiosus*. How does a teenager like Eliezer reach a state of total involvement in such a dangerous religious mission against the wishes of his father? He does so only by becoming his father's father, that is, by reversing the generations. In Eliezer's case, his identification with his grandfather took him beyond that first conflict with the father's authority and allowed him to imagine God in terms of the Father. In so doing, Eliezer made a covenant with God. Though Eliezer is surely only a teenager in these stories, his personal narrative reflects an emerging sense of religious selfhood—a "budding 'I'" as Erikson describes it—that believes he "harbors a truthfulness superior to that of all authorities because this truth is the covenant of the 'I' with God." This "overweening conscience can find peace only" through such totalistic belief and action, and by assuming that the covenant with God is "more central and more pervasive than all parent images or moralities." This, Erikson writes, is the "core of a *homo religiosus*." On this basis, Eliezer studied the Zohar and Kabala against the wishes of his father and began to "practice" the Kabala with totalistic zeal—a zeal by which he sought to solve that earlier childhood conflict. This is also the reason Eliezer was able to face the danger of his adolescent quest. The motto for such religious personalities is a kind of totalism reflected in "allness or nothingness." The covenant sealed with God allows one the ability to face danger and eventually death itself. This sense of an "I" sealed in covenant with God allowed Eliezer to stand unprotected against absolute evil in that moment of terror in Kalman's house. This is the core of Elie Wiesel's personality—the person behind the emblem, here only in embryonic form. Yet, this core reality later went on the long pilgrimage from Auschwitz to Oslo and was eventually joined with an entire generation. In this view, Eliezer's inner conflict would, in time, become the genesis for his growth and eventual greatness. In due course, one must ask how Eliezer's own individual conflicts match those of his generation.[137]

## A Second Exodus and the Tyranny of a New Egypt

On 19 March 1944, while at the synagogue, Moshe the Beadle announced to the crowd that the Germans had crossed the border into Hungary. After returning home to see his parents, Eliezer went to see his friends at the House of Study. They were skeptical. Only he was optimistic. He was convinced that it was the beginning of the great end-time battle between Gog and Magog portrayed in the book of Ezekiel. The defeat of the enemy would only mean the coming of the Messiah who would take his friends to the Holy Land. Eliezer went to see his sick friends. The status of his friends had not changed—they were not going to betray the secret. He spoke to them and declared the good news that God would soon kill the Angel of Death. But Eliezer did not know that Adolf Eichmann was at that moment in Budapest with his plans to carry out efficiently Hitler's design for the "Final Solution" of Sighet's Jews.[138]

Though it was late in the war and its outcome was already determined, Hitler continued to work tirelessly to prove that the

Germans were the "master race" and to rid the empire of the "subhumans." Strange as it may seem, Hitler gave priority to the deportation of Jews over military equipment and convoys. The Germans came at Passover. In the beginning, the Nazis acted with courtesy. It was an ironic occurrence, this invasion of the Nazis during the time of the Jewish remembrance of freedom and exodus from the bondage of Egypt. In truth, the German presence would prefigure a new exodus and a new form of Egypt.[139]

Though it was just a few weeks before the landing of the allies at Normandy, the Jews of Sighet did not know what Hitler's "Final Solution" of the Jewish question would mean for them. The orders came on the seventh day of Passover. All Jewish stores and offices were closed. All Jews must now wear the yellow star. Eliezer wore his with pride, as a way of identifying with previous generations. Jewelry and valuables had to be turned over to the Nazis. A feeling of abandonment and betrayal swept through the community. Life changed for the Jews in Sighet as if overnight. The Nazis gave orders and Creation itself seemed to collapse. Eliezer's house no longer belonged to him.[140]

One day in May, Eichmann himself came to Sighet. The next day the first convoys left for the death camps. The chief rabbi, with his shaven beard, was on the first train as were Eliezer's friends and classmates, even Yiddele and Sruli motionless on their stretchers. Eliezer and his family did not leave for several more days on a later convoy. There were 15,000 Jews from the Sighet region. Eliezer was fifteen years old. It was as if he lost his innocence that spring day in 1944 when they were ordered onto the cattle car, packed in like animals. But people continued to pray, and Eliezer opened his commentaries on the train. Eliezer's convoy stopped at a small town on the Czechoslovakian border called Kaschau. It was then that the Jews of Sighet realized that they were leaving Hungary.

# Bar Mitzvah and Approaching Tyranny

When the train came to a final stop, they were at a place called Birkenau in Poland, the reception station for Auschwitz. Immediately after arriving at Birkenau, Eliezer heard the fateful words: "Men to the left! Women to the right!" With those words, fifteen-year-old Eliezer watched as his mother and youngest sister moved away never to be seen again. Eliezer grabbed his father's arm as if to cling more tightly to him and to hold on to his past. It was there in the camps that Eliezer came to know his father. The family was then and there reduced to the two of them. As long as his father was alive, the family was alive—he was alive.

Eliezer and his father were able to stay together and to avoid the "selection" for almost a year. The first days in the death camps appeared to Eliezer as the "antechambers of Hell." Eliezer and his father stood for selection in front of the infamous doctor, Joseph Mengele. The crematories operated seemingly around the clock. In the camps he saw children burning in open pits, young people hanged, others beaten, oppressive work conditions, and virtual starvation. Yet there were human times. Eliezer studied Talmud with another inmate who was a former *rosh yeshiva* (head of a rabbinical school). Eliezer and his father got up earlier than they had to in order to stand in line to borrow a pair of phylacteries to use in prayer. Eliezer said his prayers every day. On Saturdays, Eliezer sang Shabbat songs, if for no other reason than to show his father that he would remain a Jew even there. They were at Birkenau/Auschwitz for about three weeks. Then, Eliezer's group of ordinary laborers walked to their new work camp: Buna. They stayed there until winter. In mid-January, Eliezer's foot became badly infected and required an operation. Soon thereafter, because of the advance of the Russian army, the inmates at Buna were evacuated to a camp deep in the heart of Germany. The evacuation turned into a death march. They went on a forced march in the snow to Gleiwitz. After spending three days there with no food, one hundred inmates got into an open cattle car and traveled west into Germany for ten days. When they reached their destination at Buchenwald, Eliezer and his father were among the twelve who got out. There, at Buchenwald, Eliezer watched his father die of dysentery. The date was 28 January 1945. In less than three months, American soldiers liberated the camp. Eliezer was alive physically, but he had suffered an emotional death.

## Eliezer's Adolescent Spiritual Geography: Tyranny and the Ultimate Environment

During these years, tyranny became a double *entendre* for Eliezer. These teenage years found him in a typically adolescent form of faith—conventional in the way that his faith appealed to the ways and thoughts of friends and valued teachers. But the "tyranny" Eliezer faced during this period indicates both the conformist nature of his faith as well as the event—the Holocaust—that would eventually undermine his adolescent style of making meaning. This period also indicates that the characteristics of his first world of faith continue to impinge upon his view of life. These early adolescent years give special indication that Eliezer has not only a deep-seated need to contradict the words and ways of his father but also some inner authority to do so. The earlier covenant sealed with God helps one to understand how Eliezer could take on the dangerous mission with Kalman—over the objections of his father—after the illness of his two friends. This dynamic also helps to inform the reader as to how Eliezer the child could be the father of Wiesel the man. Already in his teenage years, he was a budding innovator looking for a way to redeem Israel. The intervening period between the two—the child and the man—would, however, be long and full of struggle.

Contrary to popular understanding, Eliezer continued his conventional way of being in faith during the months in the camps. He took his religious books with him on the train and attempted to study on the way to Auschwitz. Despite the conditions of privation and human cruelty that surrounded him in the camps, Eliezer continued to pray and to study Talmud. His first act after being given freedom was to say *kaddish*—the prayer for the dead. Yet his spiritual landscape continued to be ridden with guilt and shame. His childhood fear of abandonment was now written indelibly on his ultimate environment in a manner that was beyond erasure or exorcism. His eyes were scorched by what he had seen and the vision seared in his soul. The depth of this adolescent tragedy means he will now struggle for a lifetime to understand, find meaning for, and give witness to these events. The one word that summarizes his adolescent landscape is for Eliezer a double *entendre*—tyranny.

# Chapter 5

# The Curse and the Crisis

After arrival at Birkenau and separation from his mother and sisters, Eliezer grew ever closer to his father. His immediate goal was to stay near him and to help him stay alive. The two of them seemed to know that their worlds had been reduced to each other. Now they were dependent upon each other as never before. In Sighet, Shlomo had kept busy working in the store and in the community, and Eliezer had little time to waste as a student of Jewish scriptures and traditions. But that changed in the camps. Now father and son comprised the family unit. They were each other's sole support. For almost eight months, the two avoided selection, surviving beatings and severe cold. They endured so much together that the emotional bonds they shared as father and son seemed to deepen. When Shlomo became ill and eventually died on 28 January 1945, it seemed to be more than Eliezer could take. The death of his father brought Eliezer to the point of despair. The brutal and inhumane treatment of his sick father, combined with his own inability to alter the situation in any way, stayed with him as a type of existential curse. That is, this death was etched so indelibly in his adolescent consciousness that it has continued to haunt him for a lifetime. Wiesel puts the issue bluntly: "When my father died, I died." And he remembers that "His last word was my name. A summons to which I did not respond."[141]

## The Curse and a Childhood Conflict

On the night his father died, Eliezer heard his father call his name. He attempted to go to him. But other inmates who surrounded his father were torturing the dying man because he no longer had the strength to take himself to the bathroom. The torturers prevented Eliezer from coming to the aid of his father. They beat the son, and he, too, came close to losing consciousness. Describing this scene in his memoir, Wiesel writes, "Powerless, crushed by remorse, I knew that however long I lived, I would never be able to free myself of that guilt: My father was twisting with pain, dying, and I was near him, but helpless."[142]

Eliezer experienced the death of his father in a manner similar to the way that Gandhi remembered his father's death. Gandhi, like Eliezer, had been caring for his ailing father. Even though his father was ill and apparently near death, Gandhi left his care to his father's favorite brother. Then Gandhi went to bed to sleep with his wife. After a time, someone came to Gandhi's room to get him. He got to his father only to learn that his father had died in the arms of his uncle. Gandhi later wrote that the fact that his father died in his uncle's arms—and not his—became "a blot which I have never been able to efface or to forget." When he writes about his father's death, Wiesel's words are similar: "I would never be able to free myself of that guilt."[143]

What does the "curse" mean in the life of an individual like Wiesel? It means that Wiesel carries some form of "existential debt." But the death of his father is not likely the cause of the debt. This particular episode is more likely the "cover memory," or the projection of an earlier childhood conflict onto this dramatic scene. In essence, one could say this memory is in some way tied to that earlier struggle, the Oedipus conflict. But this crisis may also be better understood as the "generational complex," that human beings experience the ultimate conflicts of life as the issues of life and death, past and future, the change of the generations. Thus, it may be that as a young man, Eliezer experienced such remorse and guilt because early in life he had already begun to sense some aspect of "originality" that in childhood seemed to him to point beyond competition with the father. Thus, Eliezer's precocious conscience and single-mindedness helped him to appear older even while young. When his parents looked to him with such expectation, Eliezer could grow with something of an obligation to fulfill parental hopes and dreams—the dream of his mother, as declared by the rabbi, that he would be a great man in Israel. Thus Eliezer's precocious conscience belied his already long-term struggle to deal with his own felt guilt of—early in life—having gone beyond his father in some way. Consequently, this dramatic scene became the repository for the burden of memories and expectation that in actuality go to childhood days. These memories and previous burdens only made the contemporary scene more traumatic and filled with guilt. His only solution, therefore, was to find a way to fulfill the original expectation. In order to do so, Eliezer, like other adolescents in similar circumstances, had a prolonged identity crisis while he searched for the moment that "he (and he alone!) can re-enact the past and create a new future in the right medium at the right moment on a sufficiently large scale." But there are other factors in Eliezer's moral and spiritual journey. What are they, and what do they have to do with Wiesel the man?[144]

## The Call to Protesting Faith and
### the Vow to Be a Witness

Eliezer spent the ten weeks following his father's death in Buchenwald in a dazed state of lethargy. A couple of friends from Sighet were there with him—Irwin Forkash and Anshi Meisner. He played chess with some of the inmates and went to Passover services held in the barracks. But Eliezer was essentially sleepwalking, living without consciousness or awareness. Toward the end, with the American army moving toward Buchenwald, the Germans made plans to kill all the prisoners. But each day the convoys filled up before Eliezer was taken. He was scheduled to leave on 11 April. That day, while the SS were driving the last group to the gate, the resistance forces attacked and the SS fled. The Americans came a few hours later. The first thing Eliezer did was to join with other Jews to form a minyan in order to say *Kaddish*. This service became, at one and the same time, a glorification of God's name and a challenge to God's ways in the universe. Then Eliezer began to eat, which he had not done in almost a week. The American soldiers shared their food with the former inmates. Eliezer was given ham. He put it to his lips, but his body rebelled. He became sick with food poisoning. For two weeks, Eliezer was in serious condition. Some of the doctors thought he would not recover. In fact, 5,000 of the 20,000 former inmates died of food poisoning.[145]

After about two weeks, Eliezer mustered his strength and pulled himself to a mirror. He did not recognize his own face. This was the first time he had looked into a mirror since leaving Sighet. As he looked at his reflection, he realized that, having survived, he had an obligation to tell what had taken place. The person he saw in the mirror was nameless, without distinctive features, face, or age; he was a person belonging to a different world, the place of the dead. A skeletal figure looked back at him. What he saw, in reality, was an image of himself after his own death. At that moment, a protest took shape inside of him, and he felt the will to live again. He shattered that mirror with his fist, but its image was seared in his consciousness. After breaking the glass, he fainted. Eliezer was in the hospital for several more days. But after that moment of consciousness in front of the mirror, his condition began to improve. During the rest of his hospital stay, he wrote the outline for an autobiographical story of testimony.[146]

The moment of consciousness in front of the mirror was an important time for Wiesel. His experience in the camps had left him psychically numb, something like a walking corpse. He had lived with the reality of death so vivid and near that his life now mirrored an imprint of death. After the war, Wiesel said, " I absorbed not only the suffering, which was not mine alone—suffering everywhere in the camps...." With that absorption of suffering around him came, ironically, a sense of responsibility for it. Eliezer lived with a powerful sense of death guilt, an undeserved residue of the camps, paradoxical in nature, yet demonstrated most clearly in relation to his father. Having cared tenderly for his father during the months in the camps, Eliezer had feelings of both shame and guilt for his own reaction to his father's death. But the key to Eliezer's survivor experience is that he had to find a way to, as he says, "do something with my memory of my death." The story of the mirror, then, implies Eliezer's beginning point of attempting to do something with the story of his death, not for himself, but as a larger vocation. This point in Eliezer's life was the beginning of his struggle for meaning in a post-Holocaust world, the beginning of his survivor mission, and his call to vocation in life. Eliezer tells us that after shattering the mirror, he began to get better.[147]

In actuality, Eliezer had sensed a "call" in some level of his being long before the incident with the mirror. What happened with the mirror and the solemn vows its image inspired is that the earlier call became wedded to new and more concrete specificity. Now Eliezer was no longer just a shy and timid though fervent yeshiva student and follower of God. He was now also a survivor. This experience must be a part of his synthesis of experiences and relationships. Therefore, as he assimilated the suffering of those around him, Wiesel also "absorbed, unwittingly perhaps unconsciously, the obsession to tell the tale, to bear witness that every single person shared and nourished and had to put forward." He knew, Wiesel says, that those who survived had to speak—had to tell the story and become a messenger. But he was afraid to take up this task immediately—afraid of not being up to the task, of saying the wrong things in perhaps the wrong way. So in 1945, Wiesel took a vow to wait ten years. Yet, that moment of consciousness in front of the mirror—the shattering of the glass—marked the moment when Wiesel decided to become a messenger, a teller of tales. What remained in his mind was the struggle of how to testify.[148]

The story of the mirror shattering clearly articulates three major themes of survivor experience: the death imprint, survivor guilt, and survivor mission. Wiesel's call to the vocation of writing can be seen, then, in relation to the profound need to reestablish some semblance of a moral universe through writing and testimony, but one also sees an adolescent integrating new and profoundly traumatic experiences into his young life. The totalism and fervor with which he had believed before Auschwitz and Buchenwald seem to presage a tumultuous crisis that awaits a bright, sensitive, and extremely zealous follower of God.

## A French Moratorium and the Rededication to Religious Fervor

The American army took control of Buchenwald. The American authorities urged the former inmates to decide what they wanted to do. Did they want to return to their homes? If not, was there some other place they would like to go? Initially, Wiesel and other Jews who did not want to go back to Eastern Europe decided to ask to go to Palestine, but because of British restrictions, that was not possible. A compromise: Belgium offered to take them. Soon came the word, however, that General Charles de Gaulle had invited them to France under the auspices of *Oeuvres du Secpirs*

*Aux Enfants*, a children's aid organization. It was a trip of two to three days. The train stopped at stations along the way, where people waited to greet them and offer them food. The group contained 400 orphans. They stayed briefly at a chateau called Ecouis in Normandy.[149]

At Ecouis, these young people who had encountered absolute evil attempted to reenter "normal" life. Wiesel, now sixteen years old, began a private journal and rededicated himself to his religious quest. In the company of a group of other young orphans, he soon recovered his adolescent fervor. Wiesel asked for the holy books—the Bible, prayer books, some tractates from the Talmud. They set aside a room for study and prayer, where morning and evening services were held. Wiesel was, by chance, reunited with his oldest sister, Hilda, who was now living in Paris. She had seen a picture of her brother in a newspaper and had called Ecouis.[150]

After a short time at Ecouis, the group was divided. The religious or observant Jews, Wiesel's group, were taken to Vaucelles and the Chateau d'Ambloy. At Ambloy, there were study groups, religious services, sporting clubs, and recreation events. The campfires at night and the vacation spirit reminded Wiesel of the mountain trips he took as a child in Borsha. Still so devoted to religious practice, Wiesel feared that his physical attraction to one of his counselors, Niny, might lead him into sin. During the services for the High Holy Days in 1946, Wiesel prayed the solemn prayers of Yom Kippur with more fervor and concentration than ever before. He imagined that his father and grandfather stood beside him. He wept and prayed for them.[151]

Then the group was moved to Taverny, one of the suburbs of Paris. The young people were encouraged to decide what they were going to do with their lives and where they would go. There were various options: America, Canada, Colombia, Australia.

Wiesel and a friend by the name of Kalman decided to stay in France, but Wiesel needed to learn a new language.[152]

In 1947, Wiesel received private lessons from a young teacher, Francois Wahl. Wahl taught Wiesel to explicate texts, to appreciate the poetry of Racine and the philosophy of Pascal. This was also the year that Wiesel began to study with a Talmudic scholar named Mordechai Shushani. Born with the name Mordechai Rosenbaum, Shushani was gifted with virtual total recall and could quote the Talmud from memory. During his childhood days in Lithuania, his father would take him to distant cities where people would pay to hear him recite. Shushani met Wiesel at a crucial time and managed to have a profound influence upon him. Wiesel later said that it was he, more than any other teacher, who was responsible for making him into the man he became. Shushani left his imprint on Wiesel's thought, language, and feelings.[153]

Wiesel was returning by train to Taverny from a session with Francois. While he was reading the book of Job, someone spoke to him in Yiddish. It was Shushani, a type of wandering Jewish teacher who was part genius and part "madman." They had met once before in a synagogue in Paris. But on this day, Shushani singled Wiesel out and began a teacher/student relationship with him. He asked Wiesel what he was doing with the book of Job. Wiesel made the mistake of telling him that he was going to give a lecture on the book. At that point, Shushani began to interrogate Wiesel about his knowledge of Job. The teacher's intention was to show the pupil that he knew nothing about Job, that he could not even translate the first verse properly. Shushani got off the train with Wiesel at Taverny and went with him to the lecture he was going to give on Job. He spoke in Wiesel's place and mesmerized the group. Thereafter, he met with Wiesel on a regular basis for a period of two or three years.[154]

Shushani had traveled the world and had taught important people who paid him large fees. One of his students was the well-known Jewish philosopher Emmanuel Levinas. What Shushani had done with the money no one seemed to know. He did not have the appearance of an intellectual. Wearing a small hat on his large, round head, he looked more like a vagabond or a clown. His glasses were thick and usually dirty as were his clothes. But he knew thirty languages and could quote the Zohar, the Vedas, or the Talmud from memory. Wiesel was attracted to him because of Shushani's immense intellectual power and the fund of knowledge that was readily apparent.[155]

Shushani's methods and mannerisms were as unorthodox as his appearance. After the first encounter with Wiesel, he forced the young man to admit that he knew little and that he really did want to learn. As Wiesel remembers that experience, he writes that Shushani "liked to demolish before rebuilding, to abase before offering recompense." His detractors described him as a Faust-like figure, one who had sold his soul to the devil in exchange for his great knowledge. Some of Wiesel's friends warned that this teacher wanted to shake their faith.[156]

Indeed, Shushani was an iconoclastic figure who used his skills to attack prevailing truths. To that end, he disturbed the traditional. But apparently, he saw himself in the role of "agitator" and "troublemaker." Perhaps he knew instinctively that the path to holiness is lined with questions. In terms of method, this pursuit of questions may be his most profound influence on Wiesel.[157]

The group did not stay long in Taverny. Soon they were moved to Versailles to a new home called "Our Place." In addition to studying the Talmud and French, Wiesel organized a choir. It was there that he got to know Hanna, his first love. As an eighteen-year-old in 1947, Wiesel did not know where to live his life, let alone what to do with that life. In reality, he lived in two worlds: the world of observant Judaism—eating kosher, saying prayers, and studying with Shushani; and in his dreams, a sexual life with Hanna. But under the influence of his two teachers, he threw himself into serious study. He read everything he could get his hands on. Philosophy caught his attention. And he read Hegel, Spinoza, *Das Kapital* by Marx, and Kant's *The Critique of Pure Reason* in Yiddish.[158] Shushani led Wiesel into a study that had long fascinated him: asceticism. Was this a necessary aspect of the religious pilgrimage? Why was such a person portrayed as a sinner in the Bible? What was the relationship between suffering, truth, and redemption? Why was it necessary to bring a sacrifice to the temple? Wiesel took many notes from his conversation with Shushani. He thought that perhaps this topic could lead to a book. Secretly, two things weighed upon his heart: the responsibility he felt to tell the story, and the issue of faith. Wiesel resolved the issue of testimony by taking the vow to wait ten years. Yet, it still weighed heavily upon him. The matter of his faith would eventually confront him.[159]

In summer 1947, the OSE held a camp in Montintin. Wiesel was invited to be a counselor. Hanna would be there, so he decided to go too. In the early mornings, he studied asceticism. Then he gave classes on Bible and Midrash. There were campfires and group discussions at night. At the end of the summer, Wiesel moved to a room in the Porte de Saint-Cloud. He was on his own, but he did not know what to do. With the help of his French teacher, Francois, Wiesel enrolled at the Sorbonne. He took classes on Plato and Freud and wandered through the bookstores. Though he subsisted on a meager subsidy of eight dollars from the OSE, Wiesel had good times as a student in Paris. Francois took him into the Latin Quarter to hear Sartre and Buber. Buber was regarded as a prophetic figure there. His audiences were always large and ready to listen. The problem was that he spoke in French, and his accent was difficult to understand.[160]

On the surface of his life, Wiesel was more concerned with material matters. How could he pay his hotel bill? When he did not have the money, he would sometimes spend the night walking along the Seine rather than going back to his room. He was somewhat afraid of his young and sexually attractive landlady. Pious and filled with taboos, he was afraid that she wanted to seduce him. But other terrifying subterranean issues raged in his soul. The conflicts within his spirit would come to the surface in fall 1947.[161]

## The Unmaking of the World:
## The Loss of Traditional Faith

While living alone in the small room, Wiesel eventually began to confront the issues at war deep inside himself. His life was sterile, filled with apprehension and remorse. The death immersion he had experienced in the camps now confronted him in manifold ways. This was the first time that the possibility of suicide entered Wiesel's mind. When he looked into the mirror, he asked himself if the time had come to end the torture. If death did not come through starvation, should he throw himself in front of a train or into the Seine? Though he was given a brief reprieve from his feelings of despondency, his body became seriously ill. He suffered intensely with frequent vomiting and migraine headaches. One day his French teacher, Francois, came by and found him. His mother was a doctor. He called her and she sent medicine. Then Francois helped Wiesel pull himself out of his desperate situation.[162]

The torment of Wiesel's inner life seemed now to be expressed in his body. The serious pain and torment reflected the confrontation in his soul and the realization that the world he lived in before was now gone forever. Wiesel's abiding concern with asceticism seemed to mean, as Elaine Scarry put it, that there was in his soul a need for a "world ridding, path-clearing logic." That is, asceticism is "a way of so emphasizing the body that the contents of the world are cancelled and the path is clear for the entry of an unworldly, contentless force." The intense pain of Wiesel's body reflected the torture of his soul and the destruction of himself and his world. Wiesel experienced the destruction of that former world of faith as the contracting of the universe to the pain-ridden body. The pain Wiesel felt during the time of suicidal thoughts reflects a human being in the process of being split into two persons—the man in ever-present, continued pain and the man's former self and world. Such intense pain also destroys language and faith. Robert Lifton's study of the survivors of atrocity indicates that with the death immersion comes a "symbolic gap" because there is no adequate way to represent the horror. One begins to live with a void at the center of existence.[163]

It is likely that Shushani's confrontational style—questioning everything—led Wiesel subconsciously to penetrate the psychic numbing that had taken place in the death camps. Perhaps, for the first time, he was confronting the reality of his religious life in a post-Holocaust world. His extreme pain brought the loss of his religious world, his traditional selfhood, and his voice.[164]

In his study of the survivor experience, Robert J. Lifton found that the "death imprint" was the basis for all other themes in the life of the individual. Thus, when Elie Wiesel later wrote about his death camp experience—that "In every stiffened corpse I saw myself"—he was giving expression to the way he had internalized the experience of death and the horrific assault perpetrated by the Nazis. With the imprint of death came a heightened sense of vulnerability that affected his understanding of the world around him. This contributed to the loss of faith. With this indelible set of images came a "death spell" and a prolonged sense of grief—deep sorrow for a lifetime: for a former world, family members, his own self, lost symbols such as beliefs now shattered, and for objects like his home.[165]

As Wiesel later writes in *Night*, Moshe the Beadle escaped from the Nazis to come back to Sighet to tell the story of his own death, and in so doing, indicated that he was no longer free. Having experienced death with the group—even though he escaped—he was now "bound to the dead" and to the telling of that story. Wiesel also felt this obligation to the dead, in part because of survivor guilt; no one can go through survival without assuming a severe form of guilt. Here, one is reminded of the narrative, already rehearsed, of Eliezer's witnessing his own father's death. Just before the death, however, Wiesel was temporarily separated from his father. He writes, "I felt ashamed of myself, ashamed forever."[166] One result of Wiesel's crisis in 1947 was that he turned his rage and anger inward. The survivor cannot help but do so—internalize the very world where he has been victimized.[167]

Wiesel's crisis was made worse because of the vulnerability of his early years. He was living in the fragile realm of the adolescent, that crucial period when a young man begins the first tentative steps to consolidate the images of life presented to him by his family and his peers. But Wiesel was devastated by the loss of his family. As Lifton writes, "Death, especially when inappropriate and premature, is the essence of breakdown and separation."[168] Wiesel wanted to share a world with his parents and his friends, but they were taken from him prematurely. Now, he had the double burden of survival guilt and the meeting of parental expectation with the parents gone, given as a cruel responsibility to a teenager with an already precocious and overactive conscience. He would, therefore, in due course seek to find a way to "atone" for his felt "guilt" and to fulfill the expectation that, in some manner, must have also multiplied with the deaths of his parents.[169] But, as Wiesel tells us, his crisis would be a prolonged struggle.

In summary, Wiesel's adolescent years ended with him in severe crisis. In happier times, those teenage years had revealed a zealous and totalizing form of faith, the center of which was a covenant sealed with God—a covenant that in its adolescent conception was more pervasive than any other image or morality. Eliezer believed profoundly. That extreme commitment continued after the war as Wiesel entered into a moratorium. But Wiesel's memories haunted him. The memory of his father's death pursued him like a curse. Perhaps, however, that haunting memory carried a more distant remembrance of how he had been called beyond that same father to take his own rightful place as a leader in Israel. Even so, that distant remembrance only added to the pain and the guilt. The deaths of his parents merged with an earlier call to instill a greater burden of responsibility and obligation. These dynamics were submerged under the weight of survival. The earlier call was given specificity in the vocational commitment to bear witness. Despite a reprieve in his time of a French moratorium, Wiesel eventually entered a severe crisis that led in due course to the emergence of a more individual and reflective form of faith.

# Chapter 6

# Wrestling Like Jacob:
# The Crying Out Years

*Religion is the transition from God the Void to God the*
*Enemy to God the Friend.*
—Alfred North Whitehead

In a reflective moment, Michael, the protagonist of Wiesel's novel *The Town Beyond the Wall*, thinks of his adolescent years and hears his Kabalistic master, Kalman, say to him: "Every man has a prayer that belongs to him, as he has a soul that belongs to him. And just as it is difficult for man to find his soul, so it is difficult to find his prayer." Kalman goes on to say that "Most people live with souls, and say prayers, that are not their own." Michael wonders about his soul. Is it his own? Michael hears Kalman say, "Question it...."[170] This is a story about a master calling a young disciple to the deeper realms of the human pilgrimage of faith. Mordechai Shushani was, like Kalman, a master who sought to lead Wiesel toward a deeper understanding of faith. In doing so, he, like Kalman, told his pupil that one must begin to question everything. But for a while, Wiesel lived with Shushani's questions and with a soul and prayers that were not his own.

Though the teacher has a role in the development of the disciple's faith, so do the exigencies of one's personal history. In Wiesel's case, it appears that the pain and anguish of his own continuing crisis along with the questions of Shushani pushed him deeper into himself, where he was forced to search for a reason to live and a re-created world in which to abide. Eventually, Wiesel moved into a demythologizing realm, where he searched for a faith that could stand the tests of his ceaseless questions. Those questions were renewed with earnest that summer in Jerusalem in 1949, when he forgot to put on the tefellin. In that summer of his twenty-first year, he would say a genuine prayer of protest for the first time.[171]

Slowly a new era began to unfold for Wiesel, and he joined a tradition of the faithful who agreed that the path to holiness was lined with questions. From Abraham to Habakkuk and Jeremiah, to Levi Yitshak of Berdichev, there was a venerable tradition of Jewish fervor cast in persistent questions and reflection. As a part of his own journey, Wiesel searched for his own appropriate questions and prayers and for a soul that he could call his own. He eventually developed a strong sense of his selfhood by first reaching what Maurice Friedman calls "a bedrock image of the human."[172] And Wiesel would go on to develop his own ideology, his own worldview to replace that of a traditional world.[173] But this seems to be, for Wiesel, a gradual transition over a period of years from fall 1947 to summer 1949.

When a group of scholars met in spring 1979 to review the life and work of Elie Wiesel, they seemed to agree that his early years as a writer reflect a "crying out against the world...." But his later years indicate a "shift of emphasis...to trying to save that same poor world."[174] This metaphor of "crying out" characterizes the lonely, despairing, and strident years that Wiesel spent from the late 1940s until the mid-1960s. During those years, he was "tormented," as he put it, by the God of his childhood.[175]

In brief, he was wrestling, like Jacob before him, with the angelic forces and the powers of the Divine. He was deeply troubled by issues of theodicy—how to understand the nature and justice of God in light of the overwhelming power of evil that he had seen first hand and that continued to haunt him daily. As he became a reflective and deeply thoughtful person of faith, he tried for a time to find a new life in another culture—Israel and later India. But the problems followed him. In Israel, he was "disillusioned" that Jews of the Diaspora, especially the victims of the Holocaust, were "treated like outcasts, victims to be pitied at best."[176] In India, the problem of evil and suffering met him in the lives of the poor and downtrodden.

In the early years after the war, Wiesel not only continued to study asceticism but to practice his own unique form. During this period, his faith came to be ceaselessly demythologizing and iconoclastic. He continued to encounter the "lure" of suicide. For the time being, two things seemed to save Wiesel from suicide: his friendship with Francois, who brought medical care and companionship at a dark hour, and his emerging vocation as a writer. But the lure of the "death instinct" would return.

## Becoming a Journalist: An Emerging Vocation

On 29 November 1947, Wiesel heard the news of one of the most dramatic events of his life. The United Nations passed a resolution that granted Israel the right to exist, the right for the Jewish people to establish a homeland. The land of Palestine would be partitioned. This event spurred Wiesel into action. He had regretted the fact that he had not participated in the war against the British. Now he must participate in the emerging life of Israel. Wiesel went quickly to the Jewish agency in Paris. He told the doorman he wanted to join the Haganah—an Israeli underground force. The doorman laughed and quickly slammed the door on the foolish nineteen-year-old. What could he do? Wiesel found a Zionist newspaper, the *Zion im Kamf*, with the local printer's address. He sat down and wrote to the editor of the paper and volunteered to help. In a few days, he got an invitation to come talk to the editor. So began his journalistic career.[177]

For a nineteen-year-old finding his way, such success brought some happiness and more money. Now Wiesel would have a salary of sixty dollars a month. This meant he could move to a better hotel closer to the center of Paris, and that he would have a sink in his room. Though this success brought a level of pleasure, it also brought more questions and a sense of guilt. Was he now turning his back on his studies, on religious observance, and, most of all, the dead? No! He did not neglect any of those things. He continued to study, to attend services, and to reflect on his status as a survivor.[178]

While Wiesel was young and enthusiastic, he was also politically naive. He dreamed about becoming an important foreign correspondent and traveling to distant places like Africa. He read the editorials of Camus and Mauriac. He looked for a cause to which he could commit himself. His emerging maturity is seen in his attempt to balance the roles of student and budding journalist. During his first days at the paper, Wiesel worked as a translator and did various errands. Later, he began to write. His first story appeared under the byline of Ben Shlomo. It was a contemporary story of two brothers in the new state of Israel who were on different sides in the struggle, mirroring the Cain and Abel conflict in that one killed the other.[179]

Wiesel's economic success was short-lived. In January 1949, the newspaper shut down, and once again Wiesel had no money. His situation was again precarious. He was able to pick up a few translating jobs. By spring, Wiesel was thinking of going to Israel for the summer. How could he do it? He had a small savings—a few thousand francs. He decided to join a group of immigrants and attempt to do write freelance articles once he got to Israel. The ship was named the *Negba*. There was little room on the deck or anywhere else to find privacy. As Wiesel crossed the

Mediterraean that summer, once again a profound sadness came over him, bringing back the urge for suicide. The "lure of death" was stronger now than before. "A sadness as deep as the ocean enveloped me," Wiesel wrote, "so oppressive that I found it hard to breathe, so powerful that I had a sudden urge to end my life, to throw myself overboard and be swallowed up and carried off by the waves."[180] At that moment, a stranger came and began a conversation with Wiesel. He talked for a while about history and religion. When he left, an attractive young girl caught Wiesel's eye. He could not speak to her because of his shyness, but he stood there with her a long time. Then, in the distance, Mount Carmel loomed.[181]

Wiesel's first trip to Israel was "like reliving...childhood dreams." He tried to record all he saw in order to write about it. He loved Galilee. In fact, he felt that he could live there with its breathtaking lake setting in Tiberias or its city of mystics, Safed. Then there was Jerusalem, the most beautiful city. Why not live there? Or perhaps the Negev, with its unique desert setting about which the poets wrote?[182]

Wiesel stayed with friends for a while. For a few weeks, he worked as a proofreader and errand boy. Then he was offered a job as a counselor in a children's home. He spent a few weeks there with adolescents from Romania and Bulgaria. This experience was not unlike his first months in France: study groups during the day and evenings of music and discussion around campfires. An idea came to him. Could he work as a foreign correspondent in France for an Israeli paper? He went to see Herzl Rosenblum at *Yedioth Ahronoth*. Rosenblum had been one of the signatories of Israel's Declaration of Independence. Wiesel got the job, but he would have to work as a freelance writer. The paper had no money for a salary.[183]

Wiesel also faced disappointment and disillusionment in Israel. He learned from recent immigrants that in Israel survivors of the camps were considered second-class citizens, outcasts, or victims who were to be pitied. As such they represented Diaspora Judaism or the dispersion of the Jews from the land of Israel across the centuries, which in the minds of some Israelis had perverted Judaism. The end result, the Israelis thought, was Auschwitz. This prevailing sentiment in Israel demoralized Wiesel, the young survivor. A mood of depression swept over him. He felt himself turning inward more and more. As a spirit of solitude weighed upon him, he yearned for the atmosphere of Paris. In winter 1949, Wiesel decided to return to France.[184]

## Looking for Myself: The Struggle for Reflective Faith

When Wiesel arrived back in Paris on that grey January day in 1950, he had fewer illusions than before. He had been hurt by the popular Israeli stereotypes about survivors of the camps. He was now somewhat less naive and learning to question everything as Shushani had taught him. Wiesel moved back into the Hotel de France. Though he had now lost contact with his two former teachers, he made a vow not to give up on his studies. Stimulated by the intellectual milieu of Paris, Wiesel poured himself into study, reading the works of Camus, Sartre, and Malraux. He introduced himself to the works of Faulkner, Cervantes, Miguel de Unamuno, and Kafka. He noted the major questions posed by these significant literary figures and compared them to the ones with which he wrestled. Can one pursue holiness outside the realm of religion? Is there such a thing as a "secular priesthood"? Where does human responsibility end? What is God's responsibility, and where does it begin? Is life absurd if God is not a part of it?[185]

Wiesel had entered a new era in his life that one could describe as a time of deeply reflective, but perhaps tormented faith.[186] His childhood faith was guaranteed by exemplars who were so beloved, and the conventional faith of his adolescence was so totalistic under a genuine "tyranny of the they," that the years in which he went about claiming his own faith after the war seem also necessarily totalistic. Erikson describes "totalism" as "a to be or not to be which makes every question mark a matter of forfeited existence; every error or oversight, eternal treason. All of this amounts to something like Jacob's struggle with the angel, a wrestling for a benediction...."[187] Wiesel's life after the war begins to demonstrate this totalizing, "either or" perspective.

In contrast to the views of his childhood where God was thought to be present in every aspect of life, he wondered about the divine presence and the divine-human relationship. In fact, he concluded that both God and humanity were against the Jewish people and that some Israelis looked down on survivors with scorn. Wiesel was deeply angry with the Germans and their accomplices in Hungary, Poland, France, Holland, and the Ukraine. How could the Germans claim Goethe and Bach and develop racist, anti-Semitic ideas? Wiesel was angry with Pope Pius XII and with the leaders of the allied countries for their complicity in silence and for their failure to act on behalf of the Jewish people, but Wiesel was also angry with the God of Abraham for abandoning the children of Israel.[188]

As Wiesel read in the libraries of Paris, he found virtually no literature on the death camps. He began to consider how he might tell the story. He also began to travel widely. In 1950, he went back to Israel to see the owner of his paper, Yehuda Mozes. Back in Paris, he met an official from the Jewish agency who invited him to drive to Morocco with him. They drove south across the border into Spain. After visiting several cities in Spain, they drove to the southern coast, took a boat to Tangier, and then on to Casablanca.[189]

The paper sent him to Germany. He went to Bonn and then to Dachau, where he was troubled because Jewish memory seemed to be at risk. The Jewish victim in Wiesel's mind was virtually left out of the memorial to the dead in this death camp—the Jewishness of the victims was barely mentioned. In 1952, he was sent to the Netherlands to cover the first of the negotiations between Israel and West Germany. The paper kept Wiesel busy full-time. He began having violent migraine headaches. Despite his increased work schedule, he was not personally satisfied. He grew disenchanted with life in the West, and decided to go to India to purse his study of asceticism on a comparative basis.[190]

## An Interlude in India: A Spiritual Quest in the East

Wiesel was searching, looking for answers outside the traditions of the West. He was drawn to the East because of the "spiritual force" as well as the intellectual tradition he found there. Wiesel loved the Indian texts—the Upanishads, the Vedas, and the Gitas, so he thought he would love being in India. Could someone like him really find himself there, find a sense of his "bearings" or maybe even "fulfillment"? He wanted to discover the foundation for human civilization. In India he could find religious traditions that seemed to date to the ancient civilizations of Mohenjo-dara and Harappa perhaps 5,000 years ago. Wiesel wanted to meet Indian sages and ascetics. He admired the writings of the Hindu tradition and concluded that there was a connection between Jewish and Hindu mysticism. The question was how to get to India and how to support himself once there. Wiesel wrote ten articles for the paper and did some translation work. Then he bought a lottery ticket and, against all odds, won. After booking passage, he had 200 dollars to put in his pocket. That would not take him far.[191]

Wiesel left for India in January 1952. He traveled by ship and stopped in Suez and Aden. During the crossing, he studied English and read the works of Kipling and Somerset Maugham,

among others. He arrived in Bombay on a wet morning in
January. As a zealous young religious seeker, Wiesel must have
been elated to be in the country regarded as having the world's
oldest living religion—a land where religion is taken seriously and
the giving of alms is a common practice. The Rig Veda makes it
clear that the wealthy have a duty to share with the lowly.[192]
Indeed, early in his travels in India, Wiesel met a rich Parsi.
Wiesel spoke with him about the connections between Indian
and Jewish culture, and the Persian influence on Judaism during
antiquity. For some reason, the Parsi was intrigued with Wiesel.
When he was about to leave, he gave Wiesel a card. He told young
Wiesel that whenever he needed to travel, he should use that
card. Later, Wiesel found out that the Parsi owned the airline,
and he now had free passage to anywhere in India.[193]

As Wiesel traveled, many questions came to him and he
talked with many people. He found asceticism alive and well in
India. Holy men punish their bodies in various ways there to this
day. Wiesel found that some took cold baths in the streams that
began high in the Himalayas while others buried themselves in
sand and put ashes on their uncovered faces and heads. The
conversation on religion might range widely from the origins in
the Indus Valley with the great civilizations at Mohenjo-daro and
Harappa to the traditions of honoring a deadly cobra for his
mystical potency—an idea derived from the Hindu folk traditions
that the hood of the snake, which spreads like an umbrella, has
the potential to shield from harm. Wiesel heard ancient chants
about the one Supreme Being, God above all gods. As a young and
searching religious person, he was intrigued to learn that they call
Brahman by many names but that finally truth is one. Passed
down orally from the original Sanskrit, this was one of the central
ideas in Vedic religion.[194] Wiesel inevitably learned about the
central concept of "samsara"—the Hindu view of karma, death,
and rebirth. He was likely intrigued with the Hindu notion of the

soul—the "atman" that seeks "moksha" or release, which comes only when there is the realization that atman is Brahman, a type of universal or world spirit. Wiesel probably listened with great interest to the stories of *The Bhagavad Gita*, his comparative mind noting that the great battlefield scene at Kurukshetra was a type of Hindu Armageddon. He learned about the conversation between Arjuna and Krishna and entered into debate about the meaning of the Gita. Does the Gita justify war? Is it to be read literally, or can it be read metaphorically? Is there a connection between the Gita and existentialism?[195]

Yet after the thrill of religious discovery and dialogue, Wiesel found that he had great difficulty living day to day in India. He saw the children of India as "God's most wretched orphans." Many had been devoured by leprosy and had missing limbs. They all seemed to have one thing in common: starvation. Wiesel questioned people as he went. "How could a civilized state like India tolerate such misery and agony?" The answers usually spoke about the Indian quest to improve, combined with the Hindu doctrine of the transmigration of the soul. Could the concept of reincarnation be a valid response to human suffering? In Judaism, it is not the next life that dominates thought or hope. Rather, the Jewish perspective emphasizes human action and a quest for justice in this realm.[196]

As he searched for an understanding of the country, the human suffering and misery he encountered greatly affected Wiesel. Tattered and torn individuals slept in the streets at night and were largely neglected by others. There seemed to be an air of indifference toward the suffering poor. He saw homeless people inundated by the monsoons of Bombay, the poor infected by rampant disease in the slums and pollution in Calcutta and the Ganges. He learned about the plight of suffering widows still being burned on the funeral pyres of their husbands in the heartland of India. Finally, he could not accept the caste system with its rigidity and unchanging rules. Though drawn to this land to pursue his own quest, eventually he had to leave because it was too different. But in a land so different, he had learned important things about himself and what he truly thought.[197]

Wiesel saw too much suffering in India. There was, he said, "an immeasurable, unnameable suffering" in that historic place. And he could not tolerate it. Confronted with such suffering, Wiesel once again wrestled with the problem of evil. For him, to walk the streets of India and be forced to step over the plundered poor was to impose a sense of guilt and remorse on himself. The thing he learned was this: "I am free to choose my suffering but not that of my fellow humans." He came to the conclusion that "not to see the hungry before me was to accept their destiny in their place, in their name, for them and even against them—or at least, like them…. Not to cry out against their misery was to make it all the heavier."[198]

Unable to accept all the suffering, he felt compelled to leave. So he went back to Paris, where he was forced to accept some of the "necessary ambiguities" of the West. Likewise, he felt the need to continue to practice an asceticism of his own. Wiesel cut himself off from the city of Paris and its life for weeks at a time. His room began to seem much like a prison cell, barely large enough for himself. The noises of the street were muffled by the time they reached him. Wiesel withdrew into himself, and his horizon grew increasingly smaller. Nothing could interrupt his solitude. He looked at the Seine, but he could not see the sky mirrored in the river. Living only in his books, he sought a more immense and ordered memory.[199]

Faith had been lost! With it went a sense of belonging and orientation. Perhaps, for a time, Wiesel thought he could find a new orientation and a sense of belonging in Israel. But his discovery of the stereotypes and attitudes toward survivors seemed to bring that to an end. Then, when he faced his disillusionment with the West, he looked for the possibility of a new life in India. After the trip there, he knew that was also impossible. Now it seemed that his faith in God, in life, and in human beings was shaken. To use an image from the Kabala, the condition of his soul was like all of Creation. It was off center and in exile. In essence, Wiesel was asking, To what can one cling? On whom can one lean? Wiesel was simultaneously fleeing from himself and seeking himself.[200]

Perhaps Wiesel thought he could find answers to his questions in Hinduism. But, in fact, Wiesel left India "more Jewish than before." He found that he could not escape the reality of the problem of evil. If God is good and all-powerful, how does one explain the existence of human suffering, especially to the extent that Wiesel had witnessed? In fact, Wiesel's dilemma in understanding the nature of evil and suffering only increased after his trip to India. It seems that the suffering of India pushed him further to find some semblance of a solution to the human dilemma in his Jewish world and in his own time. It became clear to Wiesel that the answers would not be traditional answers in either Judaism or Hinduism. He needed a new language and new forms of religious expression. He began to find that language and those forms in 1954 when he first started writing the Yiddish version of his autobiographical testimony of the death camps. This process of writing also became the landmark of a new era of faith—the creation of a new symbolic universe realized in his own voice and reflected in the creation of an ideology that marked the beginning of life in a post-Holocaust world.

The year 1954 was a crucial turning point for Wiesel both personally and professionally. Personally, Wiesel was trying to imagine himself with Hanna. She had proposed. What would they be like as a couple? Did he really love her? Two days before he left for a six-week trip to Brazil, she had asked him to marry her. Wiesel asked that the two of them take some time to think about marriage. When he returned to Paris, he was prepared to tell Hanna that he was ready to wed. But she was not waiting when he returned. She did not receive the letters he mailed from South America and left for Israel ten days before he got back.[201]

Professionally, this year—1954—was the last in his ten-year self-imposed silence. Wiesel was trying to imagine a way to give his testimony. During the trip to Brazil, he was busy writing his account of life in the camps. The account would eventually span 800 pages. During the Atlantic crossing, Wiesel worked frantically in his cabin and slept little. He wrote, as he said, "to testify, to stop the dead from dying, to justify my own survival."[202]

## Reconstructing a Symbolic Universe: Writing and the Creation of Reflective Faith

Wiesel's trip to India failed as an attempt to find an alternative faith. Seemingly, the renewed confrontation with the problem of evil within Judaism pushed him even further into his consciousness where he was forced to face the gap within his symbolic universe. Wiesel now knew that his encounter with death and evil in the camps came with such destructive force that he could no longer look at life the way he did before. Everything had changed. His world had changed. Language died in Auschwitz. Words that once symbolized certain forms of meaning were no longer adequate to express the horror of what he saw and internalized.[203] There was a gap in the traditional approach to religion that could not be bridged.[204] The only way to live in the world now was to search for a new way to symbolize the universe—to reconstruct the world through words and create a new symbolic universe.

Telling the tale became for Wiesel the task of giving shape to the void that now existed in his world. By telling the story, he gave shape and inner form to what he had experienced and gave meaning to his own life.[205] Consequently, once Wiesel had begun to write his story—and thereby to reconstruct the world—the lure of suicide went away and never returned. How does writing bring on such a change in an individual? What happened when Wiesel began to write? As Walter Ong puts it, "writing restructures consciousness."[206]

Through the power of language and imagination, writing reshapes the void within the human to create an "increasingly articulate introspectivity." That is, writing is able to create an introspective nature because writing as a human project is an "artificial" creation that allows the knower to become separate from the known. As discourse, detached from the author, writing opens the psyche for possible investigation of the interior self. Put another way, writing brings some distancing from the aspect of the self that in time allows for the evolution of consciousness.[207] Thus, when Wiesel began to write, he started the process of transformation that was the beginning of his spiritual pilgrimage after the Holocaust. For it was in the writing process that he found the necessary space from which to envision alternative destinies, and from which he could begin to remake the world.

When Wiesel began to write, he did so within a distinctively Jewish view of writing. "Our problem," he writes, "was and remains what to do with our words, with our tears. Because we did not know how to say certain things, we went back to our sources, to the past. That was the only link we had."[208] Language is now in exile—words no longer mean what they say.[209] When Wiesel talks about going back to the sources, he refers to the Jewish literary tradition of incorporating legends, persons, and events from an earlier historical period as "paradigmatic points of reference" both to measure and understand contemporary catastrophes.[210] Consequently, Wiesel writes, "We go back to our sources, hoping to find some links." And in looking back he found that Jeremiah "is the one who lived the catastrophe before, during, and after and knew how to speak about it."[211] So Jeremiah—the "pride" of Jewish literature—became Wiesel's code, his paradigmatic resource for dealing with the contemporary catastrophe.[212] Thus, when Wiesel began to remake the world, he did so with the language and literary logic of Jeremiah. The language is iconoclastic, and he sought to demythologize the myths and traditions that, from his perspective of Holocaust experience, no longer hold true. He was, therefore, in his early years a "messenger of the dead." Those first writings seek to let the "ghosts" speak.[213] As they do, their messages are, in the early tradition of Jeremiah, "shattering."

Wiesel's faith in his early twenties was restless and tormented. He sought a new worldview in India, but his sensitive spirit and precocious sense of guilt would not allow him to rest there either. He came home more Jewish than before, realizing that there were some things he must accept. When Wiesel began to investigate his own Jewish tradition for resources that would help him deal with the tragic elements of life, he was drawn to Jeremiah and his iconoclastic and reflective faith.

# II

# Disorientation/Evoking

*The shattering and forming of worlds is...done as a poet "redescribes" the world, reconfigures public perception, and causes people to reexperience their experience.*
—Walter Brueggemann

*Chapter 7*

# Writing Like Jeremiah:
# The Poetics of Memory and Justice

In 1954, Elie Wiesel was in his mid-twenties. His trip to India had been a failure. He had just lost the young woman that he thought could be his partner for life. He had made a vow in the camps to wait ten years to write his testimony. That period was coming to a close. After ten years, he was now a young, brooding, melancholy figure who continued to search his life and inner self for a way to make sense of the world and to make a difference for others. He had come to the sad realization that human history had ended in Auschwitz, but was beginning anew with his generation.[214] He felt a burden to find answers to the tragic issues of his day.

He also felt deeply the need for human companionship. How could he enter a vocation without a partner with whom to share his burdens and dreams? But his prolonged identity crisis and his lifelong integrity crisis had combined to make his relationships with young women tortuous, if not impossible for now.[215] However, Wiesel would soon meet one who would play the role of a mentor and would help him further his vocational goals.

As a reflective young man, Wiesel at this age took on an individualized faith. In order to sustain this independent self, such a young man composes a worldview characterized by critical thought and a willful choosing of his beliefs. This characteristically demythologizing strategy eventually results in the creation of a personal ideology.[216] For Wiesel, the demythologizing strategy within this ideology was a major theme in his autobiographical witness to the kingdom of night and can be described as extremely iconoclastic and shattering. Indeed, this fundamental element in Wiesel's ideology demonstrated a profound "sacred discontent" and had historic roots within Judaism traceable to the very origins of the Jewish people in and around the deserts of Sinai. [217]

## Meeting a Mentor and Giving
### Testimony to the Holocaust

Although Wiesel had already penned the Yiddish version of his testimony, an event soon took place that allowed for a revision of that original story and prepared the way for the eventual introduction of the Holocaust into Western culture in a new way. In 1954, there was renewed interest in foreign news in Israel. Mendes-France, a French Jewish politician, was running for the office of prime minister in France. Wiesel was recalled from Brazil to cover the election. In 1955, as part of an effort to meet and interview Mendes-France, Wiesel spoke to Francois Mauriac, who was "intellectual master" for Mendes-France. Wiesel's interview with Mauriac, a prominent literary figure in post-war France, turned out to be one of the most important events in his career as a writer.[218]

Early in 1955, Wiesel met Mauriac at the Israeli embassy. He asked Mauriac for an interview and, to Wiesel's surprise, was granted one. When the two met, Mauriac, a famous Catholic writer who later won the Nobel Prize for Literature, so impressed Wiesel that he forgot about an interview with Mendes-France. On the day that Wiesel went to Mauriac's home, he was very conscious of being there under false pretenses.[219] Consequently, Wiesel had difficulty looking Mauriac in the eye. He asked foolish and nonsensical questions. In an effort to put the young journalist at ease, Mauriac began a monologue about his thoughts and feelings concerning Israel. From that point, Mauriac launched into a discussion of the greatness of one particular Jew, Jesus. Mauriac's single theme seemed to be that Jesus as son of God was not able to save Israel but went on to save the world. Mauriac's discourse greatly irritated Wiesel. Perhaps he was angered by Mauriac's praise of human suffering against his own memories of the atrocities in the camps, or perhaps it was the memory of his own childhood and the anti-Semitism of Christians. Whatever the reason, Wiesel demonstrated anger and what he later admitted to be bad manners.[220]

When Wiesel attempted to respond to Mauriac, he began by summarizing Mauriac's theology: Christians place the suffering of Christ at the center of conversation. Then Wiesel said, "Well, I want you to know that ten years ago, not very far from here, I knew Jewish children every one of whom suffered a thousand times more, six million times more, than Christ on the cross." Mauriac was stunned and began to turn pale. But Wiesel continued, "And we don't speak about them. Can you understand that, sir? We don't speak about them."[221]

After finishing his brief but pointed speech, Wiesel turned and walked out of the room and headed for the elevator. As he waited, he heard the door open behind him. Mauriac came after him and implored him to come back into the room. Then, Mauriac, with tears running down his face, asked the young journalist to tell him his story. When it came time for Wiesel to leave, Mauriac embraced him and told him that he was wrong not to tell the story. As Mauriac stood at the door, he said to Wiesel, "Listen to the old man that I am: one must speak out—one must *also* speak out." One year later, Wiesel sent him a manuscript copy of the book that was to become *Night*.[222]

What happened to Wiesel during the year between his first meeting with Mauriac and the publication of *La Nuit*? Naomi

Seidman is correct when she writes that the meeting with
Mauriac was of immense consequence for the young Wiesel.
Mauriac became the first in a long line of partners in dialogue.
That conversation with the famous writer came when Wiesel was
a poor, unknown, and struggling writer, and it would remain in the
mind and heart of the budding artist and invite him to ask not
only how he could speak of what he had seen and heard but what
words he could use when language had clearly died in the flames of
Auschwitz. Indeed, how could he speak at all about the
unspeakable? In attempting to speak, would he betray the very
ones for whom he sought to give witness? Yet this meeting with
Mauriac must have intensified his burden to testify—a burden
imposed not only by survival but also by the family expectation
that he would be a great man as proclaimed by his mother when
he was but a child of eight. This generational imposition left
Wiesel with an indelible sense that he must earn his value as a
human being through his work. It must be through some
unfolding project, now only barely visible, that he would justify
himself, his life, and meet the impossible expectations his family
imposed upon him. The challenge from Mauriac was then the
challenge of a lifetime and an opportunity to respond to a
generational calling given to Wiesel from his earliest days.[223]

While he had already written an early Yiddish version
testifying to what he had seen in the death camps, Wiesel must
have known at some level of his being that with the help of
Mauriac—one of the best-known authors in France—he now had
an opportunity to reach a new audience and begin the process of
fulfilling a lifelong obligation. As a part of that obligation, Wiesel
had to discover a way to position himself within the traditions of
the Jewish people and yet find a language to speak in a modern
world about the most unspeakable atrocities. The challenge
represented by Mauriac—speak to the literary world of France
and to Christians like him—implied a response to the Western

world embodied already in Wiesel's mother, who was a fervent Hasid but who also quoted Goethe and Schiller. Yet as literary mentor to Wiesel, Mauriac invited the young man into a world that the novice could only begin to apprehend. The capacity of the young man to respond would in due course reveal both his gifts and the burden of his genius.

A special relationship developed between Mauriac and the young writer. Mauriac came into Wiesel's life at a crucial time and helped him begin to imagine himself as a writer with a sense of mission. Other meetings followed the initial interview. The older man made it clear to the young writer that he believed in him and wanted to encourage and foster his dream. In his later reflection on the debt he owes to Mauriac, Wiesel writes, "I owe him much.... That I should say what I had to say, that my voice be heard, was as important to him as it was to me." Mauriac knew that Wiesel's story would offend him, yet he persisted and urged him to write "in a display of trust that may have been meant to prove that it is sometimes given to men with nothing in common, not even suffering, to transcend themselves." Mauriac became "protector and ally" for the young Jewish man, encouraging him to write the book.[224]

The crucial question was "how." How can one write when language is dead and words are in exile? Wiesel had learned in the *Zohar* that "When Israel is in exile, so is the word." With the cataclysm of the Holocaust, word and meaning had been split apart. The language of the death camps negated all other language. Now, Wiesel says, "All words seemed inadequate, worn, foolish, lifeless, whereas I wanted them to be searing." Where could he discover a " fresh vocabulary, a primeval language"? Put another way, his problem as a survivor of Auschwitz was "how to find a secure place, somewhere between memory and imagination, for all those corpses who...cry out against the injustice of their end, but for whom no act of vengeance or ritual remembrance exists sufficient to bring them to a peaceful place of rest."[225]

Wiesel concluded that in times of the eclipse of God and the death of language, one can only go back to one's sources, in this case the classic biblical texts. From there, Wiesel found that within Judaism there was an age-old tradition of taking significant events from the collective history and turning them into paradigms or points of reference to measure and understand contemporary events. In joining this quest, Wiesel became heir to a continuous tradition that dates back to the destruction of the first temple. For more than 2,500 years, Jewish storytellers have sought to document tragedy after tragedy with an unbroken chain of liturgical poems, commentaries, and folk tales. This lamentation literature worked to preserve communal memory in several ways. The poems and stories provided footnotes in Jewish history to chronicle the past, but they also provided a medium and a language by which the contemporary generation could continue to grapple with biblical views of that past, and to add new interpretations.[226]

Consequently, Wiesel appropriated a series of images and stories with which to construct and tell his story that could not really be told. Wiesel appropriated the central core narrative of Judaism—the story of Moses and the exodus from bondage—as a central theme in his new work. But he saw the Holocaust as an anti-Sinai, so he looked for ways to reverse that core Jewish narrative. He also thought the *Akedah* narrative was an important story of suffering in Judaism that he could effectively use. It too, however, had to be reversed because of what the Holocaust had done to religious tradition.

When Wiesel went back to Jewish history to study sources, he found many eloquent voices, but none more so than Jeremiah ben Hilkiah. In a portrait of Jeremiah, Wiesel wrote that he is "the first—and most eloquent—among Jewish writers of all

times. ...We still use his vocabulary to describe our experiences."
There is much to commend Jeremiah to the survivor. Perhaps
above all, Jeremiah is a link to the Jewish past and the time of the
exile. "I love the prophet Jeremiah," Wiesel says, "because he is
the one who lived the catastrophe before, during, and after and
knew how to speak about it."[227] So his language would be
appropriate for this retelling of human history. But how could
one talk about God and the divine role in this tragic event?
Wiesel had heard Buber speak in Paris. He knew Buber taught
that God cannot be expressed, only addressed. Wiesel also knew
that the lamentation literature within Judaism worked to preserve
communal memory in poems and stories and that this literature
was addressed to God and to others. When compelled by Mauriac
to tell his story to a larger audience, Wiesel appropriated these
themes to produce a small but powerful narrative that in the
minds of some "burst forth as *suis generis*."[228]

## Between Memory and Imagination: Jeremiah
##   as Literary Logic and Groundplan

How does Wiesel tell his story? When Wiesel rewrote his
Yiddish memoir and gave it to Mauriac, that new version was
written using the language and imagery of Jeremiah ben Hilkiah,
the famous prophet of the exile. This literary imagery is found in
the "call" narrative of the prophet, which indicates that his task
is "to pluck up and to break down, to destroy and overthrow, to
build and to plant."[229] This call to "shatter" the old world and to
"form," "evoke," and "enact" a new one is a crucial theme that
appears at important junctures in Jeremiah's work and exists as a
dominant pattern in other parts of the prophetic canon.[230] It is
likely that this literary logic was also mediated to Wiesel by
Shushani in as much as Wiesel confesses that Shushani—more
than any other—helped him become who he is and left an
indelible imprint on his thought, feelings, and language. "It is to

him," Wiesel said of Shushani, that "I owe my constant drive to question, my pursuit of the mystery that lies within knowledge and of the darkness hidden within light."[231] In addition, Wiesel described him as one who "liked to demolish before rebuilding, to abase before offering recompense." The words "demolish" and "rebuild" echo the central logic of Jeremiah: to "destroy" and to "build."[232] Thus Shushani's teaching may have validated Wiesel's reading of Jeremiah and Jewish tradition.

Wiesel gets not only his literary code from Jeremiah but also his mode of autobiographical portrayal.[233] It is what one might call "religious autobiography."[234] In the book that bears his name, the prophet Jeremiah is involved in the process of literary self-construction, which is central to any autobiographical project. But in the biblical book, Jeremiah calls attention to his self-construction only in the end to move away from it or to subordinate the self. Consequently, in the book in which Wiesel finds his literary code, he also finds that autobiography should be a medium for a message rather than a form for the development of a storyline about the self. Therefore, in Jeremiah, the construction of the prophetic self becomes "an indirect route of insight for others."[235] Or put differently, the autobiographical mode in the text "mobilizes the subjective knowledge present in all kinds of readers and directs it to one particular end. However varied this knowledge may be, the reader's subjective contribution is controlled by the given framework."[236]

What does it mean that Jeremiah provides the literary code for Wiesel? In a literary sense, it must be that Wiesel found in Jeremiah the inner literary logic—the language—with which to address the crisis brought on by the Holocaust in as much as words can be found to address this profound confrontation. But more than vocabulary, Wiesel found in Jeremiah an example or model figure, a paradigm by which he could at least begin to make some sense of the broken world. It is possible that the model

Wiesel found in the portrait of Jeremiah is an extension of the formative view of moral transformation and moral character that was emerging in the Jewish community as a response to the disaster of the Babylonian Exile. That is, the book of Jeremiah can be seen as a "thick" response to the broken world, the "cosmic crumbling" of the sixth century BCE. In this narrative, Jeremiah is described as the "ideal" survivor who relentlessly portrays the poignant nature of this "domain of death." It is from this rendering of Jeremiah that the Jewish community first appropriates the new identity of "survivor," a reading in which Jeremiah becomes a paradigm for the community to follow. The book's lack of structure, however, refuses easy answers for the community and forces it to wrestle with the tough questions—to read the abyss of the moment. The lack of structure in the book actually introduces or "performs" the collapse of the world in as much in the text time is fractured and narrative meaning is ruptured. In other words, the book "reads" the abyss that surrounds the community and forces the group to face the disaster through the proclamation of a jumbled narrative. As Kathleen O'Connor writes of the book, "Its mosaic of broken pieces invites the formation of a new text, of a new world, and a new community." In following Jeremiah, Wiesel will also force readers to search for a new text and a new vision of the community and world.[237]

Ten years after the Holocaust, when Wiesel began to testify to what he had seen and heard, he found that he had a "given framework"—the paradigm of the prophets of Israel, especially as mediated in the literary framework and paradigmatic models of Jeremiah. Wiesel's own use of autobiography, with its reference to the language of the self, is in the service of another story: the prophetic paradigm as seen in Jeremiah—the shattering of pre-Holocaust reality (Sighet gone forever except in memory and imagination) and the forming, evoking, and enacting of a just and humane post-Holocaust world (Sighet reconstructed and extended to the ends of the earth).

The portrait of Jeremiah that Wiesel found in his Bible during the days of his youth in Sighet, and perhaps mediated anew through Shushani, was theologically intentional. It provided a paradigmatic portrait of Jeremiah as a poet/prophet. The portrait constructed with words offers to the reader a model of the understanding of the poet/prophet as well as a paradigm of what Israel might become. In adopting Jeremiah's language and groundplan, Wiesel adopts a similar theological intentionality. The story of his life is now projected as a public persona—a paradigm for "witnessing" to the Holocaust, living as a person of faith in the post-Holocaust age, and eventually modeling what the community of Israel may be like. Just as in the work of Jeremiah, the first of Wiesel's themes is "shattering."

## Shattering

How does Wiesel tell his story? After adopting the "code" of Jeremiah, Wiesel appropriates a series of themes and images from the Hebrew Bible and utilizes them together with Jeremiah's language and his own prophetic imagination to construct stories around the Holocaust as an anti-Sinai. He appropriates the central core narrative of Judaism, the story of Moses and the exodus from bondage as a central theme in his retelling and reworking of the new updated tradition. But Wiesel saw the Holocaust as a reversal of Sinai. So he looked for ways to reverse the core narrative. Each of these traditions was appropriated in a manner that essentially redescribed it and placed it in the service of Jeremiah's literary logic of "shattering."

## The New Torah: A Second Exodus, An Anti-Sinai

Wiesel's narrative opens with a portrayal of Moshe the Beadle. The allusion seems clear. From the beginning of his story,

Wiesel wants the reader to think of the biblical Moshe and his story, which was the core narrative of Judaism. He goes on to characterize Eliezer as a young Jewish boy who "believed profoundly" at the age of twelve. In the beginning, *Night* is a story of a young boy growing up in the midst of Hasidic fervor, in love with his family, his God, and the Torah. But then, at the time of Passover—when in the original core narrative of Judaism, Israel is liberated—Wiesel tells how the boy and his family are deported from Sighet and taken to the death camps of Birkenau and Auschwitz, where his mother and youngest sister are immediately killed; how he and his father struggle through the winter avoiding "selection"; and finally, after a long forced march in the brutal cold and snow, how his father dies shortly before liberation. As a central framework for his story, Wiesel takes the core narrative of Jewish tradition, the exodus, and reverses it in order to show the reversal of the classical paradigm of the Exodus/Sinai traditions. As in the first exodus, there is a "going out," but this time the going out is from an ordered land into chaos—a movement from the secure and ordered world of Sighet into the unspeakable horror of the death camps. The season of the year is the same as in the first exodus. Yet this time, the Angel of Death does not spare the Hebrew children. The Jews of Sighet are taken to a place where food tastes like corpses, where gallows are erected to hang young children, and where people begin to ask, "Where is God?" Wiesel's autobiography is biography in the sense that he demonstrates that the old order is now no longer. Eliezer and other inmates discover a new historical age, a new view of God, others, and themselves in the camps.[238]

## Tradition Reversed: The Eclipse of God

The original Exodus narrative is a theocentric story of the power and salvation of God who intervenes on behalf of Israel to lead her to the Promised Land. Wiesel's story told in *Night* is a narrative in which the world grows increasingly smaller, far more dangerous, and characterized by the absence of God. When the doors on the train were shut, the world became "a cattle wagon hermetically sealed." Immediately after his arrival in the reception station of Birkenau, Wiesel writes, "Never shall I forget those flames which consumed my faith forever.... Never shall I forget those moments which murdered my God and my soul and turned my dreams to dust."[239]

What had Eliezer seen and heard? "Men to the left! Women to the right!"[240] He had seen his mother and younger sister taken from him forever. Then he and his father were forced to walk into the "night"—past a burning ditch where a wagon had pulled up to dump its human cargo. The ditch? It was full of burning babies. Eliezer thought that he and his father were going to be marched into such a pit for adults. Eliezer's father began saying Kaddish—the prayer for the dead. At that point, Eliezer began to feel revolt rise up within himself. Was there any reason to bless God's name? "The Eternal, Lord of the Universe, the All-Powerful and Terrible was silent."[241] Wiesel asked, Why should I give thanks to Him? His father was weeping and his body was trembling. Two steps from the flames, they were told to take a right and then were marched into the barracks.

## The Sad-Eyed Angel and the Crucifixion of Israel

An informed reading of *Night* must now be done in the context of Wiesel's ongoing dialogue with Mauriac, whose theology found focus in the suffering of Jesus. Wiesel had responded to Mauriac by telling him that he knew Jews who had suffered more than Christ. The episode of the hanging of the child with the face of a sad-eyed angel brings this conversation to mind. This scene occurs at Buna, which was about a four-hour walk from Auschwitz. The young boy, who takes part in an attempt to blow up the power plant, is discovered and tortured for days. Having refused to give the names of those who helped him, the boy is sentenced to death by hanging.

On the day set aside for carrying out the sentence, even the SS are disturbed. It is no small matter to hang a young boy in front of thousands of witnesses. Two men stand on the gallows with the boy—all three condemned to death. The two older men die quickly. But when it comes time for the boy, his light frame prolongs his suffering. His death is slow and agonizing. Wiesel writes that he heard a man behind him ask, "Where is God now?" While the camp prisoners are made to march past the gallows to view the face of the sad angel, Wiesel hears a voice within himself answer: "Where is He? Here He is—He is hanging here on this gallows."[242]

This scene also symbolizes an age of untold Jewish suffering and the beginning of the necessary effort to redefine images of God, history, and the self. The three young men executed at the hands of the German state bring to mind the biblical narrative of the crucifixion of three Jewish men put to death by the Romans. Within the context of the dialogue with Mauriac, this episode draws a poignant analogy about the death of the six million and the crucifixion of the children of Israel.

## The Anti-Sinai as the Failure of Modernity

A second major aspect of Elie Wiesel's dialogue with Mauriac, embodied in *Night* and given as a critique for French and Western institutions, is the poignant description of the end of modernity with its naive understanding of the goodness of humankind and its myth of inevitable progress. The narrative of Wiesel's arrival at Auschwitz, described in *Night*, portrays his introduction to a world of unbelievable horror. Another prisoner came up to Wiesel and his father and began to say, "Poor devils, you're going to the crematory."[243] It seemed to be true, Wiesel wrote, because not far in front of them was a flaming ditch. A cart loaded with human cargo had pulled up to the ditch. The cart was loaded with babies, but it could not be true, Wiesel said to his father. "I told him that I did not believe that they could burn people in our age, that humanity would never tolerate it...," but his father responded, "Humanity? Humanity is not concerned with us. Today anything is allowed. Anything is possible, even these crematories...."[244]

Eliezer's naive assumption—about the goodness of humankind and the evolving of the human race—with the father's response that now anything is possible suggests the failure of modernity, the second major paradigm. This view of modernity—held in disciplines like philosophy, science, economics, and politics—suggests that human power, when properly understood, will liberate human beings and allow them to gain mastery over the world. Wiesel's memoir, *Night*, demonstrates that this paradigm, like that of his first traditional world of a God-intoxicated Sighet, is shattered also.

Yet standing before the pit, Eliezer has difficulty believing that such things can happen in the twentieth century. In describing such a circumstance, Wiesel rejects modernity as a foundational paradigm for present existence. The colossal breakdown in morality that was behind the Holocaust was, in part, brought on by relativistic and objectivistic standards together with bureaucratic ideas that made up the foundation for modern culture. Thus, the Holocaust is not so much a deviation from modern culture so much as it is a demonic expression of some of its most fundamental and powerful themes. As Irving Greenberg puts it, "It is the universalism, the efficiency, the technology, and indeed the education of modernity that made its execution possible."[245] In *N i g h t*, Wiesel demonstrates that both paradigms—that of traditional religion and that of modern secular culture—are now shattered.

## The Anti-Sinai as the Death of the Self and Human Exile

What Mauriac asked of Wiesel was, in some sense, a form of autobiography that is traditionally understood as a creation of the self through the written act—a self born of writing. In as much as autobiography constitutes an act of life, it is a book of life. But at the end of his autobiographical portrayal in *Night*, Eliezer looks into a mirror and a corpse looks back at him. Thus, under the influence of the Holocaust, autobiography for Wiesel becomes "thanatography" and involves a portrayal of the death of the self.[246] In telling the story of his own death, Wiesel gives a grim portrayal of the post-modern age: the story of Eliezer's "death" calls to memory the deaths of six million others whose corpses challenge the meaning of human history and the traditional images of society and religion. This story implies that, with the onslaught of the Holocaust, humanity entered the ultimate form of exile—ontological exile where being itself had become criminal.

## The New Torah as the Akedah in Reverse

In Elie Wiesel's hometown of Sighet, the story of Abraham and Isaac was well known. In writing his story to be delivered to Mauriac, Wiesel drew upon this imagery and made the portrayal of the father-son theme reminiscent of the *Akedah*, or "binding of Isaac," in Jewish tradition. Early in Wiesel's story, his world is reduced to his relationship with his father. After being separated from his mother and three sisters on arrival at Birkenau, Wiesel grows obsessed with maintaining contact with his father. As the larger story unfolds, one reads a narrative of reciprocal devotion in which each one is committed to saving the other. But the reality of Auschwitz, which is made central to the story, implies that father and son, like Abraham and Isaac before them, stand in

113

front of an altar of death. Yet in Wiesel's story, as Andre Neher points out, the end will reveal a rewriting of the *Akedah* and a reversal of the traditional father-son roles.[247]

In Neher's reading of *Night*, the story is the *Akedah* "singed" with the fires of a new reality—the reality of Auschwitz. It is the way the story would have been told in the Bible if there it were more than a story, and if in its pages Abraham and Isaac, bathed in sweat and blood, and clothed in life and death, could rise up from the literary setting and confront us with the question "Where is God?" and not "Where is the ram?" As an *Akedah* in reverse, *Night* is the story of a young son dragging an exhausted father to the sacrificial altar, which ironically also brought about the death of the son.[248]

## The New Torah as One Unified Outcry

If there is one word that describes the beginning of Wiesel's writing project, it is the word "lament." Starting with *Night*, Wiesel seems to give "one unified outcry, one sustained protest, one sobbing and singing prayer."[249] That is, the mood of the lament hangs over all of his early works. Wiesel knew that in the books of Exodus and Deuteronomy, the cry of distress is a part of the narratives of deliverance of ancient Israel. Thus, the lament is a cry from the depths that dates from Jewish antiquity and is a vital and inevitable part of the Jewish dialogue with God. In fact, both praise and lamentation are a part of Jewish communion with God. One of the unique contributions of Judaism to Western culture is the understanding that there are a variety of forms and avenues of approach to God. In ancient times, when God made his "face" to shine on Israel—when the blessings were manifold—she sang the hymns of praise. But when God turned his face, or hid his face, and the tragedies of life fell on Israel, then she lamented. That is, there were songs for orientation, blessing, and security, and then there were songs of disorientation, dislocation, and tragedy. The laments fall into the latter category.[250]

The lament has a three-dimensional nature. It is directed toward God, others, and the self. It includes either an accusation or complaint against God, a complaint against others (the enemy), and a statement about the lamenter. The first dimension is the theological, often addressed in the Bible by questions put to God. One of the central questions for Wiesel in *Night* is "Where is God?"[251] By making this question central in the narrative, Wiesel allows the mood of the personal and communal laments to hover over the entire story. In this way, he shows that his story is, in part, a dialogue with God that has both personal and corporate dimensions.

In composing his testimony to the atrocities, Wiesel knew also that the lament had a societal dimension because of its accusations against the enemy. When Wiesel cast the haunting and dirge-like mood of the lament over his slim volume of testimony, he created not only a cry from the depths directed toward God, but also a sustained protest against the enemy. Wiesel's testimony, sent to Mauriac, was a story in the Jewish lamentation tradition of how a people of culture turned to genocide and how the rest of humankind did nothing to prevent it. In this way, Wiesel demonstrated not only that the Holocaust is central to human history but also that it is a turning point, a watershed. Not only do human beings die in the Holocaust, but also the idea of the human as it had been conceived.

Yet as a lament, *Night* is a document of faith—protesting faith. The purpose of the lament in ancient Judaism is to restore the individual to the community through participation in this unique form, the very structure of which places one in bold conversation and dialogue with God. Thus Wiesel's use of the lament form suggests a robust quality to his faith as well as an ability to confront a deep sense of alienation even as he searches for a way to continue dialogue with God.[252]

## Night *as a Parable: The Quest for a Poetics of Justice*

As has been noted, all of Wiesel's work tends toward the parabolic. Parables have a certain logic and work toward a particular effect upon the reader. That is, parables read the reader and help the reader to choose a direction or course of action or thought. The logic of the parable is that of orientation, disorientation, and reorientation. A parable is essentially a metaphor with interactive elements in tension: the conventional way of being in the world versus the way of the kingdom. The interaction of the two results in a redescription of the possibilities of human life for the reader or listener. Wiesel begins his testimony, *Night*, with everyday life in Sighet—a small East European Jerusalem where he "believed profoundly"—and thereby portrays for the reader a virtual "promised land" motif as orientation. Then Wiesel describes how "night" fell on Sighet and his own childhood. The average reader of this text might hope to remain a "spectator," living at some distance. The deportation to the death camps embodies a perspective so radically different from the God-intoxicated milieu of Sighet that it can only be portrayed as the antechambers of hell. Such a portrayal typically disorients the spectator mentality of the average reader who now comes as close as humanly possible—given the distance of time, emotion, and circumstance—to being "an initiate into death, into the dark world of human suffering and moral chaos we call the Holocaust." Now the reader of the parable must choose to identify with the victim and thereby join the quest of understanding this new moral order and how to respond to it; or to identify with the spectators and remain at great emotional and intellectual distance, pretending that this event does not touch the circumstance of the reader; or finally one can choose to identify with the violent mode of the executioners and somehow look for a way to justify or deny the death of the six million.[253]

## Night *as a Document of Faith: The Portrayal of a Postmodern Ultimate Environment*

Wiesel's testimony, written under the seal of memory and delivered to Francois Mauriac in 1956, is not only the foundation for his future work, but also an important document for understanding his spiritual pilgrimage. It clearly records his stance of faith at the time of writing, ten years after the Holocaust.[254] In 1956, this document reveals him to be a person of faith in the historic line of Levi-Yitshak of Berditchev, going back to Jeremiah and earlier to those who first held to what Schneidau now calls "sacred discontent."[255] His view is that of protest, demythologizing questions, and lamentations for the irretrievable loss he has suffered. Gone is the naive, illusory worldview he describes in the beginning of his Yiddish memoir. At this point, he is iconoclastic and justifiably angry. In terms of ideology, in *Night*, Wiesel is the architect of a postmodern world. Pre-Holocaust reality is shattered. For Wiesel, the post-Holocaust world means that traditional life with its concepts of God, society, and the human are demythologized and cast aside. Being, itself, is now in exile. Religious traditions from the past, like the exodus and the *Akedah*, are useful now if they can be portrayed in reverse. In terms of the imagery of *Night*, Wiesel is a contemporary poet/prophet disguised as a literary figure with a complex code and strategy. Yet, there is an intensity to the dialogical nature of *Night* that can be understood only in divine-human terms. This intensity insured that the protest and dialogue would continue in future forms.

Wiesel's spiritual landscape can now be described as postmodern. The traditional and accepted forms of past

117

intellectual history are in Wiesel's judgment shattered and lay strewn across the ruins of his previous conventional map of reality. He begins his reflective worldview by demythologizing those forms and turning them upside down. The exodus, the centerpiece of the Jewish core narrative, is now an anti-exodus. The famous story of Abraham and Isaac is now an anti-*Akedah*. His intellectual, literary, and spiritual logic is "shattering"—relentlessly demythologizing and iconoclastic. His world, at all levels, is now one of questions concerning the deepest realities of existence. In other words, his ultimate environment is, at this point, a shattered landscape—his words "stutter toward a meaning that is never found." His is now a fragmented existence, a self in search for words and traditions that might convey something of the dark reality he has seen.[256] This spiritual landscape is one in which the God of his childhood chases him as if he is now an enemy, and his memories of the dark night haunt him like demons that cannot be exorcised. Religious tradition is helpful only if it can be demythologized to portray the broken reality of his post-Holocaust world.

*Chapter 8*

# Further into Darkness:

# A Very Troubled Man

In rewriting his Yiddish testimony for Mauriac, Wiesel quotes his beloved Moshe: "Man raises himself toward God by the questions he asks Him.... That is the true dialogue."[257] Then Moshe explains that in this dialogical process the human questions the divine, but human beings do not understand the answers of God because they are found only in the depths of the soul where they reside until death. "You will find the true answers, Eliezer, only within yourself," Moshe explains.[258] Wiesel's iconoclastic and demythologizing stance illustrated in the rewriting of his Yiddish testimony implies that he learned from Moshe's instruction. The writing that Wiesel would do in the future continued this "drama of interrogation."[259] And the questions that came to him seemed to move him in the direction of the nature of the self. But more importantly, in May 1955 when Wiesel met with Mauriac and in the months following when he began to rewrite his Yiddish testimony, it is clear that his faith was characterized by a reflective and questioning stance.[260]

An episode that documents Wiesel's ongoing questioning and demythologizing stance takes place in Israel, where he decided to go not long after the meeting with Mauriac. When Elie Wiesel was a child, he thought that whenever an argument occurred or harsh words came to him, he could flee to his grandfather's house or perhaps to the Holy Land. As a child, all he had to do, he thought, was climb the mountain and look for the secret door that opened to a special corridor leading right to the mountains of Galilee. But now, he made the long crossing by sea—for the third time. Like his grandfather's house, Israel was a refuge.[261]

### Searching for a Blessing for the Journey into the Profane Books

Once in Israel, Wiesel stopped in to see the "young" Rebbe of Wizhnitz, who was the son of the Rebbe from Wiesel's childhood and who now lived in the religious suburb of Tel Aviv, Bnei Brak. The Rebbe received him with a "mixture of tenderness and frustration." Since the Rebbe had not seen Wiesel for a long period of time, he asked him who he was now. Wiesel did not answer, perhaps because he was thinking of the Rebbe's father. But all at once, Wiesel began to feel guilty, and he understood why. In earlier times, he had come to the Rebbe in order that he might answer the Rebbe's questions. Now he had come to ask the Rebbe questions about the God of his childhood, the all-powerful One who had created the earth, now devastated beyond repair. Wiesel did not know, however, a proper way to form the questions. His lips betrayed him. The Rebbe smiled and gave him a chance to explain how he had changed. Wiesel replied, "Times, too, have changed, Rebbe." The Rebbe was not impressed and told Wiesel that he liked him better before. "Why? Because I wore side curls, and feared heaven?"[262]

The Rebbe did not respond but asked Wiesel to tell him about the relationship between the man he was now and the man he appeared to be. Wiesel responded with some of the philosophy he had read in Paris: "Being is not necessarily visible, and that which is visible is not necessarily part of being." In a disapproving tone, the Rebbe asked him where he had gotten such an idea. The Rebbe knew. Such an answer had come from "profane" books that now sat side by side with the sacred books on Wiesel's desk. The Rebbe asked what Wiesel's grandfather would think about him. What did the grandson of Dodye Feig want to hear from the Rebbe? That was a question Wiesel needed to answer. Had he come to seek the Rebbe's blessing for his journey into the "profane" books?[263]

Then the Rebbe told a story. It was a story passed on by the great Rebbe Nahman of Bratslav. A child is lost in the forest. Near panic, the child cries out, "Father, Father, save me!" For as long as the child cries out, there is still hope that the father might be able to come to him. But if he stops crying out, then all hope is gone. Wiesel assured the Rebbe that he had "never ceased to cry out." The Rebbe was pleased and pronounced hope but no blessing. Then he wanted to know if the stories that Wiesel wrote were true. Did they really happen? Wiesel tried to answer. "In literature, Rebbe, certain things are true though they didn't happen, while others are not, even if they did."[264]

The mood of this story reflects the nature of Wiesel's faith in summer 1955. It is indicative of a reflective stance of faith that requires independent and critical thought. Wiesel had entered a natural time of questioning, and he was restless with answers that were too easily given. While the Rebbe, like other conventional religious authorities, was reluctant to approve such a quest, Wiesel seemed to have a need for the Rebbe to bless this journey into the "profane" books, and to affirm the search for a human identity no longer defined by a traditional world. The need went unmet, and consequently Wiesel's journey into this realm took place only under the authorization of his own person.[265]

After the Holocaust, Wiesel continued his traditional faith for a time. But then Wiesel entered a period in which he wrestled with the God of his childhood and sought to understand analytically what he had previously accepted at face value.[266] The life of religious faith took on new dimensions. He shunned public prayer and tried to understand Judaism in light of a larger religious world, especially Hinduism. He asked himself questions about the value of the old traditions in light of the Holocaust. He concluded that everything had been changed by the Holocaust. It was like Sinai, an important time of revelation in human history. Ironically, it was like an anti-Sinai in terms of its nature. The covenant, for example, had been broken. Language had gone into exile and could no longer be trusted. Wiesel sought a new language, a new covenant, and new images of God and the human. The depth and dimension of Wiesel's earlier conventional world seems to dictate that this new period of suffering would be prolonged and agonizing. The story of Wiesel's confrontation with the son of the Rebbe of his youth epitomizes the confrontation with that former conventional world that goes on in his inner being. If the Rebbe would not bless his journey into the "profane" books, if he could not find answers in discussion with the Rebbe, what could he do? Perhaps he could find answers through additional writing.[267]

At the end of his stay in Israel, he was asked to go to New York as a foreign correspondent at the United Nations, representing his paper, *Yedhioth Ahronoth*. It would mean a raise to $160 a month. In December, Wiesel received the copy of his Yiddish testimony, "And the World Stayed Silent," from Brazil. In early 1956, Wiesel went to New York, where he rented a small apartment. He also took a second job at the *Jewish Daily Forward* to help his financial situation.

## Further into Darkness: A Very Troubled Man

On a hot July night in New York in 1956, Wiesel went to the *Times* office, as was his custom. Then he sent his cable with his daily report of the news to the paper in Jerusalem. Afterward, he and Aviva, a friend from Tel Aviv, began walking to the theater to see *The Brothers Karamazov*. But they did not make it to the show. As the two crossed Seventh Avenue at the intersection with

Forty-Fifth Street, Wiesel was critically injured when struck by an oncoming taxi. He was rushed to the hospital, where he was turned away because he appeared indigent. He had no money, no insurance, and he seemed beyond repair. The second hospital, New York Hospital, was more charitable. There, a brilliant young Catholic orthopedic surgeon, Paul Braunstein, saved Wiesel's life despite the forty-seven fractures. The operation lasted ten hours and left Wiesel in a complete body cast. The left side of his body had been virtually shattered. He was comatose for about a week.[268]

Wiesel was confined to the hospital for several months. During that stay, he developed a friendship with Braunstein. The doctor remembered Wiesel as a small and frail individual who was very lonely and very troubled. But he was profound, said Braunstein. Though Wiesel, according to the doctor's report, seemed at that point in his life to deny the existence of God, he talked about little else. "He was one of the most religious people I had ever met," the doctor said. Wiesel remembers this period as a continuation of his religious struggle. "I was mired in a religious crisis," he said. During this period in his life, he did not attend synagogue except for the High Holidays and the Yizkor service for the memory of the dead.[269]

At this point, Wiesel struggled with what to do with the memory of the dead. Though he had written his testimony, he did not yet know where to put the unburied dead. In fact, Wiesel's continued struggle was not just that of a survivor; it was also that of *homo religiosus*—the budding spiritual innovator who suffers from a lifelong and chronic integrity crisis. For Wiesel, the youthful problem of identity merged with the last of human questions: how to avoid betraying one's vows and commitments, and find some semblance of meaning before one dies. A young man like Wiesel extends his problem of identity to the borders of human existence and assumes that human life must start over with him. The lifelong and chronic integrity crisis not only extends the search for identity but also intimacy. This makes a young man like Wiesel very restive. He searches for a way to restate the great overstatement of his time, and he does so as he seeks to settle an earlier existential account or curse. In so doing, he merges his identity with that of the group. In other words, he seeks for the right time and place to recreate the drama of his earlier years, and there create a new future in the proper medium at the correct moment and on a sufficient scale.[270] This is in part what the doctor, Paul Braunstein, meant when he described Wiesel in spring 1956 as very lonely and very troubled.

## Crying Out to the Father:
### Orientation Theme and Quest

As Wiesel recuperated from his accident, he continued to wrestle with these issues. He began to think about writing other books. The "accident" could be used as the basis for another book, Wiesel thought. Why? What is the significance of his idea to turn this accident into a novel? In time, Wiesel would write a series of books tracing his own journey—and the identity he formulates for himself and for others. Central to his quest are some important conclusions as well as questions that seem to come to him rather early. Already in *Night*, he seems to say that the key issue of the day is indifference that leads ultimately to abandonment; the Jews of Eastern Europe are an abandoned people because of the indifference of the West.

Yet the theme of abandonment has personal dimensions for the young writer. With poignant detail, Wiesel explains ten years after the fact that he experienced the death of his father as the ultimate form of abandonment. A reader of Wiesel's later works knows that this event haunts the writer for a lifetime, that he experiences this tragedy as something like an existential curse. But Eliezer in *Night* cannot tell the story in this fashion. For him, the narrative is the story of his father's last word—which was his name, Eliezer, a "summons" to which he did not respond. Could writing be an attempt finally to answer his father? Wiesel accused and judged himself guilty of abandoning his own father—a guilt from which he would never be able to free himself.[271] But this scene, as stated earlier, is in reality a memory screen for an earlier and more primal conflict: the experience of rejection and abandonment that he feels from both father and mother, and the guilt he feels in going beyond his father as a child. His earliest memory is that of a little boy sitting on the edge of his bed crying for his mother. Without her, he felt "rejected, exiled, imperiled."[272]

It would be too easy to relegate this earliest feeling of abandonment to Freud's idea of the Oedipal crisis. It is likely that as a young child, Wiesel began to feel the "tug" of the generations, that what he experienced can be described as a "generational" crisis. A young child begins to have some elementary sense that his life will have significance beyond the competition with his father, and at a young age, he feels "called" to succeed for his family and for his generation.[273] Is this not a way of understanding the story of Eliezer and his mother visiting the Rebbe, and being told that he will be a great man in Israel?[274]

In *Night*, Wiesel demonstrates that his fate merged with that of the group. Human society turned its back on the Jews, and God "abandoned" his chosen people too. For whatever reason, God did not come to the aid of his children as in earlier times such as the exodus. Consequently, Wiesel describes the Jewish people in his testimony as being like an abandoned, rejected people, and he suffers an ultimate form of abandonment: the loss of his father and mother and sister, and six million others.

Likewise, his quest for individual identity also merges with that of the group. How does one define the self, the individual, and the group so as to answer the summons from the father and restate the previous overstatement? In his writing and in his activism and public speaking, Wiesel begins to do these things. In as much as *Night* becomes in due course the best-known and most read testimony regarding the death camps, Wiesel's name becomes associated with the Holocaust, an event with which every contemporary Jew must come to terms. For survivors, he eventually comes to represent a symbolic voice that speaks for them. For other Jews who were not in the camps, he is known as a witness. To those from a later generation, he represents a past that was often missing in their experience. To non-Jews and those embedded in a secular culture, Wiesel embodies spiritual values and a quest for meaning in the contemporary world.[275]

Writing as a response to the summons of the father? Perhaps it is only in words, only through memory reduced to writing, that Wiesel can bring back the dead and resurrect the past so as to honor the unburied. As Roland Barthes suggests, the very basis of narrative is, in this case, the son's search for the father, that narrative is "always a way of searching for one's origin...." If the thesis of this book is correct—that Wiesel is a generative religious personality whose struggle is ongoing and in quest of a universalizing perspective—then, for Wiesel "every narrative...is a staging of the...father."[276] One reason Wiesel must continue to write is that this is his only way of communicating with his father, the only opportunity to build a proper memorial. So he writes attempting to accomplish what cannot be done, but he is compelled to try.

It is not only for his father that he tries! It is also for the countless others, for the six million, and for those unborn. The existential curse is also a memory screen for the generational crisis, and Wiesel turns his own story into a vocation. He merges his quest for identity into a search for a way to restate the "genocidal mentality" so as to create an identity for his entire generation.[277] This is why he becomes known as a "moral" voice in our time, and why he comes to be understood in symbolic terms. He shares his identity with the generation as a response to one of the great problems of the day. Where and how does he do this? In writing, and later in speaking and public activity.

## Writing and the Quest for Identity:
## Wiesel's Reflective Faith and the Holocaust Novel

Why would a survivor like Wiesel be so interested in writing? Henri Raczymow, who wrote several autobiographical novels in which a protagonist participates in a fictional return to a former Jewish home in Poland, comments that writing is the process of interrogating the self about one's name and identity. For Raczymow, a post-Holocaust Jew living in France, writing is "the desire for a place, for an identity. It is the search for a connection with the past through the processes of the imagination." "Writing," Raczymow says, "turns into an archaeological and an analytical enterprise during which I reconstruct my past by imagining it. I dig out something with which to build my identity."[278]

In her book *Writing a Woman's Life*, Carolyn G. Heilbrun describes a similar process. In 1964, Heilbrun began publishing detective stories under the pseudonym Amanda Cross. As an English professor, she thought her identity as a novelist would count against her when it came time for promotion to tenured status. In addition, Heilbrun comments that before the women's movement, she and other women were so full of anxiety that they "wished to hide their authorial identity from prying eyes."[279]

In part, says Heilbrun, the use of a pseudonym was an attempt to search for a sense of identity other than the conventional one ascribed to women. But the writing process also masks the need to create a space for the emerging self. In the process of writing, Heilbrun posits, "I sought, I now guess, psychic space." In so doing, she sought a new identity and a new role. Her writing of novels was an effort to create a sense of destiny and individuality that offered more possibility than she could at the moment imagine. So in turning to fiction to create a new identity, Heilbrun created a fantasy world very different from her own everyday world. In creating her protagonists and characters, Heilbrun began to recreate herself. She desired "to remake the world and discover the possibility of different destinies for women in it." By writing detective fiction, Heilbrun came to understand that she was in fact rewriting her desired destiny for women—an alternative life etched in the feminine imagination.[280]

Wiesel's turn to the Holocaust novel demonstrates a similar quest. "The books came one after the other to answer the questions I was asking myself," Wiesel says.[281] Put another way, Wiesel says, "Reflected in all my characters...is the Jew in me trying to find himself."[282]

## Writing to Remake the World:
### Identity, Covenant, and Protesting Faith

In the fashion of Heilbrun and Raczymow, Wiesel's writing seems also to be "the desire for a place, for an identity," as well as an attempt to "remake the world and discover the possibility of different destinies." In rereading *Night*, Wiesel concluded that "to stay with the past was not enough. We must take the past and transcend it." So he began considering writing other books. In writing his Yiddish testimony, Wiesel had penned more than 800 pages. But when *Night* was finally published, it had been reduced to a little more than 100 pages. Wiesel began to think, "Since I had six hundred [unused] pages about *Night*, I must have in me other pages about other things, other times."

Wiesel was steeped in a covenant tradition that is a key metaphor for the affirmation that human life depends in some measure upon relatedness to God and to a human community. If *Night* is a new Torah that demonstrates the "shattering" of the

Jewish paradigm of covenant life, then the volumes that would follow *Night* must consider the making of a post-Holocaust covenant, along with new images of God and humankind and answers to questions on ethics and values. This covenantal heritage establishes the context for understanding Wiesel's desire to write more volumes. It is also in this context that his protesting faith can enter into dialogue through grief and rage, and seek a poetics of memory and justice validated finally through the praxis of human faithfulness.

## *Writing as Dialogue with God:*
## *Confronting Shame and Ritualizing Memory*

There are also other reasons for Wiesel, in a full body cast on a hospital bed, to ponder writing other volumes. Wiesel's first volume, *Night*, is a story of shame that is a painful experience of self-exposure—a feeling of having been seen by another in a manner that is humiliating and disorienting and forces one to see oneself in a "fallen" state, the fall of humanity and all of civilization, a "change about" for God. Wiesel's writing gives testimony to the completeness of disorientation. The theme of the reversal of religious traditions in *Night*, such as the *Akedah*, and the core tradition of the exodus as well as the use of the lament, indicate the depth of Wiesel's disorientation and sense of shame. Shame extends to God, for now the Divine also is a diminished character.[283]

The theme of shame, as embodied in the Holocaust event, helps the reader gain a new perspective on Wiesel's work. Now it is clear that as a "peddler of night and agony," Wiesel is involved in a wrenching vocation, for telling a story of shame is one of the most painful human experiences. So why does Wiesel want to continue to tell these stories? He writes and he writes and he continues to tell stories to God, in part, because this is the only way one can deal with a story of shame. This is what Augustine

129

does in his classic autobiography, *The Confessions*. He tells his story of shameful experiences to God as conversation partner. One can do this without the unnecessary fear that the story will be treated as either trivial or unimportant. Despite Wiesel's ongoing disputation with God over the issue of justice, he nonetheless portrays God, as do the prophets of Israel, as being in touch with a divine pathos, a profound feeling of grief and sympathy for the oppressed.[284] Therefore, though God's character may be diminished for Wiesel, God is still a worthy partner of robust dialogue.

But why does Wiesel in 1957 feel the compulsion to continue to write? Perhaps Wiesel has internalized the model of Jeremiah with its relentless portrayal of the story. Likely, he does so, in part, because stories of shame touch aspects of the human personality so deeply that they must be told again. Yet, Wiesel also wants to tell these stories again and again in order to ritualize the memory of these experiences that have brought trauma in his life and to the world community.[285] The only way for the community to deal with the trauma is to communalize the pain and the experience. Wiesel feels compelled to search for listeners and true readers in order to ritualize the memory of this event—in an effort to heal himself and society.

# Chapter 9

# Writing Like Jeremiah II:
# Evoking a New Universe

After a lengthy stay in the New York Hospital, Wiesel was released in a wheelchair. He went back to his hotel room and worked from there for a time. Then he returned on crutches to work at the UN, where important events were unfolding for his readers in Israel. There was the revolt by the Hungarian freedom fighters that was put down by Soviet tanks. Then there was the story of Israel's campaign in the Sinai led by Moshe Dayan. Despite his own pain, Wiesel attended the seemingly endless Security Council meetings in order to send the stories back to Israel.[286]

In 1957, Wiesel traveled across America with his friend and Israeli employer, Dov Judlowski. Together, they drove to Los Angeles on a cross-country trip that lasted six weeks. This was also the year that Wiesel met Golda Meir, the newly appointed minister of foreign affairs, who was in New York to work out negotiations for a withdrawal from the Sinai. He quickly won the confidence of this older woman who was a future prime minister and perhaps the "mother" of modern Israel. Mrs. Meir took a "maternal" interest in the young Jew who was hobbling around on crutches and trying to get a story, and she allowed him to read through her papers, including the confidential documents. Wiesel spent many enjoyable hours with her over the years listening to her speak about her childhood in Russia, her teenage years in Milwaukee, and her later experiences in Israel.[287]

In 1957, Wiesel received word from Francois Mauriac that Editions de Minuit would publish the French version of his testimony. Mauriac himself wrote a stirring foreword in which he described Wiesel as "a Lazarus risen from the dead." The book did well despite the fact that such literature was "not yet fashionable." By 1958, when the book was finally on the market as *La Nuit*, Wiesel was at work on a second volume titled *Dawn*.[288]

## Writer as Poet/Prophet and the Re-creation of the Universe

In his personal life, Wiesel continued to struggle with feelings of guilt that in part came from the fact that he was a budding "spiritual innovator" with burdens that made him feel as if he must "surpass and create at all cost."[289] But Wiesel's struggle was also, in part, what to do with the dead. As he writes in his recent memoir, "For the camp survivor life is a battle not only for the dead but also against them. Locked in the grip of the dead, he fears that by freeing himself, he is abandoning them."[290] This statement indicates that Wiesel is aware that his life is complicated by the burdens of his survivor status. When Wiesel states that the survivor battles "against" the dead, he means the survivor has an indelible death image and sense of death anxiety; a feeling of guilt for survival; a diminished capacity to feel along with the loss of "symbolic connectedness" with his world; a "death taint"—a sense of needing help from others, yet resenting that need because it confirms an inner feeling of weakness; and a compulsion to formulate or create in order to bring significance to his encounter with death and his future life experience.[291]

The theme of survivor mission—the compulsion to create—also helps the reader understand Wiesel's added burden and ongoing quest to write. It is a way of testifying and burying the unburied dead. In addition, writing becomes a way of recreating the world and bringing some semblance of order to the void left by the overwhelming nature of the Holocaust as an encounter with absolute evil and death. That encounter brought a symbolic disconnection between Wiesel and the world. He, therefore, feels compelled to create at all cost—to create a new universe for himself and for others. His sense of survivor mission increases his sense of obligation and compulsion. By the late 1950s, though he had written a testimony in two versions and in two languages, he would soon take up the writing of fiction.

As a young intellectual, Wiesel had already concluded that there are two all-important events in human history: Sinai and the Holocaust. These two events are each epoch-making, except that the Holocaust is Sinai in reverse. That is, the Holocaust as an event ushered in a new age in which all things must be understood anew. Robert J. Lifton argues in a similar vein that "the combination of Nazi genocide and the American atomic bombings of Hiroshima and Nagasaki terminated man's sense of limits concerning his self-destructive potential, and thereby inaugurated an era in which he is devoid of assurance of living on eternally as a species."[292] Put another way, these two events brought on a worldwide sense of "historical...dislocation" that includes a loss of the sense of humans' connectedness with the important symbols of their cultural tradition. This dislocation means a break in the sense of connection that people formerly had with the symbols involved with the family, religion, cultural ideas, and life itself.[293] When Wiesel in the 1950s wrestled with his own identity, he like Lifton seemed to know that he needed to search for an understanding of life and selfhood that could be projected toward an entire society. In fact, in later years, he summarized the state of world dislocation by saying, "The world has become Jewish." The identity he developed for himself and other Jews was eventually projected outward and universalized to include the world.

## The Creation of a Postmodern World:
### The Literary Artist as Prophet of Forms

The task of a survivor with a mission like Wiesel's is to search for a "form" to give shape to the horrific experience, even though it is an effort to express the inexpressible. He must find a way to symbolize the void and the radical nature of historical disarray—to provide a set of symbols that adequately portrays the "experience of desymbolization." As Wiesel began to write, he experimented with telling the tale—testifying through narrative and story as a way of fulfilling the survivor's task. That is, Wiesel perhaps had an intuition that telling the tale could be the central part of his creative struggle as a survivor to give shape to a broken world. As he became more and more successful at his developing vocation through the use of literary art, he became what Lifton calls a "prophet of forms."[294] In other words, by using the traditional images and forms of the Jewish past to tell the tale, he gives shape to what would have otherwise been a void—a break within the symbolic universe. By telling his story—utilizing images like the *Akedah*, exodus, lament, and imagery from Job—Wiesel recreates the universe. As Wiesel began to write, he created a postmodern realm where the characters are in quest of a world that is gone forever, but those same characters are given a robust form of identity to chase down and argue with God.

## Evoking: Atrocity, Irreality, and
### the Age to Come

In *Night*, Wiesel evokes a world where everything is changed by the Holocaust. The foundations for living are in disarray. Auschwitz is now no longer just a place name for a town in

Poland; it is an evocative symbol for the reordering of history. God and humans have changed places. The creation of a new universe was a part of the Nazi plot. But the new order was devastating to the survivor. Hence, Wiesel's literary project after *Night* began by continuing to follow Jeremiah's model and style, but like that of Jeremiah, Wiesel's journey was a descent further into darkness. He knew that he lived, as did Jeremiah, in a time when the forms of expression were actually breaking up; a new literature for survivors was necessary. Just as the "confessions" are central for Jeremiah, so is Wiesel's new literature of testimony crucial for reading him. The common theme for both is what Gerhard von Rad calls "questioning reflexion." Both Wiesel and Jeremiah take journeys deeper into the religious self. The common pilgrimage is actually a journey into "ever greater despair." "It is a darkness so terrible—that it could also be said that it is something so absolutely new in the dealings between Israel and her God—that it constitutes a menace to very much more than the life of a single man: God's whole way with Israel hereby threatens to end in some kind of metaphysical abyss."[295] It is clear with Wiesel as with Jeremiah that they faced questions that are not simply personal but also corporate, involving the whole nature and destiny of all Israel.

Thus in his early years as a "messenger of the dead," Wiesel's work can be portrayed as a continuing struggle with God at a new Moriah, or something like a wrestling match with angels or demons in the dark night by a new Jabbok, for nothing less than the soul of Israel. The books came in logical progression attempting to answer questions the author found in his own soul. In attempting to create new appropriate forms, Wiesel tends to condense time and action. If time is shortened to one night, action is typically confined to a closed location. Then after condensing time and action, Wiesel merges first and third person point of view. Thus for Wiesel autobiography becomes biography—personal story becomes communal. The Holocaust is portrayed as *sui generis*—as a singular event in human history that gave rise to ontological incongruity, a chasm between heaven and earth with corresponding tensions between the divine and the human. Like the Jewish writers before him in the days of the Babylonian Exile, Wiesel creates a new protagonist—the survivor—who is forever alienated from "home" and is propelled on an unending journey. Yet, even as he creates a new form of literature, Wiesel is aware that language is inadequate and paradoxical—speech is placed in tension with silence. Understanding that language can betray, and that art for art's sake is impossible with the Holocaust, Wiesel places his literary art in the service of testimony and the work of justice.[296]

Wiesel's texts are narratives of intense pain that communicate "the experience of non-interpretability and chaos." Language cannot express the depth of the experience that it is called upon to convey. Therefore, the text functions as a "metaphor of witness," crying forth the pain and the experience in mystery and inexpressibility. The stories stutter toward a meaning that cannot be found and without sustained affirmation. Thus, by its very nature, Wiesel's literature of testimony can contain "metaphors of witness," memorials to the past, and "dangerous memories" subverting the oppressor, but it finally frustrates the effort to find answers. Rather, Wiesel's work compels questions and the reliving of the experience. Therefore, Wiesel's evocative fiction moves in the direction of theological parables that seek to read the reader and compel the reader to join the quest for justice and a new definition of human society. Perhaps in an effort to validate his message, Wiesel adds an autobiographical theme to all of his work, and the final component of his poetics seems to be that of public action—the theme of enacted word that he hopes might be indelible and irrefutable.[297]

From this perspective, *Night* becomes an autobiographical story about life in the death camps—a story, however, with a collective dimension demonstrating the shattering of formerly accepted truths; *Dawn* becomes the confrontation between the ways of the "magical room" and the "cellar" with implications for the dawning of a postmodern and post-Holocaust future in which innocence has been lost; *The Accident* is the life-and-death struggle in the "hospital room," which enters into the dark abyss that is existence for the survivor; and *The Town Beyond the Wall* is the struggle for an alternative community and a search for clues to a just and humane future ironically in a "jail cell" east of the Iron Curtain. Perhaps under the weight of Jeremiah's code, Wiesel's early literature moves away from realistic fiction in the direction of theological parable with an emphasis on ultimate confrontations wherein the enclosed space becomes the world. While Wiesel's parabolic fiction establishes a contending and protesting faith as the appropriate response for the post-Holocaust era, it begins slowly to affirm the enduring qualities of Jewish existence—the founding of the state of Israel, the solidarity of the Jewish people, and the sanctity of life. But in the end, Wiesel's parabolic fiction, like the work of Jeremiah, is "unreadable" as literature—that is, "it cannot be read sensibly according to our Western habits of coherent literature that make a single, sustained affirmation." It appears that Wiesel follows Jeremiah's model not only in "shattering" but also in "evoking." By writing texts that cannot be "read," Wiesel forces his readers to confront the modern disaster and to join the quest for new understandings.[298]

## A Literature of Testimony and Justice: Recreating Israel and the People of the Covenant

As Wiesel began to read the reviews of *La Nuit*, he worked on his first novel, *Dawn*, which narrates the reemergence of Israel as a nation and portrays the newfound complexities of post-Holocaust existence. Why would Wiesel write a novel about an event that took place ten years earlier—the founding of the modern state of Israel? In modern Jewish history, there are two epoch-making events: the Holocaust and the rebirth of Israel as a nation. The two events are linked historically and philosophically. Historically, there was sentiment on the side of the creation of a Jewish state after the death of the six million. Philosophically, the creation of a homeland for the disenfranchised Jews challenged the genocidal madness with its view of Aryan supremacy and allowed the new nation to substitute a model of strength. *Dawn* celebrates the rebirth of Israel and in so doing addresses the questions associated with its new found power.

Yet as the story of the rebirth of Israel, *Dawn* contains another foundational idea for Wiesel and post-Holocaust Judaism—the reestablishment of the covenant. After the fall of Jerusalem to the Romans in 70 CE, the rabbis led the Jewish people in an important reformulation of tradition. The rabbis thought God was becoming more hidden in order that the people could take a greater role in covenant. Consequently, the covenant became more secularized and the individual became a partner with God through religious activity. The new redemptive paradigm for the post-Temple world became Purim. Now redemption comes through the activity of human beings, flawed and fallible, but nonetheless acting to save the people of Israel and to reinterpret the covenant. Purim became the event by which the Jewish people accepted anew the covenant by understanding that now both God's presence and redemption come through secular means. While the authority of the covenant was broken during the devastation of the Holocaust, the Jewish people chose voluntarily to take it up.[299]

The rebirth of Israel became a redemptive event on par with the exodus and was seen by the Jewish people to be a validation of covenant life. As in the celebration of Purim when God saves through hidden and secular ways, so once again the covenant is reestablished through human means. After the Holocaust, Jews the world over concluded that the existence of the Jewish people in the land given to them by God was a fundamental testimony to the revitalized covenant. Further, the survival of the Jewish people in an age of genocide is also testimony to the nature and existence of God who, though hidden and invisible, still works in the continuing life of the people and on their behalf.[300] Therefore, one of the major components of the post-Holocaust covenant became the endurance of the Jewish people. A second characteristic is the solidarity of the Jewish people, and, finally, the sanctification of life.[301]

The title *Dawn* is an apt metaphor for Wiesel's first work after his testimony in *La Nuit* in as much a new day does "dawn" for the Jewish people after the Holocaust. That is, for the first time in 2,000 years, they are able to live in the land granted to them by divine favor and to do so under the name "Israel." "Dawn" also signifies the "dawning" of a new age—a time of lost innocence after the Holocaust. Wiesel rejoices in the reestablishment of the Jewish state, but he is also concerned with the quality and nature of life that is possible after the Holocaust and in the land of Israel. This second book demonstrates how Wiesel's own identity merges with that of the Jewish people. To that end, the book not only mirrors Wiesel's continued search for vocation and identity but records Jewish biography and the larger search for a national identity.[302]

Through the fictive process of writing in 1958, Wiesel mirrors the circumstances of the founding of the modern state of Israel ten years before. The setting reflects a time when innocence has been lost, and the descendants of the chosen, like the ancestor Jacob, wrestle with extremely difficult questions. The post-Holocaust Jewish youth now struggle with new ways to

Elie Wiesel

secure the future for themselves and their country. This generation, like the author of the novel, is haunted with questions: Who are we? How did the Holocaust happen? Why did we not take up arms and resist? Wiesel is also personally haunted with the sad image of the Diaspora Jew: "the weak, stooped Jew in need of protection." Even in Israel, survivors were treated as "outcasts, victims to be pitied at best."[303]

In his youthful days in Paris, Wiesel longed for a cause. After the passing of the partition plan in the UN, Wiesel "volunteered" for the Haganah, a paramilitary self-defense force in Israel. When the War of Independence broke out in Israel, Wiesel attempted to enlist in the Israeli army, but was rejected for medical reasons.[304] Having been refused on both attempts to involve himself in the military and political life of the new state, Wiesel eventually found a way to be involved in Israel's life through fiction. *Dawn* is Wiesel's attempt to understand what it might be like to be involved in confronting the enemy politically and militarily, and thus search for a new identity.

In the dark kingdom of Auschwitz, Wiesel found that the Nazis sought to redefine human history—to reduce the world to killers and victims. The Jews, described through Nazi propaganda as "subhuman," were ordained in the order of the Third Reich to play the part of the victim. As such, they were to be wiped off the face of the earth. In *Night*, Wiesel portrays himself as a victim of the Nazi order. *Dawn* is a questioning of *Night*. How are Jews to live in the new order, after the Holocaust? Can Jews take on an identity other than victim? Will they become executioners in the process? As a narrative, *Dawn* restates the Jewish identity and chronicles the new covenant. Israel is a nation struggling to be born, and her citizens are searching for ways to overcome victimization. As a young writer experimenting with vocation and form, Wiesel wants to participate in the reemergence of national life in Israel. Writing this novel, then, becomes something of a sacred activity celebrating the resurrection of the national ideal, but, as the reader quickly finds out, the landscape is a postmodern realm.

## Chronicling the Survival of the Jewish People and the Reestablishment of the Covenant in Dawn

When Wiesel began to create a fictional world, he transposed the autobiographical narrative he began to write in *Night* onto the literary landscape of his first novel. His protagonist in *Dawn* continues to live out the ambiguities of the father-son relationship and the struggles of the survivor. If Elisha, Wiesel's protagonist in *Dawn,* is something of a twentieth-century Maccabee struggling for the liberation of the homeland as well as the Jewish spirit, he is also haunted by the dead. Elisha lives in a world of solitude and anguish and sees himself as more dead than alive. He becomes a stranger to himself. Living in a nightmarish realm, he wrestles with past traumas and must fight to relate at all to those around him. The gap between the dead self and the surviving self in this protagonist prevents him from distinguishing between memory and reality.[305] Elisha as a tormented fictional character mirrors Wiesel's own struggle. They both dance to the tune of a tortuous memory, what Lifton calls a "psychic *danse macabre*" encircling the dead who continue to live on inside them and dominate their existence.[306]

As the story begins, Elisha is living in Paris. He is a victim of the Nazi atrocities, a survivor of Buchenwald. He wants to enroll at the Sorbonne to study philosophy because he needs to know the meaning of his suffering. Elisha is obsessed with questions. Where can he find God? When and how is one most truly human? Where does suffering lead? What is the meaning of Hitler's genocidal madness? What is the relationship of the victim and executioner? Philosophy can provide answers, Elisha hopes.

But Elisha does not go to the Sorbonne to study philosophy. One evening a knock at the door of his hotel room interrupts his life and leads him to Palestine. His visitor is Gad, a "messenger." Gad comes to recruit Elisha for the "Movement"—a paramilitary organization fighting against the British for the freedom of Israel during the days of occupied Palestine. Elisha will eventually be asked to take the role of executioner—kill a British prisoner named John Dawson. Gad appears as a *Meshulah*—the mysterious messenger of Hasidic tradition.[307] On the night of their initial meeting, Gad walks into Elisha's Paris room and peruses the books on his table. Then Gad turns to Elisha and says, "I know who you are.... I know everything about you."[308]

In such a manner, Wiesel begins to describe and investigate a possible identity alternative to and discontinuous with his first world in Sighet. The books on Elisha's table represent continuity with the world of Sighet. But Gad brushes them aside quickly, just as his very presence represents a disruption of Elisha's solitude. The name "Gad" is a biblical one. Both Wiesel's fictional messenger and the biblical figure are warriors. Jacob calls upon the biblical figure Gad to defend the land on the eastern front—east of the Jordan River. In a similar manner, Gad will call on Elisha to defend the ancient homeland, now a refuge for the surviving Jewish people.

Gad is only the first of a series of provocative intruders who appear in Wiesel's novels. But Gad now questions Elisha, whose questions were linked to the past, and he has no sense of a quest for a future. Just as Gad questions Elisha, so *Dawn* is a questioning of *Night*, especially the idea that answers may be found within the individual. Gad pushes Elisha away from isolation and in the direction of relationship. Ironically, the relationship he creates for Elisha is that of executioner and victim.

## Dawn *as the Fall of Humankind and the End of Innocence*

*Night* had been a book of reversal. *Dawn* would be also. Elisha's name means "God is salvation." But this contemporary Elisha will bring salvation in an ironic way. He will actually reverse the action of his namesake, the biblical prophet; Elisha of biblical narrative brings a person back to life, but Elisha in *Dawn* takes the life of another man. Thus, the dawn to which Wiesel refers is ambiguous. For at the end of the novel—though the clock indicates a chronological dawn and Gad had predicted a new future if Elisha embraced political action—when Elisha looks into the window, it is still night. He sees the reflection of his own image.

Wiesel reshapes Jewish tradition in this story. Jews must find a way to overcome victimization, but perhaps their desire to be innocent actually contributed to the process of their own victimization. Yet to be an executioner is to presume the prerogative of God, for God is the source of life. During the hours before dawn, the important figures from Elisha's past come to visit him, and he cannot justify his action to them. Thus, *Dawn* is in some sense an ethical and religious exploration of Elisha's quest for a future. Elisha, the narrator, says, "'Tomorrow I shall kill a man,' I said to myself reeling in my fall."[309] Within this perspective, it appears that human action is participation in a fall. That is, *Dawn* is a fall narrative rehearsing the fall of early humankind, especially Cain.

If the survivor is to achieve a new sense of identity after the Holocaust—never again to be a victim—one must give up the illusion of innocence and be willing to "fall." The dawning of a new age is one of increased complexity in which individuals who want to act on behalf of the future will pay the price of innocence. Whether Elisha kills Dawson or not, he has learned that life is now necessarily ambiguous. The dawn is the possibility of a new human community based on the proposition that now all human beings stand together in their limited and ambiguous moral nature. It is the end of innocence.[310]

In the beginning of the novel, Elisha rehearses how he knows the difference between "night" and "day." A beggar once taught him to look at a window, and if you see a face, then it is still night. So at the beginning of the novel, Elisha looks at a window and he sees his own reflection. The beginning of Wiesel's novel, *Dawn*, is the same world as that of *Night*. At the end of *Dawn*, Elisha goes to the window again. The face he sees is his own. Wiesel has given the reader an ironic title. After the execution of John Dawson, Elisha does not say "I have killed Dawson." Rather, he says, "I've killed Elisha." Darkness still eclipses dawn.[311]

## Dawn *as Parabolic Fiction*

*Dawn*, like Wiesel's other fiction, is ambiguous and ironic and finally turns in the direction of the parabolic.[312] This second work by Wiesel is a parabolic story about terrorist activity that explores the "other" side—an examination of the meaning of killing. Wiesel's autobiographical protagonist is asked to take the role of the executioner of the British prisoner, John Dawson. The parabolic story, set in a house in Palestine, is eventually reduced to a final setting in the cellar where Elisha is alone with the victim John Dawson. The conventional perspective is embodied by Elisha's colleagues in the movement: "If we must become more unjust and inhuman than those who have been unjust and inhuman to us, then we shall do so," says Gad. Murder will be not only their profession, but also their duty in order that Jews might be truly human.[313]

Young Elisha had come to accept this orientation as his own. Yet his memories disrupt this perspective, especially the visitation of his friends and family on the night he is scheduled to kill Dawson. Elisha's own confrontation with his own former self on that night, and with all the persons who contributed to the identity of his former self, prevents the easy acceptance of the conventional view of his political action. Consequently, after having killed Dawson, Elisha realizes that he has killed part of himself. Such activity is ruled out in a morally coherent world. Is such action ever justified in a post-Holocaust world?[314]

## Dawn *as a Document of Faith: A Reflective and Postmodern Ultimate Environment*

In 1958 when Elie Wiesel began writing *Dawn*, he did so with the same reflective and iconoclastic faith with which he wrote *Night*. The novel is full of questions, as was the autobiographical testimony. The novel is continuous with the testimony in other ways as well. The testimony evokes a post-modern world where the old realities no longer exist. Gone are the sure foundations of the traditional religious world as well as the humanistic virtues of the Enlightenment such as the innate goodness of the human and the inevitable progress of civilization. In *Dawn*, Wiesel demonstrates that he envisions a new "ultimate environment" that is far more dangerous, a place where ethical decisions are much more complex and difficult. Innocence has been lost. Survivors of the horrific struggle that was the Holocaust now must entertain the possibility that they must take up arms to protect themselves. In such a context, Wiesel chronicles a new foundation for himself and others as survivors: the rebirth of Israel and the renewal of the covenant. Neither of these realities, however, is formed in the manner of pre-Holocaust reality. Israel must be established and protected through the use of force; the covenant is formed with a diminished vision of God who in some measure depends on the participation of faithful human beings. Yet Wiesel chronicles the new covenant with the writing of this novel in as much as the story celebrates the remarkable existence of Israel, the solidarity among the people, and in an ironic way

145

the sanctification of life. Wiesel will test this last characteristic further in his next novel. The ambiguity of *Dawn* forces Wiesel's readers to continue to ask questions with him—questions concerning the relationship of force and violence to a Jewish future. Does the dialogue in the magical room represent a wrestling match in the soul of the author? Does this dialogue still haunt Wiesel? Some of these questions are carried forward in the next novel, which is a portrayal of the dark abyss that surrounds the survivor.[315]

# Chapter 10

# The Poetics of Grief:
# Choosing Between Life and Death

Despite good reviews of his first book, *La Nuit*, in France, Wiesel had lingering doubts about the endeavor of writing. Such testimony should have aroused anger, he concluded. And despite good reviews in France, Wiesel had difficulty finding an American publisher. The big publishers turned it down. Some wrote back that it was too short, others that it was "too depressing." After all, Americans preferred longer and more optimistic works. Wiesel's literary agent, Georges Borchardt, did not loose heart, however. He continued the search. Eventually, a small press, Hill and Wang, decided to take the risk. In 1960, *La Nuit* was translated into English and published as *Night*. In its first two years, *Night* sold only 2,000 copies.[316]

As indicated in the previous chapter, after Wiesel wrote *Night*, he turned his attention to the writing of "parabolic novels" in which the major action comes in the pondering and discussion of theological topics by the major characters. In these novels, Wiesel begins to elaborate his view, established in *Night*, that the Holocaust changed everything. The Holocaust is the beginning of a new era—a postmodern realm where the old realities exist no longer. Since God did not come to the aid of the Jews, it appears as if now, in a real sense, God and humans have changed places. The Nazis created a new universe in the camps, seizing the prerogatives once allotted only to God, becoming the arbiters of life and death, and assuming the place of traditional deity. History was reordered. This new creation devastated the survivor.

In order to live with some semblance of coherence in a moral realm, Wiesel felt compelled to create a new world where he and other survivors could begin again. What emerges is a postmodern perspective especially for religion and faith. In this view, the pathos of God weighs heavily upon the faithful. Human beings are weighted down with numbness and indifference. The appropriate response to God, as Wiesel demonstrates in *Night*, is a contending and protesting faith. In *Dawn*, Wiesel begins to affirm the sanctity of life and the solidarity of the Jewish people, and to give witness to the enduring qualities of Jewish existence.

In his next novel, *The Accident*, published in 1961, he questions the theme of the sanctity of life. Wiesel's protagonist Eliezer says, "these people [the survivors] have been amputated; they haven't lost their legs or eyes but their will and taste for life."[317] Consequently, Wiesel pursues an understanding of this "amputation" by exploring the theme of suicide juxtaposed to the theme of self-invention. Next to idolatry, suicide is perhaps the most striking denial of covenant Judaism, but as "amputated" selves, survivors are, for Wiesel, "spiritual cripples" who have lost the will to live and the sense of identity.[318] In the novel, Eliezer says to the doctor who has saved his life, "You want to know who I am, truly? I don't know myself."[319]

Like all of his work, *The Accident* is, as Alan Berger suggests, "strongly autobiographical."[320] In this second novel, Wiesel emphasizes the continuing presence of the survivors' past experiences and calls upon them to redefine their relationship with God and others. In this work, one can see Wiesel's role as a writer who is a poet/prophet more clearly than in other places. That is, the prophetic voice that originates with Moses is less thinly disguised here. In this "border" situation of ontological exile, as in Deuteronomy and in the book of Jeremiah, one hears echoes of the voice of Moses at Mt. Nebo. Just as in Deuteronomy Moses encourages Israel to "choose life" instead of choosing death, so Wiesel calls upon his readers, and by implication himself, to resume the burdens of covenant by contending with God through the vigorous life of protesting faith and by assuming responsibility for one another.

## Choosing Life: The Creation of a Language of Grief

In the death camps, the survivor's major defense against the immersion of death was what Lifton calls "psychic numbing," the actual cessation of feeling.[321] Consequently, the inmates could become so numb that they were seen as the walking dead.[322] This temporary form of symbolic death functions in human terms to prevent permanent psychic death. Wiesel tells his readers in *Night* that after his father's death, Eliezer is unable to narrate the story any longer. Only three pages tell the events of several months. "I had to stay at Buchenwald until April eleventh," Wiesel writes. "I have nothing to say of my life during this period. It no longer mattered. After my father's death, nothing could touch me any more."[323] Wiesel's other early protagonists are like Eliezer in *The Accident*, "amputated selves" who can neither feel nor enter into positive relationships with others.

Wiesel's early writing, however, narrates the reversal of psychic numbing and lays the foundation for the restoration of some semblance of covenant life. How can a survivor so immersed in death choose life? One of Wiesel's most important achievements in his early writing is the creation of a "poetics of pain," or what Walter Brueggemann calls the "language of grief." Brueggemann argues that this language of grief alone has the power to cut through the numbness and deathliness of denial.[324] As a poet, Wiesel finds symbols—reactivated from the past—with which he brings to public expression and awareness the fears that terrorize the community. With a "candor born of anguish and passion,"

149

Wiesel as a poet/prophet speaks metaphorically about the deathliness that continues to hover over himself and other survivors.[325] In *The Accident*, Wiesel offers to the public a dark symbolic story adequate to the horror of ongoing pain. This relentless public expression by Wiesel as poet/prophet pushes the community once again to engage what has been denied and challenges the community to refuse the realities of the Nazi "royal consciousness" and engage the experience of deathliness that hovers over them.[326] In this sense, this parabolic novel will embody a prophetic act that becomes something like a clarion call to read the numbness of the abyss and to confront it.

## *The Poetics of Pain: Grief in the Hospital Setting*

Thus Wiesel's accident in New York became the background for this third work titled *The Accident*. As Wiesel recuperated in his hospital room in New York in 1956, he concluded that his own situation would be a fitting way to begin a book about a survivor's continuing search for meaning. Consequently, the book begins in autobiograpical fashion. The degree to which the early narrative implies the author's identification with his fictional character is supplied when Wiesel gives his protagonist his own name. "Eliezer," who narrates the story, is a composite of Wiesel's own life story and his fictional character Elisha from *Dawn*. He is a survivor of the camps, a veteran of the War of Independence in Israel, and a foreign correspondent for an Israeli newspaper. The accident takes place near Times Square in New York, just as with Wiesel in 1956. As Eliezer recovers in his hospital room, the reader learns that the "accident" was no accident. It was an attempted suicide. Eliezer has lost the will to live.

In the initial scene, Eliezer and his friend, Kathleen, are walking across Times Square in New York City on a hot evening in July on their way to see the movie *The Brothers Karamazov*. A speeding taxi strikes down Eliezer. The car with its screeching brakes leaves Eliezer lying on his back in the middle of the street. After being taken to the hospital, Eliezer undergoes an operation that lasts more than five hours. Five days later, the patient regains consciousness. Feeling abandoned and isolated, Eliezer says, "Deep inside I discovered a regret: I would have preferred to die."[327]

The entire novel—except for flashbacks to earlier times and relationships—takes place in the hospital room where the doctor named Paul Russell, Eliezer's friend Kathleen, and another friend named Gyula attempt to bring the reluctant patient back to life. Eliezer is aided in his quest for identity by long conversations with each of the three. But the cast that covers Eliezer's body, like the hospital room itself, encloses Eliezer in an impenetrable world and expresses the numbness that covers his being.

When Eliezer is taken off the critical list, Dr. Russell comes by to visit and talk. At one point in their conversations, the doctor asks, "Why don't you care about living?" Then he informs Eliezer that "During the operation.... You abandoned me. I had to wage the fight alone, all alone. Worse. You were on the other side, against me, on the side of the enemy." What you don't understand, Eliezer thought, is that survivors "aren't normal human beings." They are "the living dead."[328]

The tortuous relationship Wiesel's protagonist has with Kathleen mirrors the writer's own painful and poignant journey to rebuild a human world. Kathleen is a "charming" young woman who is devoted to Eliezer and patiently looks for ways to help him rebuild his life.[329] Yet Kathleen knows that the love Eliezer promises lacks integrity. Finally, her words to Eliezer demonstrate that she knows the true nature of their relationship: "You claim you love me but you keep suffering.... You're still living in the past.... The truth is that I am nothing to you."[330]

Eliezer tries to respond in a way that Kathleen will understand. He explains that, during the time in the death camps, he took vows that prevent forgetting the past. But even if he had not taken the vows, "our stay there planted time bombs within us. From time to time one of them explodes." When those explosions occur, a survivor becomes nothing but "suffering, shame, and guilt." Eliezer goes on to tell himself that "suffering pulls us farther away from other human beings. It builds a wall made of cries and contempt to separate us."[331]

In the face of his dilemma of alienation and suffering, Eliezer's friend Gyula tells him he must invent himself. Gyula, a Hungarian painter described as a "living rock," is a virtual lifeforce whose energy is directed against the dominion of death that rules in Eliezer's soul. As a close friend of Eliezer, he comes to visit and banter every day. Gyula is similar to Gad in Wiesel's *Dawn*. Both function as the messenger/teacher of Hasidic tradition. Gyula's words of wisdom are aimed at nourishing Eliezer's soul. As he talks to Eliezer on his daily visits, Gyula also paints a portrait of Eliezer.

In the portrait, Gyula attempts to objectify the dead self of his friend. On the day before Eliezer is to leave the hospital, Gyula unveils the painting for Eliezer. The portrait is a picture of death and sets up a violent confrontation. Eliezer says, "My whole past was there, facing me." The background of the portrait is a black sky with a dark gray sun. Eliezer's eyes are "beating red"—eyes belonging to one "who had seen God commit the most unforgivable crime: to kill without a reason."[332]

As the portrait is unveiled, a silent dialogue begins to take place between the two men. Gyula understands that the accident was no accident. "Maybe God is dead," he says, "but man is alive. The proof: he is capable of friendship." To that Eliezer responds with the heart of a survivor: "But what about the others? The others, Gyula?" Gyula begins to tell Eliezer that the dead must be chased away. They have no place on earth. Where there is suffering, it is one's duty, Gyula says, to make it stop. But Eliezer protests. What if one cannot do that? "Man must keep moving, searching, weighing, holding out his hand offering himself, inventing himself," says Gyula. One must invent oneself anew.[333]

If a realistic view of life is too much to bear, one should invent a new way of being: fictionalize the self. Eliezer assumes that Gyula is suggesting that he should take up another mask. The portrait has demolished his former one. So he says he will learn to lie and to make Kathleen happy; "It's absurd: lies can give birth to true happiness." Yet Gyula will not allow Eliezer to invent a self without integrity. In a parabolic yet violent act of friendship, Gyula strikes a match and holds it to the portrait, demonstrating that an inauthentic mask of solitary suffering must be rejected.[334]

This story, appropriately set in a hospital room, reflects Eliezer's struggle with the forces of life and death. Gyula's portrait of Eliezer reflects back to the patient his own attempts at self-destruction and invites a response demanded by Deuteronomy: choose between life and death. As a survivor, Eliezer's life is bound inextricably with the dead. Eliezar's deceased loved ones can be seen in his eyes in Gyula's portrait. When Gyula begins to burn the portrait, Eliezer calls out in despair: "Don't do that! Gyula, don't do it! Don't burn Grandmother a second time! Stop, Gyula, stop!" The ashes fall to the hospital room floor. Eliezer cannot hold back his tears. He cries for a long time.[335]

## Tears and the Possibility of Renewal

Wiesel's first two novels explore what he calls the "other side." In *Dawn*, Wiesel examines the meaning of killing. He concludes that murder of another also brings a form of death to the murderer. In *The Accident*, Wiesel investigates the possibility that life may not be worth living and that suicide might be a possible solution. Eliezer, like Job, comes close to rejecting life. Yet this book plays an important role in Wiesel's journey toward an affirmative view of life. In the hospital setting, Eliezer begins his movement toward both physical and spiritual healing.

Eliezer thinks tears "open all doors." Yet at the end of *Night*, Eliezer has no more tears. In Wiesel's fictional world, the tears begin again fifteen years later in the hospital room in New York City. Tears, for the survivor, are "linked with hope and the possibility of renewal."[336] The writing of this book seems also to be associated with the strengthening of the voice of testimony. For Eliezer not only loses his ability to cry at the end of *Night*; he also loses his ability to speak. There are no more words after his father's death. But in the hospital, Eliezer begins to have flashbacks about his grandmother. Those reflections lead him to say, "Suddenly I felt a strange need to speak out loud. To tell the story of my Grandmother's life and death...."[337]

Another important thing happens to Eliezer. As he is called to consider an affirmative view of life through the rejection of his own numbness, to choose life rather than death, Eliezer is also challenged to redefine and renew his relationship to God and covenant Judaism. Eliezer's bantering friend, Gyula, bids Eliezer to join him in contending with God and others in a renewed form of covenant community characterized by a robust and reflective faith. Eliezer admits that human suffering creates alienation and walls that separate individuals—walls built of the cry of agony. Yet Gyula affirms that "man is alive," and one must continue to "invent" oneself and in spite of the pain build relationships and community beyond it. Wiesel picks up this theme in his third novel, *The Town Beyond the Wall*.[338] In this book, Wiesel tests Gyula's affirmation that through faithfulness to the other, one can be faithful to—and in relationship with—God.

## The Parable of the Choice

As a parable, *The Accident* is a story about choosing between life and death. Suicide as a rejection of life is in Jewish tradition a rejection of God and one's human relationships. To investigate this theme, Wiesel makes his protagonist Eliezer like Camus's Meursault in *The Stranger*—they both live with the absurdity of life. This portrayal makes *The Accident* one of Wiesel's darkest and most somber works. For Eliezer, happiness is dead. That is the conventional view of the story as a parable: human existence is without meaning and happiness is not possible. The Holocaust has made it so, and the train cannot move backward.

Yet Gyula, Eliezer's bantering friend, disrupts this perspective that provides Eliezer's orientation throughout the novel. Gyula barges into the Eliezer's room at the end of the novel, completely disregarding hospital policy and Eliezer's sense of self-pity. Then Gyula confronts Eliezer with an objective appraisal of the "accident"—it had been an effort to choose death. But "man is alive," Gyula announces. It is so, he affirms, because "he is capable of friendship." Despite Eliezer's continuing pessimism, the parabolic confrontation between the two ways of being in the world have taken place. Eliezer is now aware that friendship is alive. He experiences it in the mature relationship he shares with Gyula.[339]

## *The Accident as a Document of Faith: Grief and the Portrayal of an Ultimate Environment*

In his second novel, Wiesel continues his quest for identity and faith. The nature of this novel when read as a document of Wiesel's faith in 1960 and 1961 indicates that the author is still the reflective and iconoclastic literary artist and religious figure who wrote *Night*. Yet the nature of this volume indicates growth on the part of the author. Wiesel's concern with the poetics of pain suggests that he sees the need to deal with the psychic numbing that grips the survivor. This implies a deepening of selfhood and a quest for a more mature religious selfhood. Wiesel's spiritual landscape in the early 1960s seems to be an introspective and sensitive horizon where the survivor knows he must attend to the trauma that has numbed his inner being and the consciousness of survivors. This landscape continues to be a place for contending with God, addressing the call to the sanctity of life, and wrestling with the demons who would keep the survivor in the realm of the dead. Yet Wiesel's ultimate environment in the early 1960s continues to be a sacred region dedicated to growth.

The creation of a poetics of pain implies that as an author Wiesel is continuing to write himself toward a type of prophetic awareness and selfhood. Wiesel's now relentless portrayal of Nazi crimes and Jewish struggles begins to help the reader see beyond his modern disguise as a writer. Wiesel's identification with the work of a poet/prophet with echoes of Moses and Jeremiah is clear in the parabolic novel, *The Accident*. As he writes about the psychic pain involved in being a survivor, Wiesel also demonstrates the deep religious contours of his reflective faith, all of which implies a growing complexity to his own journey of faith. Will Wiesel be able to move beyond the tortured stance that his faith has taken now for more than ten years? The tears on the face of Wiesel's character in the hospital room anticipate some form of renewal not yet visible and a possible deepening of faith, for both the protagonist Eliezer and the author Eliezer.

## Confronting Evil: The Eichmann Trial

*The Accident* was published in 1961. That same year, Wiesel accepted another painful assignment—covering the Eichmann trial in Jerusalem for his newspaper. Eichmann was head of the Gestapo office dealing with Jewish affairs. He had written the protocols of the Wannsee Conference and had been the chief SS official in charge of the deportation of Jews to the death camps. He had been captured in Argentina and brought to Israel for trial, which began in August 1961. Wiesel went daily to the courtroom in Jerusalem, where he listened to the proceedings. Eichmann sat in a bulletproof glass cage. He appeared to be an ordinary person who, according to reports, "ate heartily and slept normally." Eichmann was, therefore, both an "enigma" and a "challenge."[340]

Wiesel was irritated by the thought that Eichmann was somehow "human." He would have preferred him to be somewhat "like a Picasso portrait with three ears and four eyes." Wiesel stared at him for hours. And even though Eichmann could not harm Wiesel while locked away in the glass case, nonetheless, Wiesel was frightened in his presence. The whole experience raised some of the old questions with which he had struggled. How does one explain the Holocaust and the nature and power of evil? How does one explain the complicity of other people and nations? How does one understand God and humankind in lieu of this event? Against a background of questions like this, Wiesel wrote his fourth work titled *The Town Beyond the Wall*, in which he outlines "one survivor's itinerary—religious childhood, deportation, arrival in France; faith, rage, and friendship."[341]

# Chapter 11

# A Town Beyond the Walls:

# Creating an Alternative Community Beyond

# Suffering and Pain

In an interview in fall 1961, Wiesel indicated that he was still struggling with those old questions. He declared, "I have made an oath to myself. ...In every book I write, I must go back over this period—if only for a chapter. And I must continually ask: what is there lacking in man, that he allowed it to happen?" He further stated, "Until we ask why men can act the way they do, everything is in doubt: God, man, morality, life." There is a "circle of guilt," Wiesel said. While "No one was untouched," somehow this experience passed over humankind and did not leave much of a mark on the human conscience. "The most fascinating thing about Eichmann," he noted, was that "he is human." His encounter with Eichmann seemed to push Wiesel further in his ongoing wrestling match with the nature of religion and humankind. Speaking of the Holocaust, Wiesel wondered out loud, "How can such things happen?" "What is there about man that we don't know—but must find out before we destroy each other?" Wiesel went on to say that "If there is any value in man, it's only when he faces up to these questions and answers them honestly."[342]

In October 1961, *Dawn* began serialization in the *New York Post*. At that time, Wiesel had lived in New York for five years.

He was thirty-two years old, unmarried, and living in a residential hotel on Riverside Drive. He spent his time writing, listening to music, and thinking. Literature and art must be moral, he thought. It must be "the result of cumulative silence." Before writing, "The silences must become so full that they finally break out. There must be a tremor that reaches the hand. Then you start writing."[343] His third novel, *The Town Beyond the Wall*, published in France in 1962, seemed to imply the articulation of a new covenant society—the creation of new relationships, ethical requirements, and a vision of life. Indeed, by 1962 a reader of Wiesel's work might speculate that he was proposing a new form of religion complete with a new view of God, the covenant, and appraisal of the human—all in the context of post-Holocaust life.

In *Night*, Wiesel had shown—through his reversal of the exodus narratives—that the covenant was broken. In *Dawn*, Wiesel chronicled the survival of the Jewish people and the creation of the new state of Israel. In *The Accident* along with *Dawn*, Wiesel had affirmed the sanctity of life while indicating the loss of innocence and the moral ambiguity of the human plight—all in the context of the ongoing struggle of the survivor to find a way to give meaning to life in light of the burdens of Holocaust survival. Now, in *The Town Beyond the Wall*, Wiesel describes the solidarity of the Jewish people and the importance of friendship and faithfulness in the post-Holocaust era even while giving new definition to the nature of God and humankind. The sum of these four works is the articulation of a new beginning among Jews after the Holocaust. Though these works describe an ideology in its original phase, the personal philosophy will eventually deepen and be extended to become more inclusive.

*Friendship and Faithfulness Tested:*
*Wiesel's Journey to Solidarity*

Wiesel linked his two novels, *The Accident* and *The Town Beyond the Wall*. At the end of *The Accident*, Eliezer declares that suffering builds walls. But Eliezer's friend Gyula tells him that his duty is to overcome suffering, invent himself anew, and commit to faithful friendship. In *The Town Beyond the Wall*, Wiesel tests this affirmation by Gyula, making the "interrogation" process central to the action of the novel. The entire story is told as the Hungarian police interrogate pilgrim-protagonist Michael as to why he entered the country illegally. The police have a well-known way of breaking the resistance of their prisoners: they make the prisoners participate in "prayer." Called the "prayer" because the Jews stand to pray, this form of torture involved placing the prisoner in front of a wall and forbidding him to touch the wall or to cross his legs. This means the prisoner was made to stay on his feet until he passed out or gave the information requested. Most prisoners were broken within twenty-four hours.

Michael's story is related from within the confines of this imprisonment experience with flashbacks to his earlier life and the details that explain why he is now in Hungary. As a protagonist, Michael is much like Wiesel's earlier characters, Elisha and Eliezer. Michael also comes from a small village in Eastern Europe and grows up as a pious Jew. He has a teacher named Kalman, reminiscent of Shushani, who instructs his pupil to question everything. After liberation, Michael makes his way to Paris. There, he enters into the depths of his own solitude where he seeks to "create a new skin...a new life."[344] Michael spends an entire year in Paris "seeking his God, tracking him down.... questioning himself."[345] Here the protagonist's stay in Paris mirrors Wiesel's own "crying out" years in Paris and New York. Yet, as in the previous two novels, Michael finds his solitude interrupted by a friend who calls the protagonist from this state of indifference to a more human way of being in the world, perhaps just as some of Wiesel's friends were speaking to him while he was writing the novel.[346]

Since the end of the war, Michael's one desire has been to return to his city, Szerencsevaros—the city of luck. With this dream of returning to the lost city, Michael embodies a major autobiographical theme in the life of the author and prefigures Wiesel's own return to Sighet two years later. Pedro, whose warm and human relationship calls Michael to know friendship once again, makes it possible for Michael to go back to his hometown, yet, having made the visit to his hometown, Michael is discovered by the local police and jailed for crossing the border illegally.

Now Michael, the interrogator, is interrogated by the police concerning his trip through the "Iron Curtain." Philosophically, the major theme is faithfulness in friendship. Can Michael be faithful to his friend Pedro, who is responsible for Michael's illegal entry into Hungary and whose life is in danger if Michael cannot be a faithful friend? Theologically, however, this is a story about establishing the ethical requirements of covenant life, for in this novel, Wiesel transmutes faithfulness in the divine-human relationship to action in the immediate human situation. Pedro, as the unsuspected stranger, provides an image of the transcendent present. He says to Michael, "He who thinks about God, forgetting man, runs the risk of mistaking his goal: God may be your next-door neighbor."[347]

## The Return to Szerencsevaros: A Fictional Journey Through Home

Michael's journey to his town is an important turning point not only for the protagonist but for the author as well. The return to his city, Michael thought, would allow him to "see himself, know himself, compare himself." His prayer was "God of my childhood, show me the way that leads to myself."[348] Robert J. Lifton demonstrates the importance of this journey homeward, if only in fiction, when he notes that "the survivor cannot formulate from a void. He requires the psychological existence of a past as well as a present, of the dead as well as the living."[349]

Yet as a stranger in his own home, Michael finds that the way back leads not to a physical town, but to memories and other human beings. On one hand, the "town" to which Wiesel's protagonist returns is very different from Michael's original city. But in other more fundamental ways, it is the same: a place where one discovers that the transcendent is revealed in the mystery of one's relationship with a neighbor, and it is that relationship that ultimately exemplifies the "town" as community. Not only does Michael refuse to betray his friend and mentor Pedro when tested by the local police, but he also remains faithful to Pedro when placed in a cell with a catatonic prisoner. In this circumstance, Michael attempts to "resume the creation of the world from the void" by repeating with the silent prisoner what Pedro had done with him—call him to the creation of a town/community beyond the wall of pain and despair.[350] How does Michael move so far beyond Eliezer in *The Accident*? Somehow, Wiesel's protagonist is undergoing a transformation, which suggests that the author as well is going deeper into himself. Can Wiesel find the personal resources now to create a more inclusive world for himself? Will he, like Michael, come to the personal conclusion that he too is called to "resume the creation of the world from the void"? Will Wiesel begin to live with the understanding that the transcendent is revealed in the mystery of one's relationship with a neighbor? What does the long section on the "spectator" mean for the author?

## Ethical Requirement, Moral Transformation, and the Struggle with Indifference

The background for Michael's transformation is shown in his confrontation with the "spectator." While in Szerencsevaros, prior to his interrogation by the police, Michael encounters and confronts the "spectator" who had watched with indifference as he and his family were led away by the Nazis. After the confrontation with the spectator whose indifference led to the abandonment of the Jews of Sighet, Michael makes a startling statement. He no longer has a need to speak. He has delivered the message. Now he can return to normal life. The past has been "exorcised." He can marry and have children. He is "whole" again.[351]

In this key text, Michael makes some important claims. He is a messenger of the dead who is unable to live with a split between being and action, either within himself or others. To live with indifference to moral evil is only to subsist on the margins of existence—not really living at all. "You're a machine for the fabrication of nothingness," Michael tells the spectator. Michael cannot pretend that an authentic life leads only to indifference and ultimately to the position that the deaths of men, women, and children are of no consequence. Michael's confrontation with the spectator implies that, for Wiesel, the possibility of moral neutrality ended with the Holocaust.[352]

One of the striking characteristics of this entire narrative about the spectator is its resolute nature. Wiesel's protagonist has moved from his reflective and questioning stance to the position of affirmation—affirming a certain way of being in the world. That way of being in the world leads ultimately to courageous action to save the life of another. How does this transformation come about?

163

Elie Wiesel

## Grief, the Politics of Confrontation, and the Creation of an Alternative Community

In *The Accident*, Eliezer lives with a sense of the absurdity of life. For him, happiness is dead; human existence is without meaning. The Holocaust has made it so, yet this bitter and pessimistic novel is followed by one filled with passion for justice, moral courage to withstand a harsh interrogation of the self, fidelity to friendship, and a claim of human wholeness. What is the difference? How does Michael make the moral journey so far beyond Eliezer?

The key comes from Pedro, who, like Gyula, is a teacher/ guide and who serves as a link with Wiesel's past. Pedro teaches Michael that "what you must say is 'I suffer, therefore you are.'" As the hero of the novel, Michael is determined to live out this maxim. To that end, he dedicates himself to overcoming his hopelessness in prison by saving his catatonic-like cellmate. In the process, Michael is able to accept the Talmudic injunction to become partners with God in the ongoing process of creation. In living out the maxim, "I suffer, therefore you are," Michael is learning to grieve, which is the only emotion that can penetrate the psychic numbness brought on by the madness of the Holocaust. Ironically, in learning to admit his suffering, he is freed for a survivor mission that goes beyond his own pain.[353]

In learning to grieve, Michael finds the freedom to embrace the politics of confrontation—confrontation with the spectator. The spectator, in this case, is not just external but also internal. That is, Michael's confrontation with the spectator is, in part, a conversation within the self of the protagonist as well as a dialogue within the author himself. Wiesel's "poetics of pain" serves several functions. In writing such a story, Wiesel is able to continue to confront his own memories and story and thereby to search for aspects of a new and just human community. And, in the writing of his own story through fiction, Wiesel is able to call others to contribute to the building of a moral community.

In the Exodus narrative of the Torah, the children of Israel, who feel the weight of their heavy burdens under the oppression of the pharaoh, first "cry" out to God. Then the pharaoh, who wants to continue the "royal" consciousness of the status quo in imperial Egypt, seeks to continue the politics of oppression. The Israelites learn eventually to demythologize this strategy and proclaim an "alternative" consciousness that frees them from the pharaoh's control.[354] The title of this volume, *The Town Beyond the Wall*, is suggestive of the prophetic task to create an alternative community in opposition to the dominant and oppressive forces of society, and implies Wiesel's ever-deepening journey of religious selfhood. Michael's embrace of Pedro's dictum, "I suffer, therefore you are," indicates the transforming power of Wiesel's emerging vision—a vision that will be clarified and strengthened as the author learns from his own journey back to Sighet.

## The Parable of the Spectator

As a parable, the complex narrative of *The Town Beyond the Wall*, filled with its "prayers" and flashbacks, is a severe testing of Gyula's affirmation in the previous novel. Gyula had shouted to Eliezer that friendship is possible. Now Wiesel examines that pro-position. In this story, Michael must act on his friendship with Pedro or his friend will be in great danger. The "spectator," who had witnessed the Jewish departure from Sighet in spring 1944, embodies the conventional attitude. The spectator's position is detached and noninvolved—a popular and "safe" existence. Michael as protagonist is led back to Sighet to confront this man and his attitude. This confrontation is one of the most intense in all of Wiesel's work. Michael tells the spectator that to live with indifference is only to subsist on the margins of existence, not truly living at all. "You're really a machine for the fabrication of nothingness," Michael tells him. The central position of this confrontation in Wiesel's work is illustrated when Michael says, "I shall return to the life they call normal. The past has been exorcised." It seems to be Michael's own courageous action in confronting the spectator that leads Michael later to attempt to save the life of a cellmate. As a parable, this narrative is a story of courageous action and commitment to friends and the larger human community. Philosophically, the story seems to ask not only can one be faithful to a friend, but what is the way from solitude to solidarity? As an autobiographical text, this story also charts the author's journey.[355]

## Writing as Spiritual Journey:
### The "Town" and Faith Transition

The writing of *The Town Beyond the Wall* marks an important transition in the spiritual journey of Elie Wiesel. His first three works are a part of his "crying out" period in which he is clearly a "messenger of the dead." All three of these works end with stark images of death. In *Night*, Eliezer looks into a mirror and a corpse looks back at him. At the end of *Dawn*, Elisha looks out the window and, because of the darkness outside, sees a reflection of his own face, which means the "night" still reigns. And at the end of *The Accident*, Gyula's experiment does not work, for he had not taken the ashes with him. Eliezer's grandmother's ashes remain on the floor just as they have continued to fly all over Europe. The past has not been exorcised, and Eliezer's face has not been changed from a face of death.[356]

Yet the ending of Wiesel's fourth work is different. In *The Town Beyond the Wall*, in a jail cell with a catatonic prisoner, Michael is living out Pedro's dictum: "I suffer, therefore you are." Michael, who has identified with Pedro and the catatonic prisoner, has undergone a transformation. "Before him the night was receding, as on a mountain before dawn."[357] This is a transitional book for Wiesel's corpus in as much as it marks the beginning of his new era as a "messenger of the living." It is also a transitional book in that it indicates a movement in the spiritual journey of the author.

The writer of the Holocaust novel is one whose life has been torn from him. His creation of a protagonist in the novel is in actuality part of the dialogue he has with himself in his concerted effort to regain selfhood.[358] In his early works, Wiesel's protagonists are "shattered" selves torn between the tie to the realm of the dead and the part of life that is a surviving self and bears the burden of living after the Holocaust. These protagonists are ridden with survivor guilt, alienated from the world around them, and haunted by their memories of a world that is no longer. One literary technique Wiesel uses to facilitate the dialogue with himself is the creation of a second self for his protagonist—a double who appears in the story as something of a spiritual guide or perhaps kabalistic master from his childhood.[359] It is possible to read this double as a reappearance of the lost father. Otto Rank and Sigmund Freud tended to view this ancient notion of the invented double as an effort to preserve life in the face of possible extinction, as an effort to defend the self against separation and loss of selfhood.[360] It seems clear that Wiesel's use of a fictionalized double is part of his ongoing effort to combat the fragmented self that resulted from the Holocaust. Wiesel's quest, in utilizing the double, is reintegration and expansion of the self. In utilizing the double, Wiesel can dialogue with the self and seek to recover some semblance of wholeness by bringing the past and present together. The significance of *The Town Beyond the Wall* in Wiesel's own growth is that in this work Wiesel seems to be attempting to work out some new relationship between the "dead" self and the "surviving" self.[361] Pedro helps Michael in the reintegration of his own selfhood in the novel, and one could argue that by extension the same is true for the author as well.

That is, the spiritual growth of Wiesel's characters in his novels reflects his own journey and the way he writes himself forward in his spiritual pilgrimage. By the time Wiesel finishes writing a novel about a protagonist who makes a physical journey toward home, he himself is ready for such a pilgrimage. What Wiesel finds in his physical journey to Sighet will make him go even deeper into himself and prepare him for another stage of his spiritual journey.

Wiesel's literary journey in *The Town Beyond the Wall* implies the nature and direction of his inner spiritual journey. Michael's journey home leads Wiesel to suspect that Sighet is not Sighet—that a journey to the place of his birth will yield only a trip to nothingness and the embrace of his true identity of the homeless pilgrim destined to roam the earth in continuing exile. A new quality of restlessness slowly begins to emerge in Wiesel. The author who in 1961 was content to sit reflectively and write in his apartment on Riverside Drive in New York turns into the pilgrim-protagonist he had written about in his novels. He, like Michael, is compelled to go back to his village in search of his origins. This journey "through home," both literary and later physical, eventually means that Wiesel, the religious pilgrim, is forced to redraw the nature and dimensions of his ultimate environment—the map by which he makes sense of the world, for he eventually discovers that the only place he feels at home in Sighet is the cemetery. There is nothing left in Sighet. His journey must turn inward where he attempts to rebuild the town in terms of human relationships, setting the stage for a complete reworking of his spiritual geography.[362] The journey inward, however, has external consequences. Wiesel's redefinition of his spiritual geography sends him around the world to what might appear to the reader as the most unlikely places, all in search of a more communal understanding of life and faith.

# III

# Reorientation/Enacting

*My life is a commentary on my books, not the other way around.*
                                                    —Elie Wiesel

# Chapter 12

# The Return:

# Re-envisioning God and Faith

*God of my childhood show me the way*
*that leads to myself.*

—Elie Wiesel

The publication of the novel *The Town Beyond the Wall* in France in 1962 marked a "decisive phase" in the literary-spiritual journey of Elie Wiesel. His first three books had described his pilgrimage away from his roots. But in *The Town Beyond the Wall*, Wiesel began to fictionalize his return. Here, the pilgrim-protagonist begins to make the painful journey home in search of his roots and an understanding of who he is in relationship to that past.[363] What is decisive about this turn toward home is that it is a journey deeper into the self in search of a redefinition of selfhood, vocation, and relationship. For Wiesel, this would be a "proleptic" return. That is, he would experience this event in writing prior to his actual return two years later. But the fictional account is an important indicator of his journey inward and a helpful clue to the events in his life that follow the writing of this book.

A survivor like Wiesel cannot create from a void. He requires a past, and he must come to terms with that past.[364] But at age thirty-four, Wiesel was approaching mid-life, that time when persons often revisit the past and seek to reclaim and rework images of previous years. With this journey into the deeper self comes energy to commit oneself to a larger cause, to work for the welfare of a larger group while maintaining a more inclusive and communal perspective.[365]

Wiesel's book *The Town Beyond the Wall* was received favorably in France. It won the Prix Rivarol, a prize given each year to a foreign novelist who writes in French. But still there were those who could not understand the attention Wiesel gave to the Holocaust. One reporter from the Belgian Radio asked Wiesel in a rather crass manner, "How much longer are you going to wallow in suffering?"[366]

## Re-envisioning God:
### A Legend about Divine Transformation

Despite this reporter's misunderstanding, *The Town Beyond the Wall* can be seen as a genuine point of new beginning for Wiesel. In the last pages of the novel, his protagonist re-creates a world as he reaches out to the young catatonic prisoner. In reaching out to this Silent One, the protagonist reaches deep into his inner resources and begins to touch his own life. By saving another, he begins to save himself. In a world where God may be found unexpectedly in one's neighbor, Wiesel has transformed the divine human dialogue into a program of solidarity with the needy, the oppressed, and the unfortunate children of God.

In a brief epilogue, Wiesel drives home the point of what has happened to both God and the human who now requires a quest for human solidarity. Legend has it that one day, a man spoke to God and asked that the two change places. Reluctantly, God agreed and granted the man's request. But after the two had changed places, the man refused to change back. So neither God nor human was ever the same again. As the years passed, "the liberation of the one was bound to the liberation of the other [and] they renewed the ancient dialogue whose echoes come to us in the night, charged with hatred, with remorse, and most of all, with infinite yearning."[367]

## The Call to a More Communal Faith: Voices from Without and from Within

This book became an important guide for Wiesel when he decided to go back to Sighet in 1964. It seems also to be an important blueprint for mapping his new version of the "ultimate environment"—that charting of the spiritual geography, for in the coming years, Wiesel's life will increasingly unfold as that of Michael in *The Town Beyond the Wall*. He will begin to search with renewed intensity for traces of the divine in the most unlikely places, in the midst of the voiceless and downtrodden the world over.

In the 1960s Elie Wiesel met a series of people whose dialogue with him can be seen as part of the call to deeper selfhood and faith. Three of these persons were Abraham Joshua Heschel, Rebbe Menahem Mendel Schneersohn of Lubavitch, and Saul Liberman. Wiesel met Heschel in the early 1960s.[368] Heschel was a Yiddish poet and theologian who taught at the Jewish Theological Seminary in New York. He was the great-grandson of the Rebbe of Apt and bore his name. In the 1930s, Heschel followed Martin Buber at the Institute of Jewish Studies in Frankfurt. A man of immense learning, Heschel was motivated by Hasidic fervor as well as civic virtue. His life's work was an attempt to synthesize the traditional faith of Hasidism with Western philosophy. Within Hasidism, his work attempted to bring together the inward-looking perspective of Rabbi Menachem Mendel of Kotsk with the views of the Baal Shem Tov, Rabbi Israel ben Eliezer.[369]

Heschel's involvement in social issues began in the early 1960s when he was rewriting his doctoral dissertation for publication. He became involved in the civil rights movement and in the struggle for Soviet Jewry. Writing the book, *The Prophets*, helped Heschel to understand that his involvement with religious issues could not remain in the study. Rather the truly religious person must also be involved in the lives of people.[370] For Heschel, the prophets were not simply subjects to be studied but models for living. "God is raging in the prophet's words," Heschel wrote.[371] In 1965, Heschel went to Selma to march with Martin Luther King, Jr. He returned home telling his family that he felt as if he had been praying with his legs.[372]

Heschel and Wiesel spent many hours together, often walking up and down Riverside Drive. There, they discussed "God, prayers, Polish Hasidism compared to Hungarian Hasidism, Lithuanian Yiddish folklore, and Polish Yiddish literature." One senses that Heschel's conversation with the younger Wiesel was one of the primary influences that became an outward call toward a deeper humanity.[373] In time, Heschel and Wiesel began to share a zeal for many of the same social issues. The voices from without, like those of Heschel, would eventually be orchestrated with Wiesel's inner voices so that his life would in due course move in new directions.

Two other dialogue partners who spoke to Wiesel about different aspects of his Jewish past were Saul Lieberman and Menahem Mendel Schneersohn, the seventh Lubavitch leader. Like Heschel and Schneersohn, Lieberman was a rabbi. He was born in Belorussia and studied at the University of Kiev and Hebrew University in Jerusalem where he later taught Talmud. In 1940 he was invited to come to the Jewish Theological Seminary in New York where he eventually served as dean and rector. Lieberman became Wiesel's revered teacher of Talmudic studies for seventeen years until his death in 1983.[374]

Schneersohn was born in Russia and educated in mathematics and engineering at the Sorbonne in Paris. He led the Lubavitch community in New York from 1951 until his death in 1994.

While discussions on the Talmud with Lieberman must have taken Wiesel back to his childhood days as a yeshiva student in Sighet, it was with Schneersohn that Wiesel spoke about the issues of faith that concerned him after the Holocaust. Wiesel's first visit to the Lubavitch court in Brooklyn lasted an entire night and became a model for his description of a Hasidic celebration in his fourth novel, *The Gates of the Forests*.[375]

In the mid-1960s Wiesel met another person who would in due course have an impact on his life. Marion was a young Austrian with delicate features and a broad understanding of art, music, and the theater, and she spoke five languages. She had a beautiful little girl named Jennifer. Like Wiesel, Marion had been in Europe during the war years. Her family had fled from Austria to Belgium, then to France, and finally to Switzerland. Now she was in the process of getting a divorce. She and Wiesel became friends and began to see one another more often.[376]

## The Return to Sighet: A Journey through Home

At the end of the war, young Eliezer could not and did not want to go home.[377] But twenty years later in 1964, he felt compelled to make that journey. As in his narrative *The Town Beyond the Wall*, Wiesel's return would be linked to re-creation. He had left by train in spring 1944. In fall 1964, Wiesel returned by car. During that intervening time, his town had "haunted" him. Over the years, he heard contradictory voices. Sometimes he told himself that he had never really left home, as if he were living in a dream world. Or perhaps the town never really existed beyond his imagination. Yet again, maybe the whole world was nothing but a projection of this town; maybe the world was turning into Sighet.[378]

His return was an effort to answer those voices and more. Wiesel describes his journey in search of his home in an essay titled "The Last Return." This was a journey, Wiesel writes, that "was to take me back to where everything began, where the world lost its innocence and God lost his mask." The preparation for the journey took twenty years of anguish. He knew the trip would be a "watershed," and it was. There would be a "before" and an "after." "Despair" would be a natural consequence of this journey. For "one cannot dig up a grave with impunity."[379]

As in the novel, the first place Wiesel wanted to visit was the cemetery. There, he wanted to find his grandfather's grave and meditate. Ironically, this would be the only place where he felt at home. Though the town had changed little, it was difficult to "orient" himself there. So Wiesel roamed the streets filled with people. But there were few Jews in Sighet now. As he walked he looked for his adolescent comrades filled with a messianic dream. But they were not there. They too had been "swallowed by the night." Wiesel found the movie house and the hospital. He walked down the "Street of Jews" where he had lived as a child. Now it was an area of small apartments with shutters closed over the windows and doors nailed shut. He marveled at how small the houses seemed now, how poor the Jews of his hometown had been. Bits of memory came to the surface of his consciousness—a widow begging for credit in the family store, images of an anxious father worried over debt, the lined face of his mother who spent long days in the store.[380]

Wiesel visited all the places that had once filled a familiar landscape—his grandmother's house, his uncle's store, his teacher's house. He went to the synagogues. Most of them were closed, but one was open. There Wiesel found hundreds of sacred books covered with the dust of time. Apparently, the books had been collected from the homes and deposited at the synagogue. Wiesel shuffled through them with impatience and was rewarded by finding a few books of his own. He even found some yellowed and worn sheets of paper that he himself had written more than twenty years before when he was perhaps thirteen or fourteen years of age. Wiesel described the script as "clumsy" and the thinking as "confused."[381] Nonetheless, it must have been a priceless treasure—an artifact from a world that no longer existed.

He found his old home and entered the yard. But he was a stranger there as in the town. An old terror of a dog attack invaded his spirit, so he bolted out of the yard and ran down the street. He reached the main street where he sat on a bench and dropped his head into his hands. He was "blinded by pain, by rage, by shame—especially by shame." As he sat there, he later wrote, "a new day began to dawn on the summit of the mountain."[382]

How does a new day dawn from pain, rage, and shame? Wiesel's response to Sighet is obviously complex, but on some level of his being he is confronting the realization that Sighet is not Sighet. There are no Jews there now. Painfully, with rage and shame in his soul, Wiesel has to admit that Sighet is not his home anymore. The Sighet of his youth can be found only in his memory. The only way to deal with the pain and trauma of this understanding—the shame of this experience—is to tell the story over and over again so that it is ritualized in communal memory. Poignantly, however, a new day does dawn. As a survivor of this tragedy, Wiesel is free to find a "town beyond the wall" of pain in the form of human relationships with other victims of tragedy the world over.

## The Gates of the Forest:
### A Flight from the Self to the Self

In the same year that Wiesel made his "return" to Sighet, he published his fourth novel, *The Gates of the Forest*. He described it in a variety of ways, including as a song of remembrance for Maria, who was the family housekeeper in Sighet, and as a "flight from myself into myself." Wiesel also tells the reader that he pursues a theme in this book that he had already "touched on" in

*The Town Beyond the Wall*: the call of God.[383] The last two
items—the flight from self into self and the call of God—indicate
something of the nature of Wiesel's journey of faith as an ever-
deepening journey into religious selfhood. The novel is
autobiographical, like Wiesel's other early works, in the sense
that it is a story about a young Hungarian Jew who is on a quest
for meaning after the Holocaust. The protagonist, Gregor, is
hiding from the Nazis in the forests of Transylvania in Eastern
Europe. Eventually, a fellow refuge named Gavriel joins him and
in time gives his life so that Gregor might continue to be free.
From that point on in the story, Gregor struggles to find his own
redemption and to learn the meaning of his failure and guilt as
well as God's role in suffering, especially the suffering of the
Holocaust.

As a part of his continuing quest, Gregor, like Wiesel, makes
his way to America and finds himself in Brooklyn in conversation
with a Hasidic rabbi. Gregor asks the rabbi if anything has
changed. "Nothing," says the rabbi. What about Auschwitz?
Gregor asks. The rabbi responds, "Auschwitz proves that nothing
has changed, that the primeval war goes on." By this the rabbi
means that the human being is capable of both love and hate,
murder and sacrifice. Auschwitz means the human being is both
Abraham and Isaac, but God—God has not changed. Gregor is not
convinced and asks, "After what happened to us, how can you
believe in God?" To this the rabbi responds with a knowing
smile and the dictum "How can you 'not' believe in God after
what has happened?" The rabbi later admits that God is guilty of
becoming an "ally of evil, of death, of murder." Still, the rabbi
concludes, this does not solve the issue, for, he says, "I ask you a
question and dare you answer: 'what is there left for us to do?'"
Gregor eventually asks the rabbi to teach him to cry. But the
rabbi says it is better to teach him to sing. Beyond suffering and
mystery, God still awaits us.[384]

Gregor's quest for meaning and understanding has taken him a long way since Gavriel gave his life for Gregor's freedom. Finally, Gregor's pilgrimage leads him to America, where he continues the effort to find some form of understanding that will give meaning to his experience. At the end of the novel, Gregor is still torn between two worlds: his Jewish heritage and the dislocating experience of the Holocaust. His quest for meaning has taken him to the Hasidic rabbi in Brooklyn. Knowing that humankind continues to endure what seems to be intolerable suffering, the rabbi and his fellow hasids persevere in believing that beyond the pain, one is called to a life of affirmation and holy joy.

## The Gates of the Forest *as a Document of Faith*

Published in 1964, *The Gates of the Forest* is the culmination of Wiesel's early period of writing and indicates a coming transition in both his writing and his faith. This first period was dominated by Wiesel's "crying out" and by his role as a "messenger of the dead." It corresponds with a period of iconoclastic, demythologizing, and reflective faith consumed with questions of identity. All of his works to this point have one major theme—the Holocaust was an utterly unique event in human history, and because of that event the world has been so contaminated that neither God nor human will be as before.[385] For ten years and with a series of different plots, Elie Wiesel interrogated God, history, and the Holocaust, searching for answers that could not be found. He demythologized the classical paradigm of Judaism and put the God of his childhood on trial. But in *The Town Beyond the Wall* and in *The Gates of the Forest*, the reader is given clues that Wiesel's literary landscape and the "ultimate environment" of his faith world is in the process of change. The reader is given intimations of the call of a more mysterious God who may be found in one's neighbor and who may be experienced and worshiped in community beyond the pain of tragedy.

When Elie Wiesel published *The Town Beyond the Wall*, he was thirty-four years old and nearing the midpoint of what was long considered the human lifespan. For some persons, especially like Wiesel who was so steeped in religious tradition in his childhood and youth, the stories and symbols of the past beckon one to a new and more dangerous way of making sense out of the world, a more communal and paradoxical vision. The call to this new perspective comes not only from friends like Heschel and Lieberman, but also internally from the memories of one's past. This means that as Elie Wiesel walked down Riverside Drive talking with Abraham Heschel, he was "called" by his friend and by the inner compulsion to rethink and rework the myths, images, and religious traditions of the storied past that continued to haunt him. As he began to make this journey—a pilgrimage traceable in his writings—he moved from being a "messenger of the dead" to becoming a "messenger of the living." Wiesel began to see truth in more complex and paradoxical ways, which meant he was given a new freedom to re-envision the religious traditions of his past and his own role in both religion and society.[386]

The very next year, Elie Wiesel had a life-changing experience when he journeyed to the Soviet Union in search of the "Jews of Silence." His "ultimate environment" expanded to include Russian Jews. Wiesel found Sighet no longer in Sighet, but in the Soviet Union. His literary focus changed to include a new motif—"the miracle, the majesty, and the mystery of Jewish life in our time."[387] He discovered a new passion, telling the story of the living.

# Chapter 13

# Man and Event:

# Becoming a Great Man in Israel

Elie Wiesel has lived for a lifetime with an unusual burden—a sense of generational obligation to become a great man in Israel. As mentioned earlier, when he was a child, his beloved mother took him regularly to see the Rabbi Israel of Wizhnitz. On one particular occasion when Elie was eight years old, something unique happened. The rabbi asked to speak to the child privately. Then later he spoke to his mother by herself. In that secluded moment the rabbi told Elie's mother that her child would grow up to be a great man in Israel, but the two of them would not live to see it. Elie's mother came out "sobbing violently." Twenty-five years later, Elie Wiesel learned why his mother cried that day.[388]

In the early 1960s, Elie Wiesel was living in New York as was his cousin Anshel Feig. A family member called with the urgent news that his cousin was very ill, and requested that Wiesel come. Wiesel went quickly to Anshel's bedside. His cousin had what Wiesel considered an odd request. He wanted Wiesel's blessing before he underwent surgery. Wiesel did not understand. Anshel had been far more pious and faithful to tradition than he. But the cousin would not take no for an answer. So Wiesel prayed the same blessing that he had received as a child when he had gotten ill. After Anshel's surgery, Wiesel went back to visit his cousin and asked him why he had insisted on a blessing from him. It was then that for the first time Wiesel learned the unusual story of the rabbi's comments. Though Elie's mother had not told him, she had told the family and no doubt treated him in a special way, expecting the growth and development of a great man in Israel.[389]

What does such a story mean in the life of Elie Wiesel? This childhood story is, in fact, a clue to understanding the life and work of Wiesel the man. It implies that he is what Erikson would call an "uncommon man" who goes on to become a spiritual innovator—a leader in his time. According to Erikson, this special young person grows up to make his own identity prototypical for the young people of his time. The solutions he finds to current issues are projected onto the youth of his day. Erikson says the question is "why certain men of genius can do no less than take upon themselves an evolutionary and existential curse shared by all, and why other men will be only too eager to ascribe to such a man a god-given greatness surpassing that of all others." The key to such a pattern of growth is that the uncommon men " *have* to become their fathers' fathers while not yet adult." For a budding spiritual innovator like Wiesel, this meant special conflicts would arise early in childhood in which he would experience "filial conflicts with such mortal intensity just because he already senses in himself...some kind of originality that seems to point beyond competition with the personal father."[390]

This is in part why Erikson describes this uncommon young man as having a precocious or "early and exacting" conscience. It is also for this reason that the child both appears and feels "old while still young." Likewise, the child at times may appear older with regard to single-mindedness than his parents, who perhaps tend to treat the child as a "potential redeemer." This gifted young person grows up with something of an "obligation beset with guilt, to surpass and to create at all cost." These dynamics tend to prolong "identity confusion" because this uncommon man searches for a way and a time when he can reenact the past and reverse the overstated identity of his era. The prolonged identity confusion "may invoke a premature generativity crisis that makes him accept as his concern a whole communal body or mankind itself and embrace as his dependents those weak in power, poor in possessions, and seemingly simple in heart."[391] If this is a plausible way to understand the complex journey of Elie Wiesel, however, where is the origin of his efforts to embrace the poor, the oppressed, and the downtrodden? What pushes a young man like Elie Wiesel to include all humankind in his quest?

Extraordinary themes began to develop in Wiesel's life and in his literature during the 1960s. He began that decade leading a rather quiet, sedate life writing books, listening to music, taking walks on Riverside Drive, and sending cables for news reports. In fall 1965, Elie Wiesel had a life-changing experience. For some reason he was no longer content with his quiet life and found it no longer possible to be satisfied with "gestures of solidarity."[392] He made plans to spend the High Holy Days behind what was then the Iron Curtain investigating the status of the Jews in the Soviet Union. When he came back to the United States, his life took on a frenetic pace. What happened to Elie Wiesel, and what is the meaning of this experience for an understanding of his life?

## Man and Event: Becoming a
## Great Man in Israel

Despite the publication of several books, in the mid-1960s Elie Wiesel continued to ask himself a "harrowing" question: Had he "made something" of his life, of his survival? The trip to the Soviet Union was in 1965 "an unexpected journey," arduous and "more dangerous than it appeared." The background for this trip is not completely clear. In his memoir, Wiesel gives only a few details of his decision to embark on this life-changing experience. He met two young Israelis who were working in the Israeli

Ministry of Foreign Affairs. Meir Rosenne worked in New York and Ephraim Tari in Paris, both overseeing "clandestine activities on behalf of Soviet Jews." They reported directly to the prime minister. The plight of the Soviet Jews was not well known. No one seemed to know what the Soviet Jews wanted the Western Jewish community to do for them. It was a delicate matter. Israel could not risk arousing the Kremlin's ire. Both Meir and Ephraim worked tirelessly attempting to find a way to communicate with the Jews of the Soviet Union. These young men encouraged Wiesel to go and investigate the situation.[393]

After much preparation, Wiesel found himself in the Soviet Union in fall 1965 for the High Holidays. The purpose of his journey was to attempt "to penetrate the silence" of the millions of Jews who had lived apart from the rest of world Jewry since the events of 1917.[394] He would search for the "Jews who held no position in society." They would be able to give him the information he needed. Wiesel went to Moscow, Leningrad, Kiev, and Tbilisi where he used his considerable journalistic and investigative skills to search for the truth about the Soviet Jews. In the streets and in the synagogues of these cities, Wiesel came face to face with the Jewish eyes that communicated a language all their own about life under political tyranny.[395]

On his first night in the Soviet Union, which was the eve of Yom Kippur, Wiesel went to the Great Synagogue in Moscow. There, under the suspicious and examining eyes of the faithful, Wiesel was told not to talk. "Talking is dangerous," said another. "Just pray. That is enough." So he prayed. Wiesel later wrote, "Never in my life have I prayed with such a sense of devotion."[396] This is an extraordinary statement coming from a young man whose religious life had been so troubled that he gave up on prayer and attending services. How does one explain such a development?

Wiesel celebrated the Feast of Sukkot under a small Sukkah somewhere in Leningrad. There, an old man was shouting, "The Holy Presence dwells not among the sad of heart! ...If there is no joy, let us create it from nothing, and bestow it as a holiday gift upon our Lord!" Wiesel watched this old Hasid with wonder and envy. "Everything he touched took fire. When you shook his hand, you felt strengthened and purified...protected." He ordered the other Jews to rejoice and encouraged them not to submit. "Where did they get their prodigious courage, where did they find, how did they ever preserve, the hidden power of their faith?" In the presence of the Hasidic faithful of Russia, "You feel moved to emulate them," Wiesel later wrote. "Not for their sake, but for your own."[397]

Wiesel stayed with the Jews of Leningrad for several hours and celebrated Sukkot with them. He ate and drank with them and joined in their singing. Yet a mood of depression stayed with him. He envied them. They were able to overcome their melancholy. "Why them and not me?" Wiesel asked. They made him promise that he would give witness to how they had fulfilled the commandment of joy, and tell of their dancing and singing.[398]

Despite a pervasive sense of persecution and an "overwhelming and irrational fear" that characterized the Jews of the Soviet Union, Wiesel also found tremendous courage and an unusual capacity for celebration. Russian Jews were caught, Wiesel wrote, in an "unending ring of terror." They continued to endure efforts "to annihilate the Jewish soul by eradicating all memory of its historical identity." Assimilation was being forced on the Jewish young. There were no teachers of Hebrew, and many of the younger generation were not circumcised. Despite these circumstances, however, Wiesel found that these Jews had a fervor that managed to overcome their melancholy and that the Jewish young had found ways to remain Jewish.[399]

While in the Soviet Union, Wiesel heard of many acts of heroism. In the town of Kutaisi, Georgia, where Jews have maintained an "active Jewish life," state authorities attempted to close and demolish a synagogue. On the day set for demolition, a large group of Jewish men, women, and children laid themselves down in front of the building. No demolition work was possible. A leader of the synagogue in Leningrad gained the reputation for educating Jewish children—in opposition to state law—in the ways of Jewish tradition. He was arrested and put in prison. Clandestine lessons on the Bible and Hebrew were being taught.[400]

On Simchat Torah, Wiesel saw thousands of young Jews dancing defiantly just ten minutes from Red Square. Almost fifty years after the Revolution, Jewish young people in Moscow were still finding ways to demonstrate their Jewishness. One dark-haired girl stood in a circle and led a large group in a series of chants: "Who are we? …What are we? …What shall we remain?" The answer was a loud and enthusiastic answer—"Jews!" The dancing and singing stunned Wiesel. On this night, gladness was overcoming fear, song overcoming silence.[401] The young people continued to dance until midnight. They rejoiced even though there was no reason to rejoice, and their dancing became an act of definition—"to let the city know that they are Jews."[402]

For Wiesel the experience was like a second trip to Jerusalem: "Caught in the frenzy of the dance, they seemed to float on air, transfigured, torn from their shadows, rising above the buildings, above the city, as though climbing an invisible ladder, Jacob's ladder, the one that reaches into heaven and perhaps higher still." For a moment, Wiesel forgot time and place. He envisioned himself as a pilgrim to the holy city of Jerusalem, jostled by a celebrating multitude seeking to claim land and city. Wiesel had not been "so strong" or "so proud" for a long, long time. In a dreamlike state, he allowed himself to be carried by the crowd.[403]

Wiesel had a similar experience in Moscow at the Great Synagogue on Simchat Torah. More than 2,000 people had gathered there that night despite threats from the government. The Torah scrolls were taken from the ark, and the people were invited to dance with the scrolls. Wiesel participated in the dance. The people proclaimed their unity. Each member of the congregation had at one time stood at the base of Sinai and heard God's word. "We held the scrolls tightly to our chests and tried to make our way through the congregation," Wiesel wrote. But the people rushed in toward the scrolls. A "sea of faces" surrounded Wiesel. He went on to say, "I have never in my life received so many blessings, never in my life been surrounded by so much good will and love." The experience reminded him of when he was young: "We used to surround the holy rebbe in this fashion begging him to intercede for us before the heavenly tribunal."[404]

### Searching for Sighet Beyond Sighet: Wiesel's Recovery of Community and Tradition

When Wiesel returned to New York and began to reflect on his journey, he realized that he had been changed by the experience. He later wrote, "Something happens to the man whose travels bring him into contact with the Jews of Russia." Wiesel went there to carry words of hope and encouragement, but to his surprise he came back strengthened and encouraged by the Russian Jews. He found a resiliency and authenticity that was in some strange way transforming. As he looked into the eyes of the Russian Jews he met, he was reminded of his own childhood. Wiesel's trip to the Soviet Union was the continuation of a "journey through home" that he began when he went back to Sighet. This time, though, he found Sighet beyond Sighet. He found the warm community of fervor and tradition that he had hoped to find in Sighet, where he actually found no Jews. What happened in Russia? The Jewish community still knit together by the "covenant of kinship" surprised him; the people welcomed him with warmth and affirmation.[405] Against all odds, he found a community of Jews that many thought had disappeared, and he embraced it as his own.[406] He "immediately felt close" to them. The interchange that took place between Wiesel and the Jews of the Soviet Union helped to transform him from being a messenger of the dead to becoming a messenger of the living.[407]

When he began to speak and write about this community, he did so in terms of his own past as an effort to rework his situation and that of the Jews of Sighet: "They feel forgotten and abandoned."[408] Wiesel has used these words to describe his own circumstances as a young child, and he uses them to portray what happened to the Jews of Sighet. For Wiesel, the West forgot about Eastern European Jews and Hitler declared them to be subhuman, life unworthy of life. With his campaign for the Jews of Russia, Wiesel attempts to restate the great overstatement of his time, and to right the wrongs done to his generation. Wiesel affirms the Soviet Jews as being a people of dignity, courage, and transforming faith. Because no one came to help the Jews of Sighet, he went to the Jews of Russia.

This move outward to embrace the Jews of the Soviet Union also signifies a move inward by Wiesel. That is, his faith now begins to take on new qualities of connectedness, a more communal nature—what James Fowler calls "conjunctive faith." Wiesel's move to embrace the Soviet Jews and to work on their behalf signifies a widening of his faith horizons. His spiritual landscape has a larger realm, and with it comes greater concerns and commitments. To put this in Wiesel's literary terms, the journey back to Sighet led to a great discovery of a "town beyond the walls." He disovered that "town" in the Soviet Union, and it was a community of the covenant realized in authentic solidarity with the Soviet Jews. Elie Wiesel had gone home, but it was Sighet beyond Sighet.

*Accepting a People's Burden:*
 *Becoming a Witness for Soviet Jews*

The energy required for Wiesel to be a person of faith also expanded. After he returned to the United States, Wiesel wrote, "I threw myself into the struggle for Soviet Jews." Again and again while in the Soviet Union, various people asked Wiesel to carry a message, to speak on their behalf. So with Abraham Heschel, Wiesel began to travel across the United States and Canada telling the story of the Soviet Jews. They were "distant" and "invisible" but now needed help. They had refused to give up. Wiesel pleaded with audiences "to help them overcome the unutterable spiritual dangers which threaten their future." Wiesel met with groups in various cities, wondering how he could mobilize and awaken the powerful Jewish community to the needs of their Russian cousins. He visited with rabbis in Toronto, Miami, Los Angeles, and New Jersey. He gave interviews, appeared on radio and television programs, and wrote articles for various magazines—all to little avail. "We had to do something else, we had to do more," he later wrote.[409]

Wiesel had promised not to forget the Soviet Jews and that he "would try to be their spokesman." He tried his best in the United States, France, and Canada. Part of his testimony about his first trip appeared in magazines in France and America, and the larger work was published as *The Jews of Silence* in 1966. Yet the effort to support the Jews of the Soviet Union remained, for the most part, "lethargic," and he began to think that he had failed.[410] But perhaps Wiesel was being overly harsh. His published testimony, *The Jews of Silence*, brought world recognition and reaction to the plight of Soviet Jews. Many humble Soviet Jews wrote to him telling their stories and pleading for him to use whatever influence he had for their desperate plights. Wiesel became engaged on their behalf and spoke for them in whatever way possible. He organized meetings and rallies. He wrote articles and spoke to heads of state from France to the Soviet Union. In the following years, many Jews from the Soviet Union were able to emigrate to Israel. Wiesel himself became increasingly recognized as a leader in human rights.[411]

The trip to the Soviet Union, then, had been for Wiesel a "turning point." He came back renewed in spirit and strength. What happened to Elie Wiesel in the Soviet Union? In his embrace of Soviet Jews, Elie Wiesel established himself in the terms of Erik Erikson as *homo religiosus*—that spiritual innovator who joins his own personal and existential struggle for meaning and identity with the quest of the group. In working for the liberation of the Jews in the Soviet Union, Wiesel shared his own hard-won sense of identity and drew strength from the group in the process. In finding Sighet beyond Sighet among the Soviet Jews, Wiesel was able to go through home again and begin to be a leader in Israel. Perhaps for the first time in his life, he was able to see his vocation merge with the sense of generational obligation he had felt in some level of his being since his earliest days in Sighet.

It is no wonder that Elie Wiesel followed the plight of the Soviet Jews from his first discovery in summer 1965 until they were allowed to emigrate to Israel. In 1965 no one knew about the Jewish tragedy in the Soviet Union. No one wanted to know. But Elie Wiesel, along with others like Abraham Heschel, attempted to awaken the Jewish conscience and the world consciousness.

Wiesel naturally followed the story from the beginning. But why in 1971 and 1972 did he "go as often as possible to a remote section of Lod Airport to witness the arrival of the first Soviet Jewish immigrants"? They came on "predawn" flights by way of Vienna. Wiesel watched the "stirring reunion" of family members and looked on as they knelt "to kiss or just touch the ancestral soil."[412] As Elie Wiesel stood in the Tel Aviv airport in those pre-dawn hours, what role did he play in the poignant drama? Was he aware of a generational obligation? Did he have any sense that perhaps for the first time he was close to fulfilling the rabbi's prediction those many years ago—that he would grow up to be a great man in Israel?

# Chapter 14

# Re-envisioning Faith and Tradition

Elie Wiesel's journey to the Soviet Union was a turning point. But in truth, that turning point was part of a gradual process that began years earlier when Wiesel first started to take walks down Riverside Drive with friends like Abraham Joshua Heschel. Since then, Wiesel had been on an ever-deepening journey into the soul, hearing voices from within and without beckoning him to a more communal and paradoxical view of the world. He had been "crying out," as some of his readers put it, for more than ten years. This "crying out" was the characteristic mode of his writing then and typical of his iconoclastic way of being in the world. For Wiesel, the world was in those years a "shattered" universe where fragmented selfhood existed in a demythologized realm. The trip to the Soviet Union represents a move away from this place to a realm where he could practice a "restorative" form of interpretation and more communal style of faith.[413]

Now Elie Wiesel began to reread and rework many of the traditions of his past religious heritage. Wiesel's early books represent a "stage" from faith in the sense that they are relentlessly demythologizing. But with its new vision of faith for Elie Wiesel, *The Jews of Silence* represents a "stage toward faith"—pointing to its communal form of faith and its restorative style of interpretation.[414] So the journey to the Soviet Union was both a journey from and to a stage of faith—away from the crying-out years with their "individuative" and "reflective," somewhat tormented style of making meaning to a more "paradoxical" and "consolidative" effort to re-envision tradition and faith.[415] After his trip in 1965 to the Soviet Union, Wiesel began to write more about the ironic, mysterious, and majestic aspects of Jewish life.[416] For example, in a report on his trip, Wiesel began his second paragraph by saying, "this may sound paradoxical, but then Jewish life everywhere is full of paradoxes—and even more so in Russia."[417]

Wiesel's writing from this era demonstrates a new awareness of the complexities of life, yet there is also a new level of commitment to what he values and holds dear. After publishing *The Jews of Silence*, he went back to the Soviet Union in 1966 in order to learn if what he reported was actually so.[418] Wiesel also heard that his new efforts at solidarity with the Soviet Jews came with a price. While in the Soviet Union on his second trip, he learned that the KGB had orders to arrest him on the slightest provocation. They were aware of who he was and what he had done with the publication of his book. Consequently, Wiesel needed diplomatic help to leave the country.[419]

Wiesel also published *Legends of Our Time* in 1966. It is a collection of essays on material both before and after the Holocaust. This volume contains especially poignant essays on the death of his father, reflections on his teachers, the story of the "orphan" who shared *heder* with him, thoughts on his beloved Moshe, the story of his return to Sighet twenty years later, a record of a second visit to Moscow, and thoughts about the Eichmann trial. Yet one of the most revealing pieces is the short introduction, which is part autobiography and part fiction.[420] It is based on a true story that has been changed to suit Wiesel's purpose—apparently to introduce this volume of essays. As revised, the story is also a good introduction to Wiesel's "re-envisioning of faith and tradition" at the time the volume of essays was published in 1966. The event upon which this story is based is described in his memoirs (and also in chapter 8 of this book) and took place in 1955 in Bnei Brak outside of Tel Aviv. Wiesel had just met Mauriac but had gone to Israel. Wiesel writes, "I had a sudden desire to see the 'young' Rebbe of Wizhnitz, for he represented an essential part of my past to which I need to cling." The young Rebbe's father was the one whose blessing Wiesel's mother cherished for her son and who pronounced that young Elie would grow up to be a great man in Israel. The old Rebbe was dead, leaving the young Rebbe as Wiesel's only connection to the one who blessed him. So he went to the young Rebbe seeking a blessing for his journey into the profane books. The visit went badly and Wiesel did not get the blessing. In his memoirs, Wiesel ends his description of that episode with these words: "I would have loved to have received his blessing."[421]

Ten years after this visit took place, Wiesel rewrote the story and placed it at the front of *Legends of Our Time*. Instead of meeting the young Rebbe, in the story Wiesel meets the old white-bearded Rebbe in the Tel Aviv suburb. Wiesel fictionalizes a conversation with the rabbi of his childhood—Rabbi Israel of Wizhnitz. It has been twenty years since he last saw him. In both the event and the story, the rabbi sits in a chair and studies Wiesel, and eventually the narrative turns to questions of identity. Likewise, the event and story emphasize the work of Wiesel the writer, and each one contains an effort by Wiesel to explain what his work with fiction means. But the fictionalized version in *Legends of Our Time* ends differently. The two figures stare at one another for a long moment. Then the rabbi's face lights up again. He invites Wiesel to come closer. At that point, the rabbi says, "Dodye Feig's grandson should not go away empty-handed. Come and I shall give you my blessing." Wiesel wants to remind the old rabbi of how long he has worked to achieve a name of his own that also needs to be blessed. But he does not. Instead, after he leaves the rabbi, Wiesel realizes that perhaps now is the time for Dodye Feig's grandson to begin to take his place at the typewriter.[422]

The comparison of the event and the story is striking, and the results are telling. The actual event from 1955, more prosaic and matter of fact, was an encounter between a young man and a staunch Hasidic rabbi whose stare accused the young man of reading the "profane" books and whose questions insinuated that he may have been writing lies. It was a confrontation between the tradition of conventional ways and the quest of a young reflective pilgrim. In the fictionalized account, Wiesel takes a journey "through" home again to rethink and revise the realities of his experience at mid-life. He feels the need for affirmation from the religious authority of his childhood and, in a dream-like episode, he creates the experience wherein the Rebbe blesses him. Yet this blessing is connected to another insight and commitment. It is time for the grandson to honor Dodye Feig by sitting down at the typewriter in his grandfather's name. For all these years, Wiesel had worked hard to establish his own name. Now, strangely, he felt the need to work in a way that honored his grandfather!

In the same year Wiesel published this fictionalized account of meeting the old Rebbe, he began what in time became an annual and much-celebrated event—his lectures on Scripture, Talmud, and Hasidic lore at the 92nd Street Y in New York City. These presentations were eventually published as collections in works like *Messengers of God*, in which he explored biblical material anew, and *Souls on Fire*, which was dedicated to his grandfather and in which he sought to recover Hasidic tradition.[423] In these materials, more than any other, Wiesel demonstrates what it means for Dodye Feig's "grandson" to sit down at the typewriter. During the presentations at the 92nd Y, Wiesel entered into the realm of the "second naiveté" and began to demonstrate a " postcritical desire to resubmit to the initiative of the symbolic"—to remythologize the narratives of biblical and Hasidic lore and show the multidimensional nature of these texts.[424] Specifically for Wiesel, these texts were now reread in light of the Holocaust.

## Rereading the Bible, Reworking Tradition

When Elie Wiesel sat down at the typewriter in his grandfather's name, he remembered that throughout Jewish history, events and literary representations have long been utilized as paradigms or reference points by the faithful both to measure and understand tragedy. Yet Wiesel had lived through an experience for which he thought there were no adequate words or language. Thus, he turned to another traditional idea: when the archetype of the past is understood to be inadequate for the current situation, the old tradition can be reread and reworked in light of the experience, giving way to new meaning and significance.[425]

Beginning in October 1966, Elie Wiesel started what became his annual lectures at the 92nd Street Y—lectures on the Bible and Jewish tradition. Wiesel wrote in his memoir that there were two speakers on that first program in 1966: novelist Jean Shepherd and himself, and most of the crowd left after Shepherd spoke.[426] In the years that followed, Wiesel developed a large following and each fall prepared lectures on biblical characters and Jewish tradition, the first of which were collected in *Messengers of God*. "His aim," Wiesel says, "is not to plunge into historical exegesis...but to re-acquaint himself with the distant and haunting figures that molded him. He will try to reconstruct their portraits from Biblical and Midrashic texts, and eventually insert them into the present."[427] In each of these lectures, Wiesel demystifies the characters, then rehumanizes and reinvigorates them. As he rereads and reinterprets the figures, he represents them in light of the Holocaust. All of Wiesel's biblical portraits and legends are, therefore, redrawn in his own image and in the likeness of his experience of the Holocaust.[428]

## Re-envisioning the Torah:
### A Post-critical Reading of the Scriptures

In as much as Wiesel portrayed the Holocaust as an anti-Sinai in *Night* and therefore set the stage for a reworking of the Torah in light of the Holocaust, his book, *Messengers of God*, appears to be the beginning of a new Talmud—a new collection of rabbinical teachings and commentaries. The book begins with Adam, followed by Cain and Abel, Abraham and Isaac, Jacob, Joseph, and Moses. Only Job at the end, on first reading, appears to be out of sequence. Why place Job in a book that seems to be a rewriting of the Torah? First, an ancient view in the Talmud says Moses is the author of Job, and in the apocryphal appendix to the Septuagint Job is the grandson of Esau, and the great-great-grandson of Abraham.[429] Perhaps more telling, however, is the midrashic legend that Wiesel himself cites. As the story goes, since Elijah ascended into heaven, his assigned task has been to go around the world collecting stories of Jewish suffering. When the Messiah comes, Elijah will present this collection of Jewish suffering as a New Torah—the Messiah's Law. In this way, the Messiah will be able to remember Jewish suffering, and not even one tear will be lost.[430] Perhaps this is Wiesel's reason for adding Job to the New Torah. It parallels the work of Elijah in creating a new book of the Torah.

Thus, while the Holocaust is never referenced explicitly, the shadow of that dark experience looms behind most of Wiesel's rewritten stories. As James Young puts it, "Brooding questions of theodicy and human suffering pervade nearly all his portraits...." In that sense, just as Nathan Rapoport's statue of Job is a fitting monument near the entrance to the Yad Vashem Holocaust Memorial in Jerusalem, so is Wiesel's portrait of the ancient figure appropriate in his rereading of the Torah. Rapoport's statue of Job has an inmate's number tattooed on his left arm, and Wiesel makes "Job: Our Contemporary."[431]

## Adam and the Mystery of
### Beginning or Beginning Again

Adam is a universal figure for Wiesel—contemporary and companion of all people in every generation. With an echo of the dark night, Wiesel writes that every person "yearns to recapture some lost paradise, every one of us bears the mark of some violated, stolen innocence." Here is an illustration of Wiesel's "second naiveté"—an ability to portray Adam in multidimensional terms both as a universal figure and as a character who can be understood in light of the Holocaust, having lost paradise and living beyond a "violated, stolen innocence." Wiesel writes that "all men, in every age, resemble Adam: every man recognizes himself in him.... His problems are ours....We share his fears, his disappointments." Here is Adam as universal man. Yet that multidimensional character, now seen with greater clarity by Wiesel through the lens of his post-critical vision, allows the writer to portray Adam in a way that is especially poignant and recognizable to the survivor: "After the fall he was a broken man. One part of him remained in paradise while the other continued to dream of it in nostalgia. One part of him yearned for God, the other for escape from God."[432]

Adam's fall was the most dramatic aspect of his life. It brought him closer to Eve. In the years that followed the two of them tried to keep the memory of the past alive by telling stories about the former years. The original couple refused to give in to resignation but rather decided to find meaning for life. Though Adam was defeated by God, he did not participate in self-denial. "Despite his fall, Adam died undaunted. As long as he lived, even far from paradise, even far from God, victory belonged not to death but to him." Thus in Jewish tradition, Creation does not end with Adam as one might think. That is, "When He created man, God gave him a secret—and that secret was not how to begin but how to begin again." So it is that every time one "chooses to defy death and side with the living," one lives out this ancient secret.[433]

## Cain and Abel: The First Genocide

It strikes one as "reminiscent of the theater of the absurd," writes Wiesel. It is a "gloomy story" with no beauty, though it does contain a threefold confrontation: between Cain and God, between Cain and his brother, and between Cain and his own soul or self. It is also a "curious and frightening tale" of ultimate conflict and jealousy, "senseless brutality," "evil on its lowest, most primitive level." This "disquieting story" is told in the most sober and spare style. The reader finds only the bare essentials—name, vocation, conflict. There is mystery in this text. "Why did Cain choose violence and his brother resignation? Why did neither resist the role assigned to him: Cain that of executioner and Abel that of victim?"[434]

For Wiesel, the place of this first genocide is "everywhere, anywhere," for Cain and Abel are "mankind." This genocide foreshadows more than one conflict; the impulses of these early humans "prefigures" our reactions in times of stress. That is, in some unknown and obscure way, humankind is involved in the fate of Cain and Abel. "Ultimately we are confronted by them, or rather by their image...." God is also involved as judge, participant, and accomplice. One of the unknowns from this story is why it should be passed on to later generations.[435]

The story is told in three acts: the brothers bring sacrifices to God, God rejects Cain's sacrifice, and Cain kills his brother; God confronts Cain about his brother; and finally, Cain is cursed and exiled. It is a story on more than one level. "Cain and Abel are symbols, examples meant to illustrate the main motivations that drive individuals to hate, bloodshed, war and, ultimately, self-destruction: sexual obsession, material power and religious fanaticism—or just plain fanaticism." The word "brother" keeps returning in the story—not only to remind the reader that the two were brothers but to stress the basic principle that "whoever kills, kills his brother; and when one has killed, one no longer is anyone's brother. One is the enemy." The leitmotif of the story is "responsibility."[436]

How could the story have ended differently? Wiesel insists that if had Cain spoken vigorously to God, history could have been different. "Had Cain chosen to bear witness rather than to shed blood, his fate would have become our example and our ideal, and not the symbol of our malediction." Yet with those words, one understands Wiesel's own midrash differently. It is clear that Wiesel has retold this story in his own experience, making Cain and Abel figures in his own drama. This "midrash is as much about Wiesel's reservoir of figures as it is about the Cain and Abel story."[437]

## Abraham and Isaac: A Survivor's Story

One of the most enigmatic stories in the Bible is the Abraham and Isaac story known in Jewish tradition as the *Akedah* or "binding of Isaac." Wiesel, however, rewrites the story into a core narrative of the Shoah by bringing the history and meaning of the Holocaust to interpret this classical Jewish text. James E. Young puts it this way: "Where the Akedah has traditionally been invoked as a paradigm for unexplained tragedy and test of faith, Wiesel now invokes (if implicitly) a new referential paradigm—the Holocaust—to explain the Akedah." In so doing, he clearly demonstrates his own reorientation toward the ancient archetypes and how he rereads and tells them again.[438]

Wiesel is aware of the enigmatic nature of the *Akedah*. As a child, Wiesel read this narrative with his "heart beating rapidly" and with "dark apprehension." He did not understand the text. Why did the three characters—God, Abraham, and Isaac—act as they did? Why would God make such a demand? Why would Abraham and Isaac accept their roles in this drama? In those days, the text was for Wiesel "an unfathomable mystery." Yet Wiesel seems to have understood the *Akedah* in later years after the Holocaust. For he writes in his first paragraph of this midrash, "here is a story that contains Jewish destiny in its totality, just as the flame is contained in the single spark by which it comes to life." Jewish destiny? "It is all there," he writes. "Every major theme, every passion and obsession that make Judaism the adventure that it is, can be traced back to it."[439]

As a literary text, the *Akedah* is for Wiesel unmatched in the Bible. The text itself is "austere and powerful." The words reverberate across time, "evoking suspense and drama, uncovering a whole mood based on a before and continuing into an after, culminating in a climax which endows its characters with another dimension." Wiesel writes, "this very ancient story is still our own and we shall continue to be bound to it in the most intimate way." All have a part to play in this drama at one time or another. Will it be Abraham or Isaac? But how does one read or reread such an opaque and mysterious text? It is for Wiesel a "double-edged" test. God tested Abraham, but Abraham also tested God. Abraham returned the challenge to God, essentially saying "Isaac is your son too!" In that sense, Abraham with his bold sense of faith won the challenge. God relented. Yet, in another sense, in such a confrontation there are no winners, only losers. [440]

Though Wiesel reads this key text as a testing of both Abraham and God, he also finds in his rereading that the narrative is deeply typological. "All the programs, the crusades, the persecutions, the slaughters, the catastrophes, the massacres by

201

word and the liquidations by fire—each time it was Abraham leading his son to the altar, to the holocaust all over again." And this text continues to be "the most timeless" and "relevant" for the present generation. Yet the story continues. Isaac survived—he could not stay in the past. He had to take his experience and make something of it, do something with his memories. Though Isaac was not able to free himself from the trauma of his youth and despite the fact that "the holocaust had marked him and continued to haunt him forever," he, like Joseph later, learned that he could "transform" his suffering into prayer instead of rancor.[441]

## Jacob Who Becomes Israel and Who Fought the Angel

Of the great patriarchs of Israel, Jacob at first reading seems the least interesting. Most of his life lacks greatness. There appears to be little that is exceptional about the man. For much of his life—as child, as adolescent, and even as adult—he appears near tears. "We get the impression," Wiesel writes, "of a big child yearning for love and protection." Perhaps that comes from having a "possessive" and "dominating" mother who attempted to spoil him. In his childhood, Jacob was more weak and frail than his brother. So he needed the affections of his mother and the buffer she could provide him. Yet his father played a part in molding the character of Jacob as well. Isaac was a distant fellow, "uncommunicative." So "It was not easy for Jacob to be the son of the first survivor in Jewish history, the first witness of a holocaust."[442]

Furthermore, Jacob's father preferred his brother, Esau. One does not know why. One does know, however, that without the ruse engineered by "Rebecca," the blessing would have gone to Esau. Consequently, Jacob was a young man filled with self-doubt that must have tormented him. He had deceived his own father and cheated his brother. Encouraged by his mother, he was playing a role in life. There was no authentic life for him. Yet at Beth-El, God gave Jacob "dreams of consolation." But in those early years this man who was to become Israel lacked imagination and the deeper sense of life. In fact, one must admit that there was initially no discovery or heroic act that could in any way be attributed to Jacob.[443]

Yet in a dark, anxious night filled with fear and self-examination by the side of the Jabbok River, Jacob's life changed. The biblical writer tells the episode with "majestic sobriety." For some unexplained reason, a stranger attacks Jacob in the middle of the night. Their struggle is silent. Few words are exchanged, but the two wrestle until daybreak. At the dawn, Jacob's attacker tells Jacob to let him go. Jacob refuses unless the stranger will bless him. The refusal means finally the gift of a new name, Israel, which in the course of generations would "symbolize eternal struggle and endurance, in more than one land, during more than one night."[444]

The great change in Jacob's life took place on the night before he would meet his brother after twenty years of absence. But who was this strange aggressor that came to fight the reluctant Jacob and provoke him into becoming another person? An angel? Jacob called the place Peniel—"the face of the divine." Wiesel likes the hypothesis that the aggressor was Jacob's own guardian angel. Jacob was attacked by his own "split self"—"the side of him that harbored doubts about his mission, his future…." In other words, at Peniel the two Jacobs came together—"the heroic dreamer and the inveterate fugitive, the unassuming man and the founder of a nation clashed at Peniel in a fierce and decisive battle." It was naturally a "turning point." At daybreak, Jacob became Israel and went forth to meet his brother as a different man. The primary meaning of this episode:

"Israel's history teaches us that man's true victory is the one he achieves over himself."[445]

## Joseph and Becoming a Tzaddik

In terms of genre and style, the story of Joseph appears unique. It is almost modern with its emphasis on psychological intrigue, political dimensions, and lack of a theological or metaphysical perspective. Perhaps this final aspect (the lack of a theological or metaphorical perspective) is meant to "illustrate that in a situation where brothers become enemies, God refuses to participate and becomes spectator." It is an unusual story with a wide range of human fortunes and misfortunes and a wide array of human emotion and expression. Its list of heroes is also extensive: shepherds, warriors, slaves, prisoners, beggars, kings, and princes. They are all searching for understanding and destiny. It is a story filled with disappointment, love lost, tension, arguments, years of silence, and most of all waiting. In Sighet, this drama was performed in the synagogue at Purim and became the "sublimation of the Jewish child."[446]

In Sighet, the story of Joseph, a young Jewish man who became a prince, was juxtaposed to the narrative of the pagan king Ahasuerus in the book of Esther who marries a beautiful Jewish girl. On Purim, when the Jews celebrated victory over the enemy, young Jewish boys and girls could dream of becoming a prince or princess and appreciate stories of transformation. That is the theme of the Joseph story—the human capacity for transformation or, better, a series of metamorphoses. Joseph's story is a family narrative in which a young son falls victim to his own choices; a social portrayal of a lowly immigrant who achieves success in his new country; a political story of a slave who is elevated to the post of high office and changes the socioeconomic fortunes of the land; a Jewish transformation wherein a refugee without resource or connection ascends to one of the highest offices in the land and uses his office for the common good.[447]

But Joseph was also a new kind of hero. He was Israel's first hero to link his life to secular history. Yet, even though God is very much a spectator or in the background of this narrative, Joseph's life takes on a religious dimension toward its end—that of a saint or a Tzaddik, one who learns to live out his beliefs. How did Joseph achieve such status? In the beginning Joseph was an egocentric young man, a long way from being a Tzaddik. His family did not withstand scrutiny well either. His brothers were resentful, envious, and plotting against him. His mother died early and tragically, leaving him as an orphan and perhaps feeling abandoned. His father loved him with partiality, which only worked against him. In Egypt, Potiphar's wife tried to seduce him. For his failure to comply, he was thrown in jail. Is this the pilgrimage of a Tzaddik? It appears in the Midrash that God was an accomplice to Joseph's demise. Beyond the silence of the narrative, another story unfolds. As Wiesel puts it, "Joseph had to overcome inner obstacles not in order to come closer to God, but to his fellow-men." He had good reason to turn away from them all—father, brothers, women, and perhaps even God. How did Joseph become a Tzaddik? Through transformation—he learned to "forgive without forgetting." He "succeeded in mastering his grief and disappointment and linking his fate" to others. So he learned to reconcile his love for his people with the love for other nations. He worked to overcome his bitterness and attempted to transform it into inspiration. Therefore, Joseph illustrates one is not born a just or righteous person—a Tzaddik. Rather one works to become one.[448]

## Moses: Fierce Prophet, Powerful Hero

In Jewish tradition, Moses is the greatest of the leaders of the Bible. He is the "most powerful" hero. His task was immense and his accomplishments commanded the admiration of those who come after him. Because of these things and more, Moses by tradition is "Moshe Rabbenu, our Master Moses, incomparable, unequaled." He is the only one about whom it is said that he saw God face to face. The power of his authority is that the word of Moses from Sinai closes any debate. Yet the writers of the Bible do an unusual thing in the history of religion: they refuse to make Moses or the other leaders of biblical history into an icon to be worshiped. Consequently, "Judaism does everything to humanize Moses." In the Bible, no failure of Moses is ever concealed. He is shown in his full humanity.[449]

God spoke to Moses at Sinai of human relationships, specifically how one should treat another human being. Rather than speak of theology, the God of the universe spoke to Israel about how to relate to another person. Yet Israel did not want to accept the Torah, so God threatened Israel and she accepted. But Moses was not happy because he wanted Israel to accept the Torah freely. Thus, when Moses came down the mountain with the tablets of stone and saw the people worshiping a golden calf, he was so angry that he was ready to take vengeance. Moses did not get along well with Israel. They were jealous of him. On the other hand, Moses was disappointed in the people on many different levels. On the night that Moses was negotiating with the pharaoh about the release of the people, Aaron was trying to convince Israel to accept freedom. "Nothing is more painful than the sight of victims adopting the behavior and laws of their executioners." Moses had expected other things—another kind of loyalty. No sooner had the people departed Egypt than they wanted to go back. They were a "flighty, ungrateful people." Moses had much reason to grieve and despair over Israel.[450]

Moses was finally able to lead Israel out of Egypt and toward the Promised Land. But Moses could not enter that land. He came to his final hour on Mt. Nebo on the border of the land promised to the ancestors. When Moses learned that his last hour had come, he refused to accept God's dictate. He wanted to continue—to go on living despite being tormented by this "unhappy and flighty" group. So Moses the "fierce prophet" entered into a long dispute with God. How could Moses dispute the divine will? Could it be that Moses sought to teach by example and to tell later generations "that to live as a man, as a Jew, means to say yes to life, to fight—even against the Almighty—for every spark, for every breath of life?"[451]

## Job: Our Contemporary

The last biblical figure in Wiesel's rewritten Torah is Job. This model of human suffering is important for Wiesel because "we know his history from having lived it." If we want to express "anger, revolt, or resignation," Wiesel writes, we turn to Job who is a part of "our most intimate landscape." In fact, in the years immediately after the war, "I was preoccupied with Job," Wiesel said. Job could be found on every highway in Europe. Consequently, "whenever we attempt to tell our own story, we transmit his." Job is the conscience of the ancestors—Abraham, Isaac, and Jacob. Wiesel had long been interested in him. He was on his way to give a "lecture" on Job when he first met Shushani in Paris shortly after the war.[452] Wiesel knew well the philosophical ramifications of the book and the struggle with the problem of theodicy—how to understand the goodness and justice of God in light of the problem of evil. It was an "eternal problem." Job—like the Jewish people—did not deserve the fate delivered by human history.[453]

Beginning with the prologue of the book, Wiesel narrates the tragedy of Job—the dialogue between God and Satan, the debate with the three friends, the revolt of Job speaking in outrage and grief, Job's repentance, and the epilogue with its restoration of the great man. This traditional ending of

Job—living in peace and reconciliation with God and others—seems to trouble Wiesel the most. "Much as I admired Job's passionate rebellion," Wiesel writes, "I am deeply troubled by his hasty abdication." Job appears far more human in demonstrating his grief and cursing the day of his birth than he does in the later reconciliation. In fact, Wiesel writes, "I was offended by his surrender in the text. Job's resignation as man was an insult to man." In Wiesel's opinion, Job should have continued his protest and not have given in so easily.[454]

Wiesel's preferred reading is that the original ending was lost. In the original, Wiesel thinks "Job died without having repented, without having humiliated himself; that he succumbed to his grief an uncompromising and whole man." How did he face God in that supposed scene of repentance? He only pretended to repent. His confessions were "decoys." "Thus," Wiesel writes, "he did not suffer in vain; thanks to him, we know that it is given to man to transform divine injustice into human justice and compassion."[455]

## Re-envisioning Faith and Tradition: Rereading Wiesel's Ultimate Environment

What does Wiesel's rereading of Scripture mean for an understanding of his faith and the man behind the mask? Rereading is not unusual. In fact, literary theorists commonly hold that one's reading of a text naturally implies an inferred meaning drawn from one's understanding of the world. Put another way, every reading is a rereading and a rewriting, if only subconsciously. What makes Wiesel's work unique at the outset is that his work in *Messengers of God* is a conscious and deliberate rereading and, therefore, a post-critical effort involving the use of a "willed" or "second naiveté" illustrative of a post-critical style of faith. This work is also restorative in nature. That is, Wiesel seeks to reread tradition after the symbols and narratives have been eviscerated by the tragedy of the Holocaust.[456] Wiesel's reading of these biblical texts is essentially autobiographical in nature. He rereads the Bible in light of his own experience of the Holocaust. In terms of an autobiographical reading, Wiesel's rereading and rewriting of these texts become a rereading and rewriting of Elie Wiesel.

That is, in as much as autobiography is an expression of selfhood created by its metaphors, then the metaphors of autobiography become a reflection of selfhood at the moment of writing.[457] Who is Elie Wiesel in these rewritten texts? He is a person who cares deeply about the ancient texts and the traditions that surround them. But he is a postmodern, post-critical individual who knows that meaning has been sundered, as Ricoeur puts it. For Wiesel, the Holocaust has shattered the meaning associated with earlier readings. But he cares enough about the text to attempt to recapture meaning through the re-writing of the stories. In so doing, Wiesel is essentially rewriting the Bible and extending the Talmudic reservoir of midrashic commentary. Yet to some extent, the Bible as now retold is rewriting Elie Wiesel. His stories tell us much about who he is.[458]

The theological frame of Wiesel's reworked texts seems to be the *Akedah*, the Abraham and Isaac narrative. In his mind, this is the most relevant biblical story for this generation. It retells the story of the Holocaust and how Isaac had to struggle to transform his suffering into prayer. Adam, like the survivors of the Holocaust, lived with a lost paradise, but he was given a secret—how to begin again. Cain, the originator of the first genocide, could have had a different impact on human history if he had known and exercised the ability of bold faith to speak vigorously to God and learned the important lesson of responsibility. Jacob, like Adam, was a before-and-after character. He had a split personality, but the two Jacobs came together in a turning point. The lesson of Jacob is that the greatest victory is the one self achieves over self. Joseph became a Tzaddik; he learned to forgive without forgetting, to master his own grief, to link his fate to others, and to live out his faith. Moses, the fierce prophet, left the example of saying yes to life by fighting against the Almighty for every breath of life. Job, like Moses, is a bold example of faith, refusing resignation by fighting to transform divine injustice into human justice and compassion.

What is the composite image of Wiesel, the autobiographer, behind these rewritten texts? What is the landscape of his ultimate environment? This is a more mysterious and paradoxical place that requires a deeper and more communal faith and a profound respect for tradition. Yet it is a place that begins to look to the universal dimensions found in the depths of Judaism. Wiesel would in due course, like Joseph, learn to link his fate to others beyond tribal and ethnic boundaries. Consequently, this land is inhabited only by those with essentially bold styles of faith—post-critical in nature. This is also a spiritual landscape where one must be willing to face the dilemmas of the day, to confront the Holocaust and God's role in it and the need to protest to God and to transform divine injustice. Yet this is also realm where one realizes the need to grow in faith by overcoming one's grief and by understanding human responsibility and the interrelatedness of human communities. Here one must know how to begin again, realizing that one's most important victory will be the one won over the self, and that now beliefs must be lived—enacted. There are in these texts indications that Wiesel had grown way beyond the "crying-out" years and that he was now on the border of a new realm—beginning to look toward the universal aspects of human experience and his role in that world.

*Chapter 15*

# A Poet/Prophet for the Nations:
# The Quest for a Universalizing Faith

*Everybody's suffering involves me,*
*indicts me in a way.*

—Elie Wiesel

In spring 1967, Elie Wiesel was invited to give the commencement address at the graduation ceremony for the Jewish Theological Seminary in New York City. Chancellor Louis Finkelstein told Wiesel that the seminary wanted to grant him an honorary doctorate. Wiesel accepted the invitation and began to prepare a speech titled "To a Young Jew of Today." When he spoke to the graduating class in June of that year, Wiesel also attempted to speak to teenage Jewish youth who struggle with what it means to be Jewish. He recalled how his mother would often take him to see the Wizhnitzer Rebbe and that her requested blessing for her son was always the same—"that I grow up to be a good Jew, fearing God and obeying His commandments."[459]

He continued to speak to young Jews, telling them that of the three elements in the blessing, the one that troubled him the most was being a "good Jew." Fearing God and keeping the commandments one understands. Ultimately, Wiesel seemed to say that the task of being Jewish comes down to the issues of working for Israel and by that extending oneself to all people.

First came particularism—working for fellow Jews. "To be a Jew," Wiesel said, "is to work for the survival of a people—your own—whose legacy to you is its collective memory in its entirety." What is most significant is "the relationship between the individual and the community." A Jew's "I" includes the Jewish past; others have had the name before. The young Jew was at Sinai—at the destruction of the temple and the fall of Masada. One may call this "historic consciousness" or a "spirit of solidarity," but for young Jews, "kinship" must include those who have gone before them as well as those who live in their generation.[460]

Yet particularism does not preclude universalism. The Jewish Scriptures teach the obligation of coming to the aid of any person—regardless of background—who is in need.[461] It is only by being Jewish that one can learn to serve the larger human family. "Only by accepting his Jewishness can he attain universality. The Jew who repudiates himself, claiming to do so for the sake of humanity, will inevitably repudiate humanity in the end." So how does one understand the relationship of particularism to universalism—one's love for and loyalty to Israel over against a devotion to the larger common good to humankind itself? "By working for his own people a Jew does not renounce his loyalty to mankind; on the contrary, he thereby makes his most valuable contribution." That is, for Wiesel, working for oppressed Jews in the Soviet Union is a way of struggling for the rights of all persons everywhere.[462] Ten years later, Wiesel was even more specific: "At the core of our being there is only one 'I' and when we reach that 'I' it is *the* 'I,' *the* man. When I say 'I,' I speak for all men who say 'I.'"[463] Yet even more pointedly, "Everybody's suffering involves me, indicts me in a way."[464]

By the time Wiesel had finished speaking to young Jews that night in June 1967, it was clear that he had an expanded view of the world and a spiritual geography that was grounded in his understanding of Judaism and its relationship to humanity. There was a creative tension between particularism and universalism—his love for Israel and his commitment to the well-being of human kind. Wiesel finds it necessary now to live out his vision of the ethical that has come down to him through tradition and that he has constructed through fiction and biblical midrash. That is, for Elie Wiesel, life is an enacted word—an extension of his vocation as a writer. His orientation is that of praxis, the holding together of spoken word and the lived word of action.

Wiesel began his career as a writer telling Jewish stories. Yet there came a time when he understood that his vocation was larger than being a writer. In time, he developed a theory of praxis for his work: the Jewish story is, for Wiesel, the central symbol but appears as a metaphor for the human. Thus, by collapsing the conventional categories, Wiesel created a fictive world in which he could envision work for justice and human solidarity. In so doing, he focused on final realities. By telescoping characterization and setting, his localized stories became narratives of the world—a universe in which human community became a possibility and solidarity with victims a foundational premise.

## Enacting: Lived Faith and the Poetics of Justice

Wiesel's praxis orientation—his life as an enacted word—came as a natural consequence of his literary career and his Jewish background. Following the trip to the Soviet Union, Wiesel became increasingly involved in public life. The theory of an enacted word that Wiesel described at the Jewish Theological Seminary in June 1967 demonstrated a praxis orientation that would be the final act of his testimony and the completion of his poetics of memory and justice, which provides validation and authenticity to his vision. If Elie Wiesel had taken the time to tell the young Jewish students of the background influences for

213

his speech that night, perhaps he would have talked more about childhood influences, like those of his mother and the early teachings about the necessity of "doing" *mitsvoth*, about his understanding of Jewish messianism, or about the work of the prophets of Israel or, perhaps, some of his discussions with Abraham Joshua Heschel.[465]

But he did not. Yet by early summer 1967, one listening to Elie Wiesel could tell that his view of the world was comprehensive yet interrelated. It required a love for Israel that branched out to a regard for all humankind. Already by 1967, Wiesel's view of the world was profound. Yet it eventually deepened into a more "concentrated" and "urgent" effort to save the world. His love for Israel remained devout, but his commitment to the universal—the human family—would in the years ahead become more visible. Interestingly, having children brought about this change.[466]

## Faith Against Faith and the Rise of a Universalizing Perspective

Beginning in the 1960s, Elie Wiesel's life began to move in new directions both in terms of his particularistic devotion to Jews and in a more universal direction toward suffering non-Jews. This expanded worldview essentially coincided with an important social event in his personal life—the meeting of Marion Erster Rose, a "beautiful and daring" young Austrian. The attraction was immediate, at least for Wiesel. Within a week of having met her, Wiesel asked Marion out for lunch. He was so caught up in listening to her, however, that he did not eat his meal. She told about her childhood in Vienna, visits with her grandfather, and the story about fleeing during the war to Western Europe—Belgium, France, and Switzerland. Marion was well educated and cultured, multilingual, and very attractive. Her smile was warm and genuine. Despite her experiences during the war years, there was a sense of softness in her face that held the promise of a close and intimate relationship.[467]

In the first volume of his memoir, Wiesel describes Marion as having daring qualities. Perhaps she proved that by continuing to see Wiesel. In a revealing interview with the *New York Times*, Marion described her memory of Elie Wiesel when they first met—he was a melancholy fellow. Wiesel had what one writer called "the dark, somber intensity of a Dante or a Savonarola."[468] He would sometimes go "days without sleep, sometimes forgot to eat and frightened many women including her, with his distance." When Marion entered Wiesel's life, however, she brought change. Some who have known the couple from the early days say that she brought some sense of "serenity" to his life, and that he even looked healthier after the two established a relationship. Perhaps the biggest change Marion brought to Wiesel was in terms of having children. Prior to Marion, Wiesel saw the world as an unfit place for raising children. "I was convinced," Wiesel wrote, "that a cruel and indifferent world did not deserve our children." But Marion helped Wiesel to see differently. "It was wrong to give the killers one more victory," she argued. "She was right," Wiesel admitted. But for Wiesel, the commitment to a new way of seeing the world became an act of "supreme defiance and supreme faith against faith." Wiesel went on to say, "I'm convinced that if I had not been Jewish I would not have accepted the awesome responsibilities of bringing life into this world."[469] After their marriage and the birth of their son, a "profound change" occurred in Wiesel's life.[470] He seemed to develop an expanded love for the children of the world demonstrated by his commitment to causes and concerns that become worldwide in nature. To be sure, by 1967 Elie Wiesel articulated a vision of faith in which he knew of the need to act on behalf of all persons. Yet only later, in the 1970s after his marriage, did he begin to demonstrate that vision in unmistakable fashion. As argued below, Wiesel's "profound change" can in part be understood as a transition to what James Fowler describes as "Universalizing" faith.[471]

## Marriage Vows, Acts of Renewal, and New Commitment

In early April 1969, at an ancient synagogue in Old Jerusalem, Marion Erster Rose and Elie Wiesel were wed on the eve of Passover. It was an event charged with "signs of renewal." Wiesel's two sisters, Bea and Hilda, and their families, some cousins, and friends attended the wedding. Saul Liberman officiated at the ceremony. At the conclusion, all the guests shouted *mazel tov* and wished the couple joy and peace. A week before in New York, Abraham Heschel had organized a ceremony at Wiesel's House of Study in which the Hasidic men sang and danced with great fervor in Wiesel's honor. Following the tradition, Heschel praised the groom and the men showered him with traditional gifts of fertility—almonds, raisins, and candy. Elie Wiesel was forty years old.[472]

After a honeymoon in France, the couple made their new life together in New York City. Marion's daughter Jennifer joined them in establishing a blended family. Jennifer was "the best and most beautiful little girl in all the world."[473] She was, however, "often sad," and she waited anxiously while the couple was away. What impact did these new living arrangements have upon the former bachelor—now living day to day with an attractive new bride and her beautiful ten-year-old daughter? What influence did Jennifer have upon the Holocaust survivor? Likely a daily look into her eyes reminded this sensitive man that he must do what he could to make the world a better place. Such a commitment, based in part on his regard for the children of his generation, gained clarity when his own son was born on 6 June 1972.[474]

Samuel Freedman thought the birth of Elisha brought the "most profound change" in Elie Wiesel. "When he was born," Wiesel said, "I felt very sorry for him...coming into this ugly, difficult, horrible world," but after a time, Wiesel's attitude changed. Now, he said, "the urge is much stronger than before to try to do what we can to make it a little better. Because he is here, we try." Wiesel said something similar to Harry James Cargas: "I watch him sometimes for hours on end, simply thinking...'Why? What for? I've seen these kinds of children.'" Then Wiesel says to himself, "I will try now, because of him I shall try even harder to change destiny, to change the world, to make it better," but then he admitted that this was not exactly true. Perhaps he would have tried anyway for the other children, but now "it's a more concentrated effort and also a more urgent one." These matters were once "abstract," but after Elisha's birth, the issues were more "concrete." So Wiesel added, now "we *must* fight evil, we *must fight* cruelty, we must fight wars, we must fight injustices simply because there is one more life now in the world and this one more life...at least I will have to shape it."[475]

The "profound change" Freedman sensed in Wiesel was due to Wiesel experiencing his son's birth in a religious way that took him deeper into himself and into a more profound commitment to the universal traditions within Judaism. That is, because of the birth of Elisha, Elie Wiesel realized he was committed to making the world a better place for all persons. Such a stance, called Universalizing faith, is exceedingly rare. As Wiesel honestly declared to Harry James Cargas, likely he would have continued in this direction anyway, but with the birth of his son the issues were no longer abstract but personal. Wiesel came to an identification with being itself—a more concentrated effort to humanize the world—for the sake of the children. He had been pushed, pulled, and lured way beyond conventional understandings and would begin to "rattle the cages" in which the rest of the world lives. The suffering he saw through "scorched" eyes and the desire that such injustice should never happen again led him to envision a rare place—an environment where love and justice can be meted out to all the inhabitants of the earth. The universal dimensions of his faith propeled Wiesel to compose a spiritual landscape "inclusive of all being." In the coming years, he would demonstrate a unique quality that in his best moments made him seem "more lucid...and yet somehow more fully human than the rest of us."[476]

## Fighting Indifference:
### An Open Letter for Biafra

One of Wiesel's earliest and most powerful public acts of solidarity on behalf of non-Jewish victims of tragedy was an open letter written in 1970 titled " Biafra, the End."[477] Biafra was a secessionist state in West Africa comprised mostly of the Igbo people, many of whom who had been oppressed and/or killed by Nigerian forces. In September 1966, they seceded from the Federation of Nigeria. Nigeria fought to maintain national unity. Consequently, they imposed economic sanctions and attacked the Biafrans by air, land, and sea. Biafra had few resources except for the oil fields they lost during the war. More than one million Biafrans were thought to have died as a result of starvation. There were some groups organized to help by publicizing their cause and raising money. But few people seemed to care. Only five nations recognized the small state. Wiesel lamented that when "we tried to help them, nobody cared."[478]

Wiesel was provoked to respond when he saw a newspaper photograph of a young child "sitting in the middle of a road leading no where." Wiesel imagined that the "child is looking at me." He discovered Biafra in all of its misfortune and death in the eyes of this child—"the dark wise eyes of this orphan." The child's body was emaciated. His "arms and legs intertwined, [he] reminds me of all those other sick, betrayed children, all those other dead children." His large ravaged eyes seemed to invite death. Where were the hundreds and thousands to be buried? They were here in the eyes of this little child who sat in the middle of the road, and in the eyes of thousands like him.[479]

In his brief essay, Wiesel summarizes the tragic plight of the Biafran struggle to resist the Nigerian forces. It became a time of genocide, yet the world was indifferent. But because of his own suffering, Wiesel was sensitized to the struggle of his Biafran friends. His essay calls upon the people of Biafra to refuse the pity of politicians and officials who would not help in the hour of need. With Biafran children starving and the sick dying like animals in the brush, the governments of the world spoke only of diplomacy in hypocritical fashion. Wiesel wrote that if the governments of the world want to give a homily on the occasion of the end of the conflict, the Biafrans should not listen. Instead, they should tell the governments that if they want to cry, they should lament their own fate, for in betraying the people of Biafra, the leaders of the world condemned themselves.[480]

## Eyes Toward a Young Palestinian: An Open Letter Seeking Reconciliation

In that same year, 1970, Wiesel also penned correspondence titled "To a Young Palestinian Arab." After hearing Wiesel give a lecture at a university, a Palestinian Arab student came up to Wiesel and introduced himself. He was polite and courteous. Born in Jaffa, he had been a student in Jerusalem and lived for a time in Nazareth. "Professor Wiesel, we read you.... [W]hat do you have to tell me?" The young student went on to say, "because of Jews I am a refugee." Wiesel later described this encounter as "one of the most heartbreaking moments in my career as a teacher." Wiesel had also been a student dispossessed of home and country.

219

He too was a former refugee. Now here was a young man describing himself in the same way, yet in his case, the Jewish people had made him a refugee. Wiesel said, "I was so taken by him because there was no hate, no anger, simply a human attempt to make a contact." So the two talked, and Wiesel eventually wrote him a letter.[481]

Apparently, the irony and paradox of this encounter troubled Wiesel. The letter he wrote to the young man is long and complex, reflecting Wiesel's own struggles but also his obvious desire to reach out to the student with whom he had an affinity despite ethnic and cultural difference. After publishing the letter, he was asked by Harry James Cargas if his message could be given to Arabs and to "all men." To that question, Wiesel responded, "Absolutely."[482] After publishing the letter in *A Jew Today*, Wiesel was asked again about it. He responded, "I wrote it because I believe from time to time we must take stock and ask ourselves: 'Where am I?'" Wiesel went on to admit that over the years he had to rethink his attitudes toward Christians. The same is true of Palestinian Arabs. They too suffer. So, while giving the interview with Harry Cargas, Wiesel summarized his argument in the letter. Amazingly, he felt responsible for the pain and suffering of this young student. "Everybody's suffering involves me, indicts me in a way.... And this is true of the Palestinian too." Yet Wiesel admitted that he could not be responsible for what another did with suffering, for suffering confers no privileges. One must use suffering for creative ends and not destructive ones. The young man responded positively to Wiesel in the encounter. "He was a very beautiful young man," Wiesel said. "He said for the first time a human being spoke to him like a human being."[483]

Wiesel memorialized this encounter with the young Palestinian in his open letter, allowing the message to speak beyond the particular context. In the letter, Wiesel writes that the young man's pain separates them. Yet in facing this pain, Wiesel is also judged. He admits to being irritated by Arab threats but also to being overwhelmed by the young man's suffering—a suffering that concerns and involves him. Hoping for a positive exchange, Wiesel pleads with the young man not to turn away. Wiesel goes further and tells the young Palestinian that he feels responsible for his pain and sorrow. Suffering the world over involves us all, he says. It indicts us if we do not speak up and become involved. If the Palestinian suffers, then one must do something about it or accept responsibility for it. But with stark honesty, Wiesel goes on to say that suffering grants no privileged status and one cannot be responsible for what another does with suffering. And in fact, when one uses suffering as an excuse to create more suffering, then the original tragedy is betrayed. Such action cannot be accepted. Though suffering can be unjustified, it cannot in turn justify murder.[484]

Finally, Wiesel ends his letter with something like a messianic and transforming vision: "And yet the day will come—I hope soon when we shall all understand that suffering can elevate man as well as diminish him." Suffering is not an end or a means. Rather, through the human response, one can allow suffering to bring one closer to "his truth and his humanity." What we can do, Wiesel writes, is humanize suffering. We can turn away from the sword and turn to dialogue. "I yearn for this with all of my heart," Wiesel states. Then he pleads, "Help us help you...." And finally, "perhaps, out of our reconciliation, a great hope will be born."[485]

## A Trip to South Africa:
## Poverty and Humiliation without Parallel

After the publication of *The Jews of Silence* in 1966, Elie Wiesel's work began to capture the attention of the Jewish community of South Africa. Already by 1969, Wiesel was invited to come to

South Africa on a speaking tour. However, he was not able to go until 1975. When he got there, Wiesel went from town to town fighting apartheid, as he later recalled. While on this trip, he wrote a compelling piece titled "Dateline Johannesburg," later published in *A Jew Today*. A warm, generous, and fearful Jewish community told Wiesel to be pragmatic and logical. South Africa is a friend to Israel. This country—in contrast to many others—has proven herself time and time again, crisis after crisis. By the same token, the developing countries of Africa have let Israel down time and again. But for Wiesel, logic gave way to conscience, and pragmatism to solidarity.[486]

According to Wiesel, the human response one feels when encountering South Africans—when seeing their dwellings and looking into their eyes—is "shame." The white man within him feels shame. One has to look away, so strong is the emotion. One has to lower the head so as not to see South Africa completely. There is a feeling that something must be done quickly. Yet there is another feeling with a sense of finality—that it is already too late for South Africa. Outside of Johannesburg in a ghetto called Soweto, one sees poverty and humiliation without human parallel. Here, Wiesel writes, men and women struggle to keep body and soul together, and the eyes of the children testify to a world without a future and without hope.[487]

Physically, it is a breathtakingly beautiful land—an "earthly paradise." But in moral contrast to the aesthetics, apartheid is as petty as it is cruel: separate hospitals, separate restaurants, separate lavatories. One cannot avoid protesting, Wiesel says. One cannot be a Jew and continue in silence about an ideology based solely on the color of one's skin. And protest he did—against the advice of friends and acquaintances. Wiesel affirmed that the inhabitants of the Sowetto ghetto must take precedence over the whites of suburbia, and that Jews—because of tradition and because of their own suffering—must stand firm against racism wherever it is found, even if it is found among friends and supporters of Israel!

## Another Final Solution:
### Against Genocide in Paraguay

Shortly after the trip to South Africa, Wiesel published a brief epilogue to a book on the suffering and death of the Ache tribe in Paraguay.[488] This collection of testimonies, put together by the International League of Human Rights, made clear that under the reign of General Alfredo Stroessner, there was a national "development" policy that included the eradication of indigenous peoples like the Ache tribe. Indigenous people were considered an obstacle to the national interest in mining and cattle raising and should therefore be removed.

The discovery of such policies brought feelings of horror, disgust, and shame to Wiesel. His ensuing essay for the epilogue is particularly poignant because it contains recognizable and familiar signs that remind him of the Nazi genocide. The men of the tribe were murdered for sport and pleasure. Young girls were raped and then sold; children were killed in front of their parents. For Wiesel, the world was again divided into victims, killers, and spectators. "I shall not forget the killers who entertained themselves by shooting at human targets in the forests." Then, in his essay, Wiesel raises the question, "Is it a coincidence that this is taking place in Paraguay?" He answers that it is no accident that such genocide occurs in Paraguay, for the angel of death from Birkenau, Joseph Mengele, lives there as a guest of the government. Is he not happy to advise on another "final solution"? Wiesel writes that other Nazi officials are known to be there as well.[489]

He determines that it is indeed another form of a "Final Solution." The purpose is clear: "the moral and physical destruction of an entire tribe—no more, no less." In terms of the policy, no one "is meant to survive." People are dragged away from the tribe, deprived of strength and dignity, and forced to become their own enemies and to wish for death. In a country not far from ours, Wiesel says, people are still being tracked down and locked up like animals. Families are being torn apart and individuals reduced to slavery before being murdered, yet American society knows little about it. The press rarely covers it. There are no discussions at the United Nations about it. There is one excuse: we did not know. But now, Wiesel affirms, after these testimonies we all know. Now we are all responsible and, in fact, accomplices if we do not act.[490]

## An Emerging Consensus:
### Spokesman for a Generation

In March 1976, Elie Wiesel's play, *Zalmen, or The Madness of God*, opened at the Lyceum in New York City. The idea for the dramatic presentation came from his first visit to the Soviet Union. On the eve of Yom Kippur in the Soviet Union, he was sitting in a synagogue crowded with people waiting for the rabbi to begin the services. The cantor was chanting the prayers. The mood was solemn, and a "mad" thought came to Wiesel. He knew something would happen there—the rabbi would cry out with his truth, declare his pain and his rage. But the rabbi was silent. So Wiesel decided to help the rabbi do on stage what he could not do in life. This story mirrors Wiesel's life; in one form or another, his life became one long cry, an effort to speak to a silent world and make them hear.[491]

In the 1970s, Wiesel's life began to take on a frenetic pace and increased visibility. In September 1976, Wiesel became Andrew W. Mellon Professor of the Humanities at Boston University. His first class at the university was titled "The Literary Response to Persecution," and quickly grew far beyond seminar size. Students came from Harvard, MIT, and other area colleges as well as Boston University.[492] In New York, a three-day conference titled "The Work of Elie Wiesel and the Holocaust Universe" was held. Forty-one scholars came from around the world. Such a tribute to Wiesel indicates "the influence he is having on Jew and non-Jew."[493]

In early 1977, Wiesel wrote "An open letter to President Giscard d'Estaing of France" in which he expressed sadness over the "Abu Daoud affair."[494] A controversy also arose at Northwestern University in the early months of 1977. A faculty member published a book denying the Holocaust. Wiesel participated in a series of lectures titled "The Dimensions of the Holocaust." Wiesel gave a lecture titled "The Holocaust as Literary Inspiration."[495]

In March 1977, Wiesel was in Oregon on the west coast and in Toronto. At Smith Auditorium in Oregon, Wiesel told a packed crowd, "A Jew is a storyteller.... This is inclusive, not exclusive. Speaking of Judaism is my way of speaking of humanity." At the University of Toronto, he "transformed the formality of Convocation Hall into a living room as he told stories from the Bible, Hasidic Europe, his own life and related what it means especially for Jews to tell stories."[496]

The Jewish community in South Africa kept up their communication with Wiesel. A letter from Dennis Diamond expresses Wiesel's impact on the Jews of South Africa: "The powerful words which you addressed to our community still haunt me often." Diamond went on to write, "I have come to realise that you bear yet another and perhaps even more awesome responsibility, that is a responsibility which we, of my generation have ascribed to you...the spokesman of mysteries we cannot ourselves comprehend." Diamond also said that in his judgment, this role had come upon Wiesel "through no choice of your own."[497]

At the end of 1977, Wiesel was in Phoenix where he "enthralled an audience of over 1,000 with Hasidic tales and real life experiences." He was proclaimed a "voice for the six million who perished in the Holocaust." He told the audience that he had an obsession with the renewal of the Soviet Jews. Wiesel also told the audience, "Art for art's sake does not exist. Literature must have a moral thrust; the reader should be changed." He went on to say that Jewish stories with depth become universal, and "Literature can correct injustices."[498] Wiesel also spent several days in 1977 at the University of Notre Dame teaching Hasidism in a series of lectures. The university president, Father Theodore Hesburgh, wrote the foreword to the volume *Four Hasidic Masters and Their Struggle Against Melancholy*, the texts for the lectures.[499]

In 1978, Elie Wiesel was chosen as the recipient of the Anti-Defamation League's Joseph Prize for Human Rights. In celebrating his selection, Lily Edelman wrote that it has long been known that Elie Wiesel is a "rebbe and teacher par excellence for Jews of all ages and persuasions.... What is only now becoming apparent is his widening circle of influence among Protestant and Catholic clergy and laity as well." She noted that a new authentic form of Jewish and Catholic dialogue was created when Wiesel went to Notre Dame for the lecture series, and Protestant theologian Robert McAfee Brown noted, "Wiesel has helped me to see my own tradition more clearly."[500]

A new word entered Wiesel's public utterances—Cambodia. "It's scandalous," he said before a gathering at Wichita State University in Wichita, Kansas. "A million persons in Cambodia have been massacred and it is being virtually ignored by world leaders." The Communist regime under Pol Pot made the country into a virtual ghetto, and the world did nothing because of indifference. Wiesel emphasized that the Holocaust teaches us not to be indifferent. "We should fight poverty, racism, indifference, injustice." He would live out his words in Cambodia.[501]

## Against Abandonment:
### A Trip to Cambodia/Thailand

At the end of 1978, President Carter asked Elie Wiesel to chair the Presidential Commission on the Holocaust. In summer 1979, Wiesel was called to testify before the U.S. Senate on the issue of the boat people of Viet Nam. "We are outraged," he said, "at the sight of people set adrift with no country willing to welcome them ashore." He went on to implore "all countries" to extend rights and asylum to the boat people.[502] Throughout 1979, Elie Wiesel also continued to follow the situation in Cambodia, where the Vietnamese Army was poised to invade and crush any Cambodian resistance. Wiesel cut out a haunting picture found in the *New York Times* in February of that year. The picture shows two frames. The one on the right is a small, emaciated Cambodian child whose stomach has begun to swell from hunger. He sits on a mat, and his eyes have a compelling glare as if they contain the tragedy of the entire Cambodian genocide. In the left frame is a teenaged guerrilla fighter who wears the skull and bones on his wrist and chest and has a rifle slung over his shoulder.[503]

The Cambodian tragedy was brought about largely by the work of one man. Born in 1925 to a prosperous landowner, his given name was Saloth Sar, and he grew up as a member of the elite society and attended French language schools. Elie Wiesel could have seen him on the streets of Paris between 1949 and 1952 when Saloth Sar studied there. In 1952 he joined the Communist Party, attracted largely because of its anti-colonial bias. Soon after, he returned to Cambodia, where he eventually became identified with the North Vietnamese but later migrated into the Chinese orbit because of utopian ideas associated with the Cultural Revolution.

In 1970, Cambodian Prince Norodom Sihanouk was overthrown in a coup d'etat. Now known by his nom de guerre, Pol Pot had set up headquarters in the jungle and begun to gather a group of revolutionaries that came to be known as the Khmer Rouge. The North Vietnamese communists supplied them with weapons for several years, long enough to batter the government troops from Phnom Penh. This was the beginning of a brutal civil war that ended in April 1975 with the Khmer Rouge capturing the capitol of Phnom Penh. Pol Pot declared "Year Zero," in which human history would start anew in an idealized agrarian society. For a brief time the Cambodians welcomed him. But their loyalty was greatly misplaced. The cities were depopulated and the people driven to the countryside to work on collective farms. Intellectuals were killed, and the societal structure of religion and finance demolished. Pol Pot adopted a Four Year Plan to triple the agricultural output. People died by the thousands due to starvation, being overworked, and suffering without medical care. In late 1978 and early 1979, the Vietnamese Army invaded with more than 100,000 troops. Pol Pot fled to the jungles of Northern Cambodia and Thailand. Between one and a half million and two million people are believed to have died in the killing fields of Cambodia.

In early 1980, Elie Wiesel went with a large international group to the village of Aranyaprathet on the border between Thailand and Cambodia to participate in a "March for Survival for Cambodia." Organized by the International Rescue Committee and Doctors without Frontiers, this was both a relief effort and a protest. The group took twenty truckloads of food and medicine for the people of Cambodia. This march was a humanitarian effort to combat hunger and illness and was comprised of activists, artists, religious people of various beliefs, journalists, and medical doctors. Among the participants, along with Wiesel, were Bayard Rustin, actress Liv Ullmann, singer

Joan Baez, and the Soviet writer and former political prisoner Aleksandr Ginsburg.[504]

Wiesel said of his participation, "How could I have refused to go to the place where the refugees from the Cambodian massacres were dying of hunger and disease?" He had seen the pictures on television and in the newspaper. The refugees were essentially "skeletons with terror-stricken eyes." The atrocities done by Pol Pot and his guerillas, the Khmer Rouge, "had reached new lows even in the bloody annals of Communism." In "the name of a perverse 'progressive' ideology, an entire country had turned itself into a slaughterhouse and sealed the gates." The "dazed survivors" had the look of "hunger, despair, and resignation"—the same look Wiesel no doubt saw in the face of the small child whose picture he had cut from the pages of the *New York Times*.[505]

While there on the border of Thailand near Cambodia, Wiesel remembered the anniversary of his father's death in Buchenwald. It was his obligation to say a prayer in his father's memory. So there in this kingdom of the dead, Wiesel gathered a minyan—a group of ten Jews, including some rabbis and a group of Israeli doctors. There was much commotion as Wiesel prepared for the traditional prayers. His voice trembled as he spoke the words, and his heart was full of memories. While Wiesel led in Kaddish—the prayer for the dead—from behind him came the voice of a young man also saying the words to the prayers. When the prayers were finished, Wiesel turned around and asked the young man, a doctor, if he had said it for his father or his mother. The doctor said no. He pointed across to the border and indicated that it was for "them," the Cambodians. The doctor had recognized, as did other marchers, that the prayer had a broader sense of meaning and appropriateness. Saying such a prayer on the border of Cambodia also commemorated the millions who had died in this Far Eastern killing field.[506]

*The World Has Turned Jewish:*
*Wiesel and Fighting the Nuclear Menace*

In 1980 Elie Wiesel was invited to Yale as a visiting professor. The next year, 1981, Wiesel published a small book of essays on biblical figures titled *Five Biblical Portraits*, and in the following year he published *Somewhere a Master*, which continued the recovery of Hasidism begun with *Souls on Fire*. Despite the long commute, he continued his work at Boston University. New York University attempted to lure him to no avail. The year 1983 brought a new experience. Wiesel was invited to be on a panel with a distinguished group of statesmen, military men, and scientists discussing the viewing of the film *The Day After*, a dramatization of the nuclear threat.

This broadcast was something of a national event. At Boston University, hundreds of students came together to see and discuss what was called the "ultimate disaster film." In it, Kansas City and its suburbs are obliterated. One student at Boston University said, "How can you not be scared. You watch this movie and realize, hey this could happen to me at any time."[507] After the film, ABC News presented a special segment of *Viewpoint* with Ted Koppel. The guests included George Schultz, William F. Buckley Jr., Carl Sagan, Henry Kissinger, Robert McNamara, Brent Scowcroft, and Elie Wiesel.The responses were predictable. George Schultz defended Ronald Reagan's perspective. William F. Buckley Jr. theorized that people who wanted to "debilitate American defenses" made the film. Carl Sagan said, "In this country we've been sleep walking during the last 38 years, and past this problem without really coming to grips with how dire and compelling it is." Henry Kissinger thought the film presented a "very simple-minded notion" of the nuclear situation and noted that the problem of our time is "how to avoid such a war...how to create a military establishment that reduces the dangers of such a war...." On a positive note, Robert

McNamara thought "much can be done" and felt that the film demonstrates "there is a commonality of interest between the Soviets and the U.S. to avoid the use of these weapons." Brent Scowcroft added that fundamentally the issue is not a deliberate decision to launch a missile but about "miscalculations," where "each side is estimating both the posture and the will of the other side."[508]

As an adjunct to the more technical aspects of the discussion, Wiesel was invited to bring a humanistic perspective to the conversation. His response to the film and to the dialogue that ensued was to admit fear for the human species. Wiesel noted that while watching the film he had "a strange feeling that I had seen it before." The only difference was that previously this happened to the Jewish people, and now it was happening to people everywhere. Maybe, he thought, the world "has turned Jewish." Now all the world lives from day to day facing the unknown; now all the world is vulnerable and, to some extent, helpless. This is a scary phenomenon, he noted, because we know from history that "what is imaginable can happen"—"the impossible is possible." The "Bomb" has achieved a level of divinity. In summary, he said, "all this means is that the human species may come to an end, that millions of children may die simply because [of] one person somewhere."[509]

In a time of questions from the audience, a teacher stood up and asked how the next generation of students should be educated with regard to these issues. Wiesel responded that he thought the "only way to save mankind" is through memory and education, not through a weapons program. Why not try to improve humankind? he wondered. "I would like to educate our society, our young people especially, to make sure that it won't happen." Later, Wiesel responded to another question with the idea of confidence in the Russian people—not because of strength over them but because the human rights movement in Russia is an anti-nuclear movement as well. The only way to prevent the type of madness discussed in this forum, Wiesel asserted, is to remember. "If we remember that things are possible, then I believe memory can become a shield.[510]

## Speaking Truth to Power:
### Wiesel and the Bitburg Incident

In early 1984, Elie Wiesel made a grueling trip to the jungles of Honduras to meet with leaders of the Miskitos Indians who had lived formerly on the Atlantic coast of Nicaragua. They had been expelled from their homeland by the "repressive regime" of Daniel Ortega, the leftist leader in Nicaragua. Some of the Miskitos had been arrested, some had had their homes burned, and others had been executed. Finally, in December 1983, the Miskitos were forced to march north into the jungle along the border of Honduras. Wiesel, who never learned to swim, crossed the last stretch of the jungle by canoe. The Miskitos, who "succeeded in arousing the sympathy of a few journalists and intellectuals in Europe and America," were eventually allowed to return to their homes. In 1985, Wiesel participated in the first conference that explored "sanctuary for refugees from El Salvador and Guatemala." Wiesel's solution to the problem was that the sanctuary should be inside of the individual. Thus every individual is a sanctuary because "God resides there." Consequently, no one can violate such a sanctuary.[511]

On 19 April 1985, Elie Wiesel was awarded the Congressional Gold Medal for his writing and teaching about the Holocaust. The event was an extraordinary one in which Wiesel seized the opportunity to "speak truth to power" and implore President Reagan not to carry out his plans to visit the Bitburg cemetery where former members of Hitler's SS were buried. The episode became one of the most embarrassing of the Reagan presidency. He and his advisors saw nothing wrong in visiting the cemetery.

After all, as Reagan told reporters, the SS were also victims of Hitler. But in an effort to extricate himself from this embarrassment, Reagan decided to add another stop on his German itinerary—the Bergen-Belsen death camp.[512]

On the day Reagan presented Wiesel with the Congressional Gold Medal of Achievement, Wiesel seized the opportunity to speak pointedly to the president. The story made headlines across the nation. The *Los Angeles Times* gave the event more dramatic appeal by placing the United Press International photograph on the front page—a photograph of Wiesel lecturing Reagan and Bush. In the front-page article accompanying the photograph, Rudy Abramson called the incident " a dramatic face-to-face meeting" in which Wiesel gave an "extraordinary appeal." On this day when Wiesel received a high honor from the president, Wiesel turned to Reagan and "gently lectured" the president on the trip plans.[513]

This "unusual meeting" began with Reagan signing a proclamation announcing Jewish Heritage Week. Then came the presentation of the award to Wiesel. During his remarks, Reagan did not mention the controversy. When the time came for Wiesel to speak, he recognized Reagan as a "friend of the Jewish people." Then Wiesel said he was sure Reagan did not know there were SS graves at Bitburg. But now that it was known, Wiesel said, "May I, Mr. President, implore you to do something else, to find a way, to find another way, another site." As the reason for his argument, Wiesel said, "That place, Mr. President, is not your place. Your place is with the victims of the SS." Wiesel admitted that surely there were "political and strategic reasons" for going to Bitburg. But the human issues surrounding the Holocaust transcend politics and diplomacy. Wiesel argued that this was not a political issue but one of "good and evil." He insisted that these two perspectives not be confused. One should remember the "guilt of indifference." Though the Nazis killed

Jews, the Jews were betrayed by their "allies" who justified their indifference because of political reasons. Thus the Jewish people had to endure "a degree of suffering and loneliness in the concentration camps that defies imagination."[514]

In introducing Elie Wiesel, Ronald Reagan had drawn an analogy between Wiesel's work and that of the Hebrew prophets. On this day—in manner and tone—Wiesel embodied the symbolic action of the prophet by speaking truth to power and thereby demonstrating an exceedingly rare form of courage and faith. He portrayed a vision alternative to that held by the executive branch of the most powerful government in the world. While Reagan's political vision sought to maintain the status quo, Wiesel's vision attempted to undermine that view of normalcy and, through the portrayal of an alternative, sought to create a new way of being in the world. This same transformational logic of the visionary is necessary for understanding Wiesel's Nobel speech.

## The Nobel Address: A Prophet to the Nations

In late 1986, Elie Wiesel received word that he had won the Nobel Prize for Peace. In Oslo on 10 December, he delivered his Nobel Address. He addressed himself to the proper dignitaries and announced that Jewish tradition required he recite the prayer, "Blessed Be Thou for having sustained us until this day." Then Wiesel began his address by telling an autobiographical story of a young Jewish boy who discovers the kingdom of night. Now, he said, that same young boy was turning to him and asking, "What have you done with my future? What have you done with my life?" Wiesel responded that he had tried to keep memory alive, for when we forget, he said, we become accomplices to the killers—guilty like they are. At this point, Wiesel tells the young boy that he "swore never to be silent whenever and wherever human beings endure suffering and humiliation." One must always take sides because silence and neutrality help the oppressor but not the victim. When human life is in danger, then national borders are no longer important. "Wherever men or women are persecuted because of their race, religion, or political views, that place must—at that moment—become the center of the universe."[515]

Profoundly rooted in Jewish memory, Wiesel explained that he sought to make Jewish priorities his own. Yet other issues and persons were important to him. To him, apartheid was just as abhorrent as anti-Semitism. The isolation of Andrei Sakharov was a disgrace just as was the imprisonment of Josef Begun, the exile of Ida Nudel, the denial of dissent to Lech Walesa and Solidarity, and the imprisonment of Nelson Mandela. Injustice and suffering could be found in every land. The victims of hunger, racism, and political oppression cried out from nations all over the world. In nations such as Chile and Ethiopia, writers and poets, as in so many other lands, were imprisoned. On every continent, there were human rights violations. "Human suffering anywhere concerns men and women everywhere." This was true of the Palestinians as well. But violence and terrorism, Wiesel insisted, were not answers. "Both the Jewish people and the Palestinian people have lost too many sons and daughters and have shed too much blood. This must stop, and all attempts to stop it must be encouraged."[516]

## A Plan for Survival:
## Memory and Global Education

In addressing the audience of the film *A Day After*, Wiesel had declared that the only solution to the current nuclear dilemma was a program of education aided by memory. In January 1990 at a conference on "Global Survival" in Moscow, Wiesel began to lay out his philosophy of education necessary for the current age. His philosophy addressed basic issues. By definition, education for the globe "must rise above boundaries and nationalities." This type of education must "teach all children and their parents the universality of their condition"—that they "are all part of humanity." The curriculum should teach "the absurdity of war, the ugliness of fanaticism and bigotry, the inhumanity of terror." In the process, a student learns that there are no winners in war, only victims. Likewise, one learns that every person, regardless of ethnic background, race, or religion, deserves basic human respect. Anything less is blasphemous to God and dangerous to world community and preservation. Any time one despises a minority, one despises all minorities. In the noblest sense, the only kind of education is global education, the kind of education that one does in any one locale must be applicable in any location. That is, "education must be for humanity, not against it."[517]

At the conference, Wiesel emphasized that all are God's children and all are responsible for God's creation. We must envision and enact an ethical component to education. Fanaticism must be recognized for what it is—"pernicious and perilous." The truth of the fanatic is in his or her opinion absolute; it cannot be challenged. Human behavior must conform, the fanatic thinks, to that absolutist view. The fanatic wants to hold all people prisoner, including God. But God refuses such absolutism. Thus, "in fighting fanaticism we are fighting not only for human freedom on a planetary scale but for God's as well." Yet in our time the planet is shrinking. Consequently, Wiesel claimed this as the essence of global education: "whatever might happen to one community will ultimately affect all communities." Because of these things, Wiesel said, global education is becoming more and more "imperative and terribly urgent."[518]

This same perspective informs Wiesel's enlarged perspective of faith. At the dedication of the Holocaust Museum in Washington and after his return from the Balkans, Wiesel departed from his prepared remarks, turned to President Clinton, and said, "Mr. President, I cannot not tell you something." He had been in the former Yugoslavia during the previous fall. "I cannot sleep since [then]," Wiesel said. "We must stop the bloodshed in that country." Children are dying, Wiesel declared. "Something, anything, must be done." Clinton agreed that the ethnic cleansing in Bosnia is the most brutal form of evil in the world today. A number of months later, Clinton sent American troops there as part of a United Nations force.[519]

From Biafra to Bosnia, Elie Wiesel demonstrated a daring new form of faith—a universalizing perspective in which the former "messenger of the dead" began to cry out for people around the globe. He gave attention especially to the plight of suffering children. But his biography offers evidence that since 1970 his "overweening" sense of conscience has been quickened even more so that at every opportunity he has tried to awaken the senses of insensitive people to the plight of the suffering poor.[520] In so doing, in the last thirty-five years of his life, he has attempted to become a rebbe, a master teacher for the world, never forgetting Jewish memory but using that memory as a shield for future generations beyond race, religion, or ethnicity. Wiesel can never seemingly do enough to salve his own conscience, and he seems driven by some deep inner force, perhaps what Erik Erikson called "generational obligation." But in these later years of his life, Wiesel seems very much aware that his faith has a universal dimension. And, like his friend Abraham Joshua Heschel with whom he used to take walks along Riverside Drive, Wiesel seems to believe that every little deed counts and that one person can make a difference in the world.

*Chapter 16*

# Conclusion

Many understand Elie Wiesel to be *the* survivor of Hitler's Holocaust, a voice of conscience for the world, and a messenger to humankind. His rise to emblematic status involved a tortuous moral journey wherein a shy yeshiva student was stolen away from his beloved Sighet, a small town in Eastern Europe, taken by cattle car to the hellish regions of Auschwitz to confront naked terror and evil without limit, condemned to watch as parents and loved ones were taken away, and forced to observe the most profound symbolic confrontation of the twentieth century—the meeting of the human with the Nazi death camps. How did this small and sickly adolescent find the moral resolve and the human ability to become a spokesperson for the dead and eventually the living, to go beyond the immersion with death to live the kind of life wherein he could be called to Oslo to receive the Nobel Prize and be recognized as one of the world's leading spokespersons for justice and peace? In recent years, questions have arisen concerning the man behind the emblematic status. Who is Elie Wiesel, and what drives him along his frenetic pace of writing, speaking, and activism?

I have argued in this book that the way to put Wiesel's life in larger perspective is to ask if we can determine logic to his inner life. Is there a way to determine his working gifts and the effect of these gifts on human society? The thesis of this book is that Elie Wiesel's religious faith is the driving force of his life and the core of the personality that stands behind his emblematic status.

# Conclusion

Analyzed and described, this faith allows for a portrayal of the dynamics of an inner spiritual life as well as the nature of his gifts and their effect on society. Consequently, I have tried to show that Wiesel is essentially a generative religious personality, something of a modern poet/prophet, who by deepening his own particular Jewish vision came eventually to be a link with humanity, or being itself, which is a stance of universalizing faith. Over time he has come to identify with the oppressed the world over. As such, he is also what Erikson calls *homo religiosus*—a religious genius and spiritual innovator, a conflicted individual who joins his own struggle for meaning and identity with the group. In trying to resolve his own struggle, Wiesel has tried to find a new sense of identity for humankind.

A close reading of Wiesel's work suggests that the theme of his life—and the foundational logic of his inner religious or spiritual life—is separation or abandonment versus solidarity. I have traced this theme and religious logic throughout his entire life. His first memory, Wiesel tells us, is that of a little boy sitting on the edge of his bed calling for his mother. He could not understand why he had to go to *heder*, why he could not stay with his mother. He felt abandoned. A similar story is told about his "absent" father. He saw his father seldom, usually on Shabbat. They would go to services together, holding hands. But when his father dropped his hand, once again he felt like an abandoned and rejected child. It is clear that Wiesel's earliest years were formative for him—that the issues raised then have stayed with him for a lifetime and continue with him as major factors in shaping the image of his spiritual landscape. The central issue of abandonment over against solidarity arose in the first months and years of his life as part of the quest to resolve the initial fundamental crisis of trust versus mistrust. Wiesel's resolution of this issue became foundational for his pilgrimage through life. He was so sensitized to the issue of abandonment

239

that his adult response to the trauma he continued to see in the shattered existence around him was solidarity with the victim. During the trauma of the death camps, he saw the Jewish people abandoned by the allies and by God. As an adult, Wiesel continued to see the issue of the abandonment of the oppressed as a central problem, the answer to which is always solidarity with the victim.

It is also clear from the stories of his earliest years that Eliezer was a child in despair attempting to find a way to cope with a crisis that he neither understood nor was able to resolve easily. The relationship with his grandfather established the foundation for his young life and ushered in some of his most joyous memories—simply being with Dodye Feig. Yet the ensuing identification with his grandfather left him with a precocious sense of guilt even as it helped him resolve the issue of separation from the maternal matrix and propelled him on the journey of faith. The foundation of Elie Wiesel's adult spiritual landscape and the nature and direction of his faith were established in the first six years of life. His earliest years were a study in the growth and development of *homo religiosus*. The death of his father in the camps was the "curse," experienced much in the way Ghandi understood the death of his father—an existential blot that could not be removed. Yet this death was a screen memory for the earlier and more fundamental crisis already hidden in his soul of how he as a young child felt the initial threat of abandonment and was eventually called to resolve the conflict by going beyond the father, especially through identification with Dodye Feig.

As Eliezer entered his early school years, following the model of his grandfather, he absorbed the world story that his Jewish community provided for him in story, song, and ritual, and in due course began to believe profoundly. His mother and the rabbi—and perhaps others—began now, if not before, to treat him with a sense of generational obligation to become a great man in Israel. His life was being shaped by parental and community expectation. Put religiously, at a very young age, Eliezer, like Jeremiah ben Hilkiah, was called to fulfill the ways of the Torah and Israel. The overweening conscience, expressed in the stories of his need to give away presents, continued to give witness to the inner dynamics of his deep-seated sense of guilt and the eventual need to resolve the crisis surrounding it.[521] In time, he looked for a way to resolve his own crisis by merging his identity and quest with a larger group. Which group and when? For Elie Wiesel, it was initially the Jews of silence in the former Soviet Union, but it later extended to victims everywhere—a faith identified with being itself.

Wiesel's adolescent years give a clear indication of the emerging nature of his religious pilgrimage. The experience of tyranny was a double entendre for Eliezer during these years: first, in terms of a conventional alliance with teenaged friends in which he attempted to overcome Satan mystically; and second, in terms of the horrendous experience of the death camps including the loss of his mother, father, and little sister. In the first instance, Eliezer's refusal of his father's desire that he cease the study of the Kabala and avoid the danger inherent in the mystical attempts to stop Satan give special indication that Eliezer had not only a deep-seated need to contradict the words and ways of his father but also some inner authority to do so. Eliezer could contradict his father because he had a covenant sealed with God and because on some level he felt that he had gone beyond competition with his father. In this episode, he is a budding spiritual innovator looking for a way to redeem Israel. In the second instance, it was in the death camps that his childhood fear of abandonment became written indelibly onto his ultimate environment in a manner that was beyond erasure or exorcism. His eyes were scorched by what he saw, and that vision is seared in his soul so that the depth of this tragedy means he will now struggle for a lifetime to understand, find meaning for, and give witness to these events. At the time, he felt that Hitler's tyranny also meant God and society had abandoned the Jewish people.

After Eliezer was liberated from Buchenwald, he continued his conventional faith for a time. But in Jerusalem in 1949, he knew he could not continue to live or believe as before. He sought for a new life in Israel, in India, and in Europe. Wiesel went through a long period of some fifteen or sixteen years in which the God of his childhood was his enemy, and he himself became ruthlessly demythologizing. During this reflective period of faith, he reversed ancient traditions like the exodus and the *Akedah* in his writings in an effort to show the way life had changed. Wiesel, however, wrote himself toward new religious selfhood, which one can begin to detect in his books *The Town Beyond the Wall* and *The Gates of the Forest*.

But it is probably only during his trip to the Soviet Union in fall 1965 that one can finally begin to see the emergence of a truly communal self in Elie Wiesel. He came back from that trip a changed person, which is clearly evident in his chronicle of that journey titled *The Jews of Silence*. On this trip, Wiesel began to enact the solidarity with the victim that he first described in the novel *The Town Beyond the Wall*. Wiesel's writing began to change after the trip to the Soviet Union. He started to recover Jewish tradition. After his marriage and especially after the birth of his son, the theme of solidarity with the victim extended to victims all over the world. At this point, one begins to see clearly both Wiesel's gifts and their effect on society. His gifts are not only for the written word but also the recovery of religious tradition and the ability to share that tradition in both particularistic and universalizing fashion—for the identity and welfare of Jews the world over and for people in need whether they are in Biafra, refugees from the West Bank of Palestine,

Black South Africans in Soweto, the Boat People from Viet Nam, the Ache tribe in Paraguay in South America, refugees from the Khmer Rouge and Pol Pot in Cambodia, or refugees in Bosnia.

The inner logic of Elie Wiesel, as demonstrated by the tenor of his life described in written word and in indelible fashion through actualizing his commitment to the welfare of victims around the world, is that of *homo religiosus*—the religious genius whose faith is extended to a universalizing perspective. His gifts are that of a poet/prophet who works in written word, public proclamation, and the indelible script of symbolic action. As a writer and activist, he has followed the "code" of Jeremiah ben Hilkiah—shattering, evoking, and enacting. Wiesel's early writing shattered the Western conception of normalcy. *Night* evoked a world that a later generation could not imagine. Yet, having shattered the conception of normalcy and reversing the status quo in religious thinking, Wiesel began eventually to evoke a new way of being religious in the postmodern world.

Wiesel's *Night* became a new torah—a second revelation concerning the divine and human encounter. History had been reordered. The covenant had once again been broken, this time by God in refusing to come to the aid of the Jewish people. Yet after the Holocaust, just as the Torah was rewritten, so was the covenant reestablished and redescribed—beginning with the writing of books like *Dawn*. Though the covenant had been broken during the Holocaust, it was reinstituted after the Holocaust by the voluntary actions of the Jewish people. The story of the birth of Israel became the vehicle for describing how Jews took up covenant life once more, though in a secular way. Wiesel continued to reestablish covenant life through his narrative about the sanctity of life in *The Accident*, and his story of friendship and solidarity in *The Town Beyond the Wall*. After the Holocaust, a new form of faith was also necessary—a bold, courageous, and reflective dialogue with God. In his midrash on Cain, Wiesel writes that history could have ended differently if Cain had spoken vigorously to God.

The key dialectic of Wiesel's life from his earliest years has been that of abandonment versus solidarity. In his later life, Wiesel's particularism and his love for Israel provides a foundation for more universal concerns—solidarity with the victim. The final aspect of his poetics begins with the understanding that his life is a commentary on his books. With an eye toward a praxis orientation—and the universal model of the prophet of the nations in Jeremiah—Wiesel saw it necessary to hold faith and practice together and to act out his faith. It is this praxis orientation—the living out of his faith—that has pushed him to travel to the jungles of Central America, to the ghettoes of South Africa, and to the border of Cambodia in Southeast Asia, all of which is the final component of a complex poetics of memory and justice that, as an enacted word, provides commentary on all of his work.

As Wiesel's life story became known through the publication of *Night* and especially as he threw himself into the campaign for Soviet Jewry, he became a theological symbol and attained unshakable symbolic status. Further, given the autobiographical axiom that the life stories of well-known religious personalities become parabolic redescribing life, one can argue that in our time Elie Wiesel's life story has become the embodiment of a word to God, and perhaps about God—a parable of God's inaction in the midst of unspeakable evil. Such an encounter with Wiesel and his work can deform old stories and project new ones. One possible new awareness is the daring concept from Wiesel that says the world has now become Jewish. That is, solidarity must now be extended to oppressed persons everywhere.

For Elie Wiesel, God may be found unexpectedly in dealing with one's neighbor. Consequently, Wiesel transforms the divine/human dialogue into a program of human solidarity, especially with the needy and the oppressed. In his book on the prophets, Abraham Heschel wrote that these unusually gifted poets are given to a language that is "one octave too high," and that their words come as a "scream in the night" while the rest of us are at ease or asleep. Heschel went on to write, "prophecy is the voice that God has lent to the silent agony, a voice to the plundered poor." For Heschel, the prophet is a "crossing point" for God and the human; God is actually "raging in the prophet's words." Though the Jewish view is that prophecy ceased long ago, some readers of and listeners to Elie Wiesel will think they have encountered that "crossing point" and felt anew the "pathos" of the divine. While Wiesel's programmatic activity has sought primarily to emphasize human solidarity and messages to the human, it is not without an appeal to the divine. If we are correct in viewing Wiesel's work finally as an effort to address God rather than speaking about God, then it is possible that the mood of the lament eventually falls across his entire project. Thus, it is possible to see Wiesel's work presented as a daring act of an ongoing dialogue with the divine. If so, one imagines, as with Wiesel's epilogue to *The Town Beyond the Wall*, that neither Wiesel nor God have been the same since the first presentation. One imagines that the liberation of each is still tied to the other, that there continue to be dreams, echoes, and prayers in the still of the night, and that the "infinite yearning" that characterizes this dialogue is possibly equally poignant and profound on the part of the divine and on the part of the human. And yet, despite Wiesel's frenetic pace of writing and public activity, the young boy that he was in Sighet prior to deportation must still be glaring at the older man's face, continually asking, "What are you doing? Can you do more?"

# Notes

[1] Robert A. Cohn, "Elie Wiesel: The Novelist Whose Speeches Set Souls on Fire," *St. Louis Jewish Light*, 15 March 1978, 16.

[2] Stuart E. Rosenberg, "Elie Wiesel: One in a Generation," *Canadian News*, 9 June 1972.

[3] Ibid.

[4] Cynthia Ozick, "The Uses of Legend: Elie Wiesel as Tsaddik," *Congress Bi-Weekly* (9 June 1969): 16–20.

[5] Elie Wiesel, *The Town Beyond the Wall* (New York: Shocken Books, 1964, 1982) 172.

[6] Elie Wiesel, *Somewhere a Master: Further Hasidic Portraits and Legends* (New York: Summit Books, 1982) 203.

[7] President Ronald Reagan, "Jewish Heritage Week," *Weekly Compilation of Presidential Documents* 21/16 (19 April 1985) 477–78.

[8] See Rudy Abramson, "Reagan Trip to Include Death Camp: Emotional Appeal to Cancel Visit to Cemetery Rejected," *Los Angeles Times*, 20 April 1985, 1. The text of Wiesel's appeal is included on p. 22.

[9] Ibid.

[10] The letter from Bush to Wiesel, dated 30 May 1985, can be found in the Wiesel Collection of the Boston University Mugar Library, box 73, file Bush.

[11] See Edward B. Fiske, "Elie Wiesel: An Archivist with a Mission," *New York Times*, 31 January 1973; and Morton A. Reichek, "Elie Wiesel: Out of the Night," *Present Tense: The Magazine of World Jewish Affairs* (New York: The American Jewish Committee, 1976) 42.

[12] James E. Young, "The Prophet at the Y," *New York Times*, 20 October 1991.

[13] See Daphne Merkin, "Witness to the Holocaust," *New York Times*, 17 December 1995; and Michiko Kakutani, "Remembering as a Duty of Those Who Survived," *New York Times*, 5 December 1995.

[14] Wiesel, *The Gates of the Forest* (1964; repr., New York: Shocken Books, 1982) 22.

[15] Sidra Ezrahi, *By Words Alone* (Chicago: University of Chicago Press, 1980) 118.

[16] Fiske, "Elie Wiesel: An Archivist with a Mission."

[17] Cohn, "The Novelist Whose Speeches Set Souls on Fire," 16.

[18] Samuel G. Freedman, "Bearing Witness: The Life And Work Of Elie Wiesel," *New York Times Magazine* 23 October 1983, 35. See also Fiske, "Elie Wiesel: Archivist with a Mission."

[19] R. Cohn, "The Novelist Whose Speeches Set Souls on Fire," 16; and Barbara DeKovner-Mayer, "Elie Wiesel: Man in Search of Meaning," *Israel Today*, 20 January–2 February 1978, 8–9.

[20] Fiske, "Elie Wiesel: An Archivist with a Mission"; Freedman, "Bearing Witness," 40; Sylvia Rothchild, "Elie Wiesel in Boston," *The Jewish Advocate*, 16 November 1967; and Maurice Wohlgelernter, "The Beggar's Return," *The American Zionist*, May 1970, 40.

[21] Robert Alter, *After the Tradition: Essays on Jewish Writing* (New York: E. P. Dutton & Co., Inc., 1969) 153.

[22] Freedman, "Bearing Witness," 69; and John Weisman, "Elie Wiesel Brings Out the Jewish Tradition," *Los Angeles Times*, 16 April 1972, 52.

[23] See Robert J. Lifton, *Death in Life* (New York: Random House, 1967) 480–99; and Lifton, *The Future of Immortality and Other Essays for a Nuclear Age* (New York: Basic Books, Inc., Publishers, 1987) 231–41. See also Edward Lewis Wallant, *The Pawnbroker* (New York: Harcourt, Brace, & World, Inc., 1961).

[24] See the discussion of the film version of this story in Ernest Becker, *Angel in Armor: A Post-Freudian Perspective on the Nature of Man* (New York: Macmillan Publishing Co., Inc., 1969) 75 ff.

[25] Ibid., 80.

[26] This quote is from Egil Aarvik when he presented the Nobel Prize for Peace to Elie Wiesel and is taken from the Associated Press news articles released on Thursday, 11 December 1986.

[27] Ibid.

[28] See Elie Wiesel, *All Rivers Run to the Sea* (New York: Alfred A. Knopf, 1995).

[29] Bill Marx, "Monument Man: Elie Wiesel's Memoir Reveals Little Behind The Public Face," *Boston Phoenix*, 14–21 December 1995.

[30] Christopher Lehmann-Haupt, "Shy, but History Is Tugging His Sleeve," *New York Times*, 20 December 1999, E-10.

[31] Ibid.

[32] Marx, "Monument Man." This critique also seems valid for the second volume of the memoirs.

[33] See Young's review of Wiesel's memoir: James E. Young, "Parables of a Survivor," *The New Leader*, 18 December 1995–15 January 1996, 17–19.

[34] Freedman "Bearing Witness," 66.

[35] Naomi Seidman, "Elie Wiesel and the Scandal of Jewish Rage," *Jewish Social Studies* 3/1 (December 1996): 1–19. The hesitation to criticize Wiesel, if

diminished, is not completely gone because the major papers did not pick up the critique by Seidman.

[36] Seidman, "Elie Wiesel and the Scandal of Jewish Rage." See also comments by Seidman in the article by E. J. Kessler, "The Rage That Elie Wiesel Edited Out of 'Night': One Scholar's Explosive Accusation," *The Jewish Daily Forward*, 4 October 1996.

[37] It goes without saying that the writing and publication of *Night* was perhaps the foundational event in Wiesel's career as a writer. But one could argue that *ritual* gives rise to myth or, in this case, emblematic status. The articles on Wiesel seem to attach mythic status to him as a consequence of his ritualized activity as a speaker mesmerizing audiences. This begins more than ten years after the writing of *Night*.

[38] Seidman quoted in Kessler, "The Rage That Elie Wiesel Edited Out of 'Night.'"

[39] See Zipperstein quoted in Kessler, "The Rage That Elie Wiesel Edited Out of 'Night.'"

[40] Kali Tal, *Worlds of Hurt: Reading The Literature of Trauma* (New York: Cambridge University Press, 1996) 3.

[41] Ibid., 1. Compare also the critique of his failure "to speak truth to power" in Israel over the Israeli handling of the Palestinian issue. See especially Noam Chomsky, *The Fateful Triangle: The United States, Israel and the Palestinians* (Boston: South End Press, 1983) 383; Marc Ellis, *Beyond Innocence and Redemption: Confronting the Holocaust and Israeli Power* (New York: Harper & Row, 1990) 110–12; and Arthur Hertzberg, "An Open Letter to Elie Wiesel," *The New York Review of Books*, 18 August 1988.

[42] Kali Tal, *Worlds of Hurt*, 3.

[43] Erik Erikson, *Young Man Luther: A Study In Psychoanalysis and History* (New York: W. W. Norton & Co., Inc., 1958) 35.

[44] Wiesel's working gifts and his effect on society have been noted, if only in cursory form, in the opening paragraphs of this chapter. From the survey of the essays on Wiesel noted on page p. 1, it is clear that Wiesel has had a profound "effect" on Jewish identity after the Holocaust and the Jewish community generally, and that he has reached beyond that community to dialogue with Christians and other groups. It is also clear that his "gifts" are not to be understood simply as those of a writer or as a teller of tales, but that he wants also to be understood as a rebbe or spiritual model.

[45] See Wiesel quoted in Freedman, "Bearing Witness."

[46] See David Lyman, "Film Memoir of the Holocaust Years Falls Short of Elie Wiesel's Own Passion," *Detroit Free Press*, 2 November 1997.

[47] See Erik Erikson, *Young Man Luther*, 103.

[48] Perhaps one reason Wiesel's speeches mesmerize audiences who eventually see such occasions as spiritual experiences of a lifetime is because here one sees Wiesel, the spiritual innovator, in his most direct medium attempting to resolve his own struggle even as he projects his solution to the group.

[49] See Erik Erikson, *Gandhi's Truth: On the Origins of Militant Nonviolence* (New York: W. W. Norton & Company, Inc., 1969) 129–32.

[50] See Johannes Lindblom, *Prophecy in Ancient Israel* (Philadelphia: Fortress Press, 1962) 1; and C. H. Dodd, *The Authority of the Bible* (London: Nisbet and Company, 1929; rev. ed., 1960). Dodd argues that the dominant personalities of the Bible are marked by religious genius.

[51] Abraham Joshua Heschel, *The Prophets: An Introduction* (New York: Harper & Row, 1962; Harper/Collins, 2001) 3–26.

[52] Irving Greenberg, "Polarity and Perfection," *Face to Face An Interreligious Bulletin* 6 (Spring 1979): 12–14.

[53] Walter Brueggemann, "Imagination: New Approaches to the Bible," video of the 23rd National Conference of the Trinity Institute, Trinity Church, New York City, 1992.

[54] In the Jewish community of Sighet, the Torah, or Five Books of Moses, was the central authority for faith and practice and remains so for much of the world Jewry.

[55] This will be elaborated in chapter 7.

[56] See especially Elie Wiesel in Irving Abramson, ed., *Against Silence: The Voice and Vison of Elie Wiesel*, vol. 3 (New York: Holocaust Library, 1985) 284; Kathleen M. O'Connor, "Jeremiah and Formation of the Moral Character of the Community," paper delivered at the SBL, Toronto, 26 November 2002; and Sidra Ezrahi, "The Holocaust Writer and the Lamentation Tradition," in *Confronting the Holocaust: The Impact of Elie Wiesel*, ed. Alfred Rosenfeld and and Irving Greenberg (Bloomington: Indiana University Press: 1978) 133–49; Walter Brueggemann, "An Ending that Does Not End: The Book of Jeremiah," in *Post Modern Interpretations of the Bible—A Reader*, ed. A. K. M Adams, (St. Louis: Chalice Press, 2001) 117–28; and Colin Davis, *Elie Wiesel's Secretive Texts* (Gainesville: University of Florida, 1994) 180.

[57] Wiesel quoted in Abrahamson, ed., *Against Silence*, 1:48.

[58] Greenberg, "Polarity and Perfection."

[59] See Wiesel, *Town Beyond the Wall*, 179.

[60] Alter, *After the Tradition*, 160. Wiesel is also aware that his journey reflects many stages. See the interview with Wiesel titled "A Time to Speak," *Bostonia: The Magazine of Culture and Ideas*, Boston University, summer 1995, 21.

# Notes

[61] Ernst Cassirer, *An Essay on Man: An Introduction to a Philosophy of Human Culture* (Garden City NY: Doubleday & Company, Inc., 1944) 278.

[62] Albert Einstein, *Ideas and Opinions* (New York: Crown Publishers, Inc., 1954) 225.

[63] The work on which I draw here is that of James W. Fowler, a pioneer in the field of psychology and religion. His theory is better known as "faith development" theory. See especially his book, *Stages of Faith: The Psychology of Human Development and the Quest for Meaning* (San Francisco: Harper & Row, 1981). Fowler suggests that there are six possible styles or forms of being in faith throughout the life span. These stages, which comprise the composite pilgrimage, are for Fowler structural styles of faith, each of which presupposes a basic stance of the self with its own unique conceptual frame of meaning-making. This conceptual frame is an ecological metaphor or map of reality that Fowler calls the "ultimate environment." As the journey proceeds through time, the map of reality or ultimate environment naturally changes. That is, one's way of looking at life—the process of active knowing and valuing with its larger framework of how the world is to be viewed—must be redrawn or reworked when the old one becomes outdated. This process of revision is essentially a reworking of one's way of being in the world and is sometimes very painful. Because of that, many persons find a permanent way of being in faith, while others move from stage to stage throughout life. The six possible stages in Fowler's theory are (1) Intuitive-Projective (early childhood), (2) Mythic-Literal (school age to adolescence), (3) Synthetic-Conventional (adolescence), (4) Individuative-Reflective (young adulthood), (5) Conjunctive faith (midlife and beyond), and (6) Universalizing faith (very rare).

[64] Wiesel describes the life of Jeremiah in terms of this pattern in his essay on the prophet. See Wiesel, *Five Biblical Portraits* (Notre Dame: Notre Dame University Press, 1981) 101 and 124. Walter Brueggemann, utilizing the philosophical and hermeneutical framework of Paul Ricoeur, identifies this pattern as a typology of faith in the Psalms. See Brueggemann, *The Message of the Psalms* (Minneapolis: Augsburg Publishing House, 1984) 9–23. For a similar perspective on the nature of biblical narrative, see also Northrop Frye, *The Great Code: The Bible and Literature* (New York: Harcourt Brace Jovanovich, Publishers, 1981) 169–98. Likewise, the faith development theory of James Fowler utilized in this biographical study of Wiesel follows a similar pattern. See my essay titled "The Dangerous Journey Home: Charting the Religious Pilgrimage in Fowler and Peck," *Perspectives in Religious Studies* 25/3 (Fall 1998): 249–65; and also Joseph Campbell, *The Hero with a Thousand Faces* (Princeton: Princeton University Press, 1949) 30.

251

[65] For the role of "disciplined subjectivity" in such studies, see Erik Erikson, *Insight and Responsibility* (New York: W. W. Norton & Company, 1964) 53. Erikson also writes that in the study of a life, one must be able "to recognize major trends even where the facts are not all available...[and] must be able to make meaningful predictions as to what will prove to have happened." See Erikson, *Young Man Luther*, 50.

[66] See the published interview with Wiesel by Harry James Cargas, *Harry James Cargas in Conversation with Elie Wiesel* (New York: Paulist Press, 1976) 73–76; and Elie Wiesel, *All Rivers Run to the Sea* (New York: Alfred A. Knopf, 1995) 15. Wiesel tells this story with some pride, indicating that it is part of what made Sighet a special place, and reflects the construction of what James Olney calls the "myth of an earthly paradise." See James Olney, *Metaphors of Self: The Meaning of Autobiography* (Princeton: Princeton University Press, 1972).

[67] See Jerome R. Mintz, *Legends of the Hasidim: An Introduction to Hasidic Culture and Oral Tradition in the New World* (Chicago: University of Chicago Press, 1968) 74–78.

[68] Wiesel, *And the Sea Is Never Full* (New York: Alfred A. Knopf, 1999) 102.

[69] Both Erik Erikson and James Fowler work within a tradition that emphasizes the importance of childhood as a powerful influence on later adult life. In this perspective, they both posit that the early years are foundational to the individual's growth in faith and identity. Following Erikson, Fowler suggests that the child's early experiences of life—including the environment in which one lives out those first years—provide a fund of basic trust or mistrust. One's later growing and developing faith, then, builds on this rudimentary but basic fund of shared meaning. Primal faith, the name Fowler gives to this first style of meaning-making, arises in the shared mutuality of that first environment.

[70] James Olney, *Metaphors of Self: The Meaning of Autobiography* (Princeton: Princeton University Press, 1972) 18.

[71] Elie Wiesel, "Recalling Swallowed-Up Worlds," *The Christian Century* 98/19 (27 May 1981): 609.

[72] See Wiesel, *All Rivers Run to the Sea*, 3–6. See also Cargas, *Harry James Cargas in Conversation with Elie Wiesel*, 75.

[73] See Wiesel quoted in Cargas, *Harry James Cargas in Conversation with Elie Wiesel*, 76.

[74] Wiesel, *All Rivers Run to the Sea*, 22.

[75] Ibid., 6–8.

[76] Elie Wiesel, *A Jew Today* (New York: Vintage Books, 1978) 77–79.

[77] Ibid., 78.

[78] Mintz, *Legends of the Hasidim*, 25–26.

# Notes

[79] Elie Wiesel, *Night* (1960; repr., New York: Bantam Books, 1982) 1. See also the 2006 edition where Marion Wiesel translates the same phrase as "deeply observant."

[80] Mintz, *Legends of the Hasidim*, 64.

[81] Ibid., 64–68.

[82] Fowler calls this form of faith "Intuitive-Projective." It is typical in children ages 2–6 or 7. The term "intuitive" suggests the way the child envisions faith as a map of reality, and the term "projective" implies an imitative projection of this reality. See especially James Fowler, *Stages of Faith: The Psychology of Human Development and the Quest for Meaning* (San Francisco: Harper & Row, 1981) 119–34; Ana-Maria Rizzuto, *The Birth of the Living God: A Psychoanalytic Study* (Chicago: University of Chicago Press, 1979) 206–208; Eli Sagan, *Freud, Women, and Morality: The Psychology of Good and Evil* (New York: Basic Books, Inc., Publishers, 1988) 27, 159–82; and Scott Peck, *The Road Less Traveled: A New Psychology of Love, Traditional Values and Spiritual Growth* (New York: Simon and Schuster, 1978) 190–91.

[83] Rizzuto, *Birth of the Living God*, 7.

[84] Donald Capps, *Pastoral Care: A Thematic Approach* (Philadelphia: Westminster Press, 1979) 47.

[85] Erik Erikson, *Toys and Reasons: Stages in the Ritualization of Experience* (New York: W. W. Norton & Company, 1977) 85–91; Donald Capps, *Life Cycle Theory and Pastoral Care* (Philadelphia: Fortress Press, 1983) 24, 58–60.

[86] Wiesel, *All Rivers Run to the Sea*, 9.

[87] Ibid., 10. For a discussion of the significance of early memories, see Peck, *Road Less Traveled*, 191. Peck states, "Frequently (but not always) the essence of a patient's childhood and hence the essence of his or her world view is captured in the 'earliest memory.' ...It is probable that these first memories, like the phenomenon of screen memories, which they so often are, are remembered precisely because they accurately symbolize the nature of a person's early childhood. It is not surprising, then, that the flavor of these earliest memories is so frequently the same as that of a patient's deepest feelings about the nature of existence."

[88] Ibid.

[89] Wiesel, *All Rivers Run to the Sea*, 13.

[90] Wiesel, *Legends of Our Time* (New York: Holt, Rinehart, and Winston, 1968) 17.

[91] Ibid., 18.

[92] Elie Wiesel, "The Solitude of God," undated manuscript, Boston University Mugar Library, Special Collections of Wiesel, box 1, folder 17.

[93] These are the opening words of Wiesel's memoir. See Wiesel, *All Rivers Run to the Sea*, 3.

[94] Ibid., 4.

[95] Ibid.

[96] Erik Erikson, *Young Man Luther: A Study in Psychoanalysis and History* (New York: W. W. Norton & Company, 1958) 124.

[97] See Peck, *Road Less Traveled*, 25.

[98] See especially Donald Capps, *Men, Religion, And Melancholia: James, Otto, Jung and Erikson* (New Haven: Yale University Press, 1997) 4, 205.

[99] Erik H. Erikson, *Life History and the Historical Moment* (New York: W. W. Norton & Company, Inc., 1975) 165.

[100] These two themes can be found especially in his first four books.

[101] Fowler calls the first stage of the journey of faith, typical of children ages 2–6 or 7, "Intuitive-Projective." See James Fowler, *Stages of Faith: The Psychology of Human Development and the Quest for Meaning* (San Francisco: Harper & Row, 1981) 133–34. The second stage of faith is labeled by Fowler as "Mythic-Literal" and is typical of children ages 6–12. This stage reflects Wiesel's pre-bar mitzvah school years. See Fowler, *Stages of Faith*, 135–50.

[102] See M. Scott Peck, *The Different Drum* (New York: Simon & Schuster, 1987) 202.

[103] Elie Wiesel, *All Rivers Run to the Sea* (New York: Alfred A. Knopf, 1995) 11.

[104] Ibid.

[105] Wiesel quoted in Harry James Cargas, *Harry James Cargas in Conversation with Elie Wiesel* (New York: Paulist Press, 1976) 74–75.

[106] Erik Erikson, *Gandhi's Truth: On the Origins of Militant Nonviolence* (New York: W. W. Norton & Company, Inc., 1969) 132.

[107] Erik Erikson, *Childhood and Society* (New York: W. W. Norton & Company, Inc., 1963) 314.

[108] Erik Erikson, *Insight and Responsibility* (New York: W. W. Norton & Company, Inc., 1964) 66.

[109] Elie Wiesel, *Souls on Fire: Portraits and Legends of Hasidic Masters* (New York: Random House, 1972) 6–7.

[110] Elie Wiesel, *A Jew Today* (New York: Vintage Books, 1978) 79–80.

[111] For this brief study of Buber, see Donald Capps, "John Henry Newman: A Study of Vocational Identity," *Journal tor the Scientific Study of Religion* 9/1 (Spring 1970): 49.

[112] Ibid.

[113] Fowler describes this stage of faith as "Mythic-Literal." Typically the child in this stage is between 7 and 12 or 13 years of age. The child's social world

has expanded beyond the family and includes teachers and leaders in community organizations. See Fowler, *Stages of Faith*, 135–50.

[114] Wiesel, *Legends of Our Time* (New York: Shocken Books, 1982) 116.

[115] Wiesel, *A Jew Today*, 6.

[116] See Amos Wilder, "Story and Story-World," *Interpretation* 37/ 4 (October 1983): 353–64.

[117] Ibid.

[118] Jerome R. Mintz, *Legends of the Hasidim: An Introduction to Hasidic Culture and Oral Tradition in the New World* (Chicago: University of Chicago Press, 1968) 26.

[119] Wiesel, *All Rivers Run to the Sea*, 18–19.

[120] Ibid., 19. This narrative indicates that Eliezer, typical of school-aged children and those of Mythic-Literal faith, is learning the ways of the larger community from interaction with others on the streets. One also sees that he is becoming aware of the clash implicit in stories that will lead eventually to a new form of faith. See Fowler, *Stages of Faith*, 150.

[121] Wiesel, *All Rivers Run to the Sea*, 20–21.

[122] Ibid., 13–46.

[123] See Michael Novak, *Ascent of the Mountain, Flight of the Dove: An Invitation to Religious Studies* (New York: Harper & Row, Publishers, 1971) 104–108; Paul Ricoeur, *The Symbolism of Evil* (Boston: Beacon, 1967) 350–52; James A. Sanders, "Adaptable for Life: The Nature and Function of Canon," in *Magnalia Dei: The Mighty Acts of God*, ed. Frank M. Cross, Werner E. Lemke, and Patrick D. Miller Jr. (Garden City NY: Doubleday, 1976) 53; Elie Wiesel, *Five Biblical Portraits* (Notre Dame: University of Notre Dame Press, 1981); and Elie Wiesel, *Messengers of God: Biblical Portraits and Legends* (New York: Random House, 1976).

[124] See Elie Wiesel, *All Rivers Run to the Sea* (New York: Alfred A. Knopf, 1995) 28–33; James Fowler, *Stages of Faith: The Psychology of Human Development and the Quest for Meaning* (San Francisco: Harper & Row, 1981) 151–73; and Sharon Parks, *The Critical Years: Young Adults & the Search for Meaning, Faith & Commitment* (San Francisco: Harper & Row, 1986) 76. Fowler describes the form of faith exhibited here as "Synthetic-Conventional." The term "synthetic" implies the drawing together of one's faith into a synthesis, and the term "conventional" signifies that the beliefs and values are drawn from one's friends or significant others. This stage, typical of adolescents, is a "conformist" style of faith and reflects a time characterized by the power exhibited by the expectations and judgments of others. Values and beliefs, at this point, remain tacit or unexamined by critical thought. Contrary to popular understanding,

Wiesel remained in this stage until the post-war years when he began to experience a prolonged crisis.

[125] Wiesel, *All Rivers Run to the Sea*, 27–29.

[126] Ibid., 33.

[127] See Jerome R. Mintz, *Legends of the Hasidim: An Introduction to Hasidic Culture and Oral Tradition in the New World* (Chicago: University of Chicago Press, 1968) 27; and Abraham J. Heschel, "The Mystical Element of Judaism," in Louis Finkelstein, ed., *The Jews: Their Religion and Culture* (New York: Shocken Books, 1949) 155–76.

[128] Mintz, *Legends of the Hasidim*, 27. See also Wiesel, *All Rivers Run to the Sea*, 34–35.

[129] Wiesel, *All Rivers Run to the Sea*, 35.

[130] Ibid., 36.

[131] Ibid.

[132] Ibid., 36–37.

[133] Ibid., 37.

[134] See Fowler, *Stages of Faith*, 172–73; and Parks, *Critical Years*, 76.

[135] Wiesel, *All Rivers Run to the Sea*, 38–40. Wiesel identifies the clinical diagnosis of his two friends as being that of "aphasia" and "ataxia."

[136] See Heschel, "The Mystical Element," 155–76, especially 155.

[137] See Erik Erikson, *Gandhi's Truth: On the Origins of Militant Nonviolence* (New York: W. W. Norton & Company, Inc., 1969) 118. See also Erikson, *Young Man Luther: A Study in Psychoanalysis and History* (New York: W. W. Norton & Company, 1958) 103.

[138] Wiesel, *All Rivers Run to the Sea*, 53–55.

[139] This "ironic reversal" becomes a major theme in Wiesel's first and best-known book, *Night*, which details these events.

[140] Wiesel, *All Rivers Run to the Sea*, 61–71.

[141] Wiesel quoted in Harry James Cargas, *Harry James Cargas in Conversation with Elie Wiesel* (New York: Paulist Press, 1976) 76, 110. See also Elie Wiesel, *Night* (1960; repr., New York: Bantam Books, 1982) 106.

[142] Elie Wiesel, *All Rivers Run to the Sea* (New York: Alfred A. Knopf, 1995) 94. See also the translation of the Yiddish description of this event in Wiesel's original Yiddish memoir, now printed in the preface to the new translation of Wiesel's *Night* in the Hill and Wang edition (pxi-xii).

[143] See M. K. Gandhi, *An Autobiography or The Story of My Experiment with Truth* (Ahmedabad: Navajivan, 1927) 22. See also Erik Erikson, *Gandhi's Truth: On the Origins of Militant Nonviolence* (New York: W. W. Norton & Company, Inc., 1969) 128; and Wiesel, *All Rivers Run to the Sea*, 94.

[144] Erikson, *Gandhi's Truth*, 128–32.

# Notes

[145] Wiesel quoted in Harry James Cargas, *Harry James Cargas in Conversation with Elie Wiesel*, 88. See also the final chapter of Wiesel's Yiddish testimony, a portion of which is printed in Irving Abrahamson, ed., *Against Silence: The Voice and Vision of Elie Wiesel*, vol. 3 (New York: Holocaust Library, 1985) 59.

[146] Cargas, *Harry James Cargas in Conversation with Elie Wiesel*, 88. See also Wiesel in Abrahamson, ed., *Against Silence*, 3:59.

[147] Wiesel in Abrahamson, ed., *Against Silence*, 3:59. See also Wiesel in Harry James Cargas, *Harry James Cargas in conversation with Elie Wiesel*, 87.

[148] Ibid.

[149] Wiesel, *All Rivers Run to the Sea*, 97–110.

[150] Ibid., 110–13.

[151] Ibid., 116–17.

[152] Ibid., 120.

[153] Ibid., 120–30.

[154] Ibid.

[155] Ibid., 124.

[156] Ibid., 122–26.

[157] See M. Scott Peck, *The Road Less Traveled: A New Psychology of Love, Traditional Values and Spiritual Growth* (New York: Simon and Schuster, 1978) 193. Peck writes, "The path to holiness lies through questioning *everything.*"

[158] Wiesel, *All Rivers Run to the Sea*, 130–39.

[159] Ibid., 150.

[160] Ibid., 151–54.

[161] Ibid., 155–56.

[162] Ibid., 157.

[163] Elaine Scarry, *The Body in Pain: The Making and Unmaking of the World* (New York: Oxford University Press, 1985) 35–48; and Robert J. Lifton and Eric Olson, *Living and Dying* (New York: Praeger Publishers, 1974) 136–37.

[164] Scarry, *The Body in Pain*, 35.

[165] Robert J. Lifton, *Death in Life* (New York: Random House, 1967) 480–84.

[166] Wiesel, *Night*, 101.

[167] Lifton, *Death in Life*, 497

[168] Ibid.

[169] See especially Fowler's analysis of the loss of traditional faith in his *Stages of Faith: The Psychology of Human Development and the Quest for Meaning* (San Francisco: Harper & Row, 1981) 5–8.

[170] Elie Wiesel, *The Town Beyond the Wall* (New York: Schocken Books, 1964) 44.

[171] See Elie Wiesel, *All Rivers Run to the Sea* (New York: Alfred A. Knopf, 1995) 180, 293.

[172] Maurice Friedman, *Abraham Joshua Heschel and Elie Wiesel: You Are My Witnesses* (New York: Farror Strauss Giroux, 1987) 185.

[173] The transition noted here is the movement from what Fowler calls "Synthetic-Conventional" faith to "Individuative-Reflective" faith. A double movement marks the transition to this stage. There is the emergence of an "executive ego," which is a new identity separate from the circle of interpersonal relationships and the roles one plays. In order to sustain this independent self, one composes a worldview characterized now by critical thought and the willful choosing of one's own beliefs, values, and commitments.

[174] See Lily Edelman, "Building a Moral Society: Aspects of Elie Wiesel's Work," in *Face to Face* 6 (Spring 1979): 3.

[175] Wiesel, *All Rivers Run to the Sea*, 293.

[176] Ibid., 183.

[177] Ibid., 157–58.

[178] Ibid., 161.

[179] Ibid., 172.

[180] Ibid., 178.

[181] Ibid., 179.

[182] Ibid., 181.

[183] Ibid., 185–86.

[184] Ibid., 183–84.

[185] Ibid., 186–88.

[186] See James Fowler, *Stages of Faith: The Psychology of Human Development and the Quest for Meaning* (San Francisco: Harper & Row, 1981) 179–83.

[187] See Erik Erikson, *Young Man Luther: A Study in Psychoanalysis and History* (New York: W. W. Norton & Company, 1958) 103.

[188] See Wiesel, "Recalling Swallowed-Up Worlds," *The Christian Century* 98/19 (27 May 1981): 610.

[189] Wiesel, *All Rivers Run to the Sea*, 189–99.

[190] Ibid., 200–20. See also Wiesel, "Recalling Swallowed-Up Worlds," 610.

[191] Wiesel, *All Rivers Run to the Sea*, 223. See also Elie Wiesel, "Messenger for the ten thousandth," interview with Harry James Cargas, *Commonweal* 113/18 (24 October 1986): 555–57.

[192] See Amiya Chakravarty, "Quest for the Universal One," in *Great Religions of the World*, ed. Merle Severy et al. (Washington, D.C.: National Geographic Society, 1971) 34–40. See also 162–63.

[193] Wiesel, *All Rivers Run to the Sea*, 226.

[194] See Chakravarty, "Quest for the Universal One," 34–40. See also John J. Putnam, "Down the Teeming Ganges, Holy River of India," in *Great Religions of the World*, 50–77.

# Notes

[195] See especially Eknath Easwaran, trans., *The Bhagavad Gita* (Tomales CA: Nilgiri Press, 1985).

[196] Wiesel, *All Rivers Run to the Sea*, 224–25.

[197] Ibid., 225.

[198] Wiesel, "Recalling Swallowed-Up Worlds," 610–11. See also Wiesel, "Messenger for the ten thousandth," 556.

[199] Wiesel, "Recalling Swallowed-Up Worlds," 611.

[200] Ibid.

[201] Wiesel, *All Rivers Run to the Sea*, 238–42.

[202] Ibid., 239.

[203] On this point, see Paul Tillich, *Dynamics of Faith* (New York: Harper & Row, 1957) 43.

[204] See also Robert J. Lifton and Eric Olson, *Living and Dying* (New York: Praeger, 1974) 137.

[205] Lifton says some "survivor mission" is necessary for the individual "in order to re-establish at least the semblance of a moral universe. The impulse to bear witness, beginning with a sense of responsibility to the dead, can readily extend into a 'survivor mission'—a lasting commitment to a project that extracts significance from absurdity, vitality from massive death." See Lifton, *The Future of Immortality and Other Essays for a Nuclear Age* (New York: Basic Books, 1987) 241.

[206] Walter Ong, *Orality and Literacy* (New York: Methuen & Co., 1982) 78.

[207] Ibid., 105.

[208] Elie Wiesel, address to the National Invitational Conference of Anti-Defamation League of B'nai B'rith and the National Council for the Social Studies, New York, 9 October 1977. For a copy of this speech, see Wiesel in Irving Abrahamson, ed., *Against Silence: The Voice and Vision of Elie Wiesel*, vol. 1 (New York: Holocaust Library, 1985) 147.

[209] Elie Wiesel, address to the International Young Presidents organization, Madrid, Spain, April 1980. For a copy of this speech, see Wiesel in Abrahamson, ed., *Against Silence*, 1:179–83.

[210] James E. Young, *Writing and Rewriting the Holocaust: Narrative and the Consequences of Interpretation* (Bloomington: Indiana University Press, 1988) 95.

[211] Wiesel in Abrahamson, ed., *Against Silence*, 1:151.

[212] Wiesel in Abrahamson, ed., 1:176, and 3:284.

[213] Wiesel, "Recalling Swallowed-Up Worlds," 611.

[214] Such a struggle is typical of the young men Erikson describes as *homo religiosus*. Also typical of young men this age is the quest for developing a vocation, being in a love relationship, finding a mentor, and giving form to a

dream. See Daniel J. Levinson et al., *The Seasons of a Man's Life* (New York: Ballantine Books, 1978) 90.

[215] See Erik Erikson, *Young Man Luther: A Study in Psychoanalysis and History* (New York: W. W. Norton & Company, 1958) 218, and 261–62.

[216] Fowler describes the two essential features of this development as the "critical distancing" from one's previous value system and the "emergence of an executive ego." See James Fowler, *Stages of Faith: The Psychology of Human Development and the Quest for Meaning* (San Francisco: Harper & Row, 1981) 179.

[217] On the role of "demythologizing" in Jewish tradition, see especially Herbert N. Schneidau, *Sacred Discontent: The Bible and Western Tradition* (Los Angeles: University of California Press, 1976) 1–49. Schneidau argues that the first Yahwist vision of "sacred discontent," in contrast to the surrounding cultures, allowed the first Yahwists to confront the ancient world with a new mode of thought—a demythologizing consciousness that was turned against culture itself. These first Yahwists resisted the common forms of thought and disputed and overturned the routine assumptions of their time.

[218] Elie Wiesel, "An Interview Unlike Any Other," in *A Jew Today* (New York: Vintage Books, 1978) 17–23. See also Elie Wiesel, *All Rivers Run to the Sea* (New York: Alfred A. Knopf, 1995) 265–72.

[219] This is another illustration of Wiesel's overactive or "overweening" conscience typical in Erikson's theory of *homo religiosus*. For an example of Erikson's use of the term, see Erik Erikson, *Gandhi's Truth: On the Origins of Militant Nonviolence* (New York: W. W. Norton & Company, Inc., 1969) 117.

[220] It is likely that a part of Wiesel's unease originally with Mauriac was due to his "almost pathological shyness" and to the nature of his strident and iconoclastic "individuative-reflective" faith, a vision of life in which one views others with stereotypes. In Wiesel's case, his early "mythic-literal" faith (typical of school-aged children 7–12 years of age) embodied a perspective in which Christians were "alien" and "frightened" him. Some of that stereotype was justifiable in his childhood world, and after the Holocaust it was not easily dismissed. But Wiesel did move beyond this stereotype. See Elie Wiesel, *A Jew Today* (New York: Vintage Books, 1978) 3–21.

[221] Elie Wiesel, *A Jew Today*, 22.

[222] Ibid., 22–23.

[223] Ernest Becker, *The Denial of Death* (New York: The Free Press, 1973) 109.

[224] Wiesel, *A Jew Today*, 19–20.

[225] Lawrence L. Langer, "The Divided Voice: Elie Wiesel and the Challenge of the Holocaust," in Alvin H. Rosenberg and Irving Greenberg, eds.,

*Confronting the Holocaust: The Impact of Elie Wiesel* (Bloomington: Indiana University Press, 1978) 33.

[226] James E. Young, *Writing and Rewriting the Holocaust: Narrative and the Consequences of Interpretation* (Bloomington: Indiana University Press, 1988) 95. See also Elie Wiesel et al., *Dimensions of the Holocaust* (Evanston: Northwestern University Press, 1977) 6–9.

[227] See Elie Wiesel, address to the National Invitational Conference of Anti-Defamation League of B'nai B'rith and the National Council for Social Studies, New York, 9 October 1977, reprinted in Irving Abrahamson, ed., *Against Silence: The Voice and Vision of Elie Wiesel*, vol. 1 (New York: Holocaust Library, 1985) 151; and see Elie Wiesel, *Five Biblical Portraits* (Notre Dame: Notre Dame University Press, 1981) 123–25.

[228] Naomi Seidman quoted in E. J. Kessler, "The Rage That Elie Wiesel Edited Out of 'Night': One Scholar's Explosive Accusation," *The Jewish Daily Forward*, 4 October 1996.

[229] See Jeremiah 1:10.

[230] The interpretation of Jeremiah's call and distinctive work are drawn from Walter Brueggemann. See especially Brueggemann, "The Book of Jeremiah: Portrait of a Prophet," *Interpretation* 37/2 (April 1983): 130–45. Brueggemann summarizes Wiesel's call with the two terms "shattering" and "evoking." After reading Jeremiah and Wiesel, one could add a third term: "enacting," emphasizing the praxis orientation of both. That is, for each the lived word is clearly an important aspect. In his *Five Biblical Portraits*, Wiesel adds that Jeremiah offers an "example of behavior" (121). This is also true of Wiesel.

[231] Wiesel, *All Rivers Run to the Sea*, 128.

[232] Ibid., 122.

[233] See the study by Timothy Polk, *The Prophetic Persona: Jeremiah and the Language of the Self* (Sheffield, England: JSOT Press, 1984) 168–69. See also Sallie McFague, *Speaking in Parables: A Study in Metaphor and Theology* (Philadelphia: Fortress Press, 1975) 164.

[234] McFague uses this phrase, as does Donald Capps. See McFague, *Speaking in Parables*, 157; and Donald Capps, Walter Capps, and M. Gerald Bradford, eds., *Encounter with Erikson: Historical Interpretation and Religious Biography* (Missoula: Scholars Press, 1977) 142.

[235] McFague, *Speaking in Parables*, 169.

[236] Wolfgang Iser, *The Act of Reading* (Baltimore: John Hopkins University Press, 1978) 143.

[237] This reading is informed by Kathleen M. O'Connor, "Jeremiah and Formation of the Moral Character of the Community," paper delivered at the SBL, Toronto, 26 November 2002.

[238] See Lawrence S. Cunningham, "Elie Wiesel's Anti-Exodus," in Harry James Cargas, ed., *Responses to Elie Wiesel* (New York: Persea Books, 1978) 23–28.

[239] Elie Wiesel, *Night* (1960; repr., New York: Bantam Books, 1982) 32.

[240] Ibid., 27.

[241] Ibid., 31.

[242] Ibid., 62.

[243] Ibid., 30.

[244] Ibid.

[245] Irving Greenberg, "Polarity and Perfection," *Face to Face* 6 (Spring 1979): 12–14.

[246] See Cunningham, "Elie Wiesel's Anti-Exodus," 23.

[247] Andre Neher, *The Exile of the Word: From the Silence of the Bible to the Silence of Auschwitz* (Philadelphia: Jewish Publication Society of America, 1981) 217.

[248] Ibid., 216.

[249] Maurice Friedman, *Abraham Joshua Heschel and Elie Wiesel: You Are My Witnesses* (New York: Farrar, Strauss, Giroux, 1987) 113.

[250] See Walter Brueggemann, *The Message of the Psalms* (Minneapolis: Augsburg Publishing House, 1984) 9–23.

[251] Wiesel, *Night*, 61–62.

[252] See Walter Brueggemann, "From Hurt to Joy, From Death to Life," *Interpretation* 28/1 (January 1974): 3–19; Brueggemann, "The Formfulness of Grief," *Interpretation* 31/3 (July 1977): 263–75; Brueggemann, *The Message of the Psalms* (Minneapolis: Augsburg Publishing House, 1984) 18; and Claus Westermann, "The Role of the Lament in the Theology of the Old Testament," *Interpretation* 28/1 (January 1974): 20–38.

[253] See Paul Ricoeur, "Biblical Hermeneutics," *Semeia* 4 (1975): 94–128. See also Lawrence Langer, "The Dominion of Death," in Harry James Cargas, ed., *Responses to Elie Wiesel* (New York: Persea Books, 1978) 30–31. For the same essay see Langer, *The Holocaust and the Literary Imagination* (New Haven: Yale University Press, 1975) 75–76.

[254] On the significance of a demythologizing strategy and the creation of a personal ideology, see James Fowler, *Stages of Faith*, 179–83.

[255] See Herbert N. Scheidau, *Sacred Discontent: The Bible and Western Tradition* (Los Angeles: University of California Press, 1976) 1–31.

[256] On the fragmentation that comes with the onset of horrific trauma, see Judith Lewis Herman, *Trauma and Recovery* (New York: Harper Collins Publishers, 1992) 86–89.

[257] Elie Wiesel, *Night* (1960; repr., New York: Bantam Books, 1982) 2.

# Notes

[258] Ibid. See also the comments of M. Scott Peck, *The Road Less Traveled: A New Psychology of Love, Traditional Values and Spiritual Growth* (New York: Simon and Schuster, 1978) 193. Peck says the path to spiritual growth is lined with questions.

[259] See Ted L. Estes, "Elie Wiesel and the Drama of Interrogation," *The Journal of Religion* 56/1 (January 1976): 18–35.

[260] Nathan Scott's dictum seems true of Wiesel at this point in his life: "In a time of the eclipse of God the most characteristic form of the religious question becomes the question of authenticity, of how we are to keep faith with and safeguard the 'single one' or the 'true self'—in a bullying world. See Scott, *Three American Moralists: Mailer, Bellow, Trilling* (Notre Dame: University of Notre Dame Press, 1973) 221.

[261] Elie Wiesel, *All Rivers Run to the Sea* (New York: Alfred A. Knopf, 1995) 18, 273. Wiesel's meeting with Mauriac took place in May 1955. At the time of this meeting, he was involved with a young lady named Kathleen. The trip to Israel apparently came in early summer 1955 after the meeting with Mauriac and after a breakup with Kathleen. Wiesel went by ship. He had originally planned to travel by air. He gave up that ticket and later learned that the plane on which he was scheduled to fly was shot down over Bulgaria by the Bulgarian Air Force.

[262] Wiesel, *All Rivers run to the Sea*, 273–74.

[263] Ibid., 274. This theme is also explored in fiction in the work of Chaim Potok. See especially his *The Chosen* (New York: Simon and Schuster, 1967).

[264] Ibid., 275. For a general introduction to Nahman, see the translation and commentary by Arnold J. Band, *Nahman of Bratslav: The Tales* (New York: Paulist Press, 1978).

[265] See the discussion of questioning as a religious virtue in M. Scott Peck, *The Different Drum: Community-Making and Peace* (New York: Simon and Schuster: 1987) 199–200.

[266] This covers a period of approximately 15–16 years from 1949–1965 and has been labeled by some scholars as the "crying out" years. See Lily Edelman, "Building a Moral Society: Aspects of Elie Wiesel's Work," in *Face to Face* 6 (Spring 1979): 3.

[267] This period in Wiesel's life—between 1949–1965—was one James Fowler described as a time of "Individuative-Reflective" faith. It is a time when one seeks to understand one's self and the world on one's own terms, and thereby seeks to develop what Fowler calls an "executive ego." Likewise, it is a time when one searches for an individual identity, a vocation, and an ideology.

[268] Wiesel, *All Rivers Run to the Sea*, 293.

[269] Ibid. See also the essay by Paul Braunstein, "Elie Wiesel: A Lasting Impression" in Harry James Cargas, ed., *Telling the Tale: A Tribute to Elie Wiesel* (St. Louis: Time Being Books, Inc., 1993) 117–18.

[270] See Erik Erikson, *Young Man Luther: A Study in Psychoanalysis and History* (New York: W. W. Norton & Company, 1958) 218, and 261–62.

[271] See especially the preface to the new translation: Elie Wiesel, *Night* (New York: Hill and Wang, 1972, 2006) xi-xii. Wiesel once again accuses himself and confesses his guilt.

[272] See Wiesel, *All Rivers Run to the Sea*, 4, 9–10.

[273] See Erik Erikson, *Gandhi's Truth: On the Origins of Militant Nonviolence* (New York: W. W. Norton & Company, Inc., 1969) 132.

[274] Wiesel, *All Rivers Run to the Sea*, 11–13.

[275] See Edward B. Fiske, "Elie Wiesel: Archivist with a Mission," *New York Times*, 31 January 1973.

[276] Roland Barthes, *The Pleasure of the Text* (New York: Hill and Wang, 1975) 10, 47. For a full statement of the thesis, see chapter 1.

[277] This phrase, "genocidal mentality," is taken from Robert J. Lifton and Eric Markusen, *The Genocidal Mentality: Nazi Holocaust and Nuclear Threat* (New York: Basic Books, 1990). See especially chapter 2.

[278] Raczymow quoted in Ellen Fine, "Search for Identity: Post Holocaust French Literature," in Yehuda Bauer, ed., *Remembering the Future: The Impact of the Holocaust on the Contemporary World* (Oxford: Pergamon Press, 1989) 1474.

[279] Carolyn G. Heilbrun, *Writing a Woman's Life* (New York: W. W. Norton & Company, 1989) 110.

[280] Ibid., 114–19.

[281] Wiesel quoted in Ellen Fine, *Legacy of Night: The Literary Universe of Elie Wiesel* (Albany: State University of New York, 1982) 3.

[282] Elie Wiesel, *One Generation After*, 213.

[283] Donald Capps, *Life Cycle Theory and Pastoral Care* (Philadelphia: Fortress Press, 1983) 81–93. See also the legend Wiesel tells about God in the epilogue of *The Town Beyond the Wall* (New York: Schocken Books, 1964) 179.

[284] See especially Abraham Joshua Heschel, *The Prophets: An Introduction* (New York: Harper & Row, 1962; Harper/Collins, 2001) 26.

[285] Judith Lewis Herman, *Trauma and Recovery* (New York: Harper Collins Publishers, 1992) 221–23.

[286] Elie Wiesel, *All Rivers Run to the Sea* (New York: Alfred A. Knopf, 1995) 299.

[287] Ibid., 302–309.

[288] Ibid., 319–22.

# Notes

[289] See Erik Erikson, *Gandhi's Truth: On the Origins of Militant Nonviolence* (New York: W. W. Norton & Company, Inc., 1969) 132.

[290] Wiesel, *All Rivers Run to the Sea*, 298–99.

[291] Robert Jay Lifton, *Life of the Self* (New York: Basic Books, 1976) 114–15.

[292] Robert Jay Lifton, *Boundaries: Psychological Man in Revolution* (New York: Simon and Schuster, 1967) 95.

[293] Robert Jay Lifton, "Protean Man," *Partisan Review* 35/1 (Winter 1968): 16.

[294] Lifton, *Life of the Self*, 113.

[295] Gerhard von Rad, *Old Testament Theology*, vol. 2 (New York: Harper & Row, Publishers, 1965) 193, 204–205.

[296] For an introduction to Wiesel's fiction, see especially Lawrence Langer, *The Holocaust and the Literary Imagination* (New Haven: Yale University Press, 1975) 75–120; Robert Alter, *After the Tradition: Essays on Jewish Writing* (New York: E. P. Dutton & Co., Inc., 1969) 151–60; and Colin Davis, *Elie Wiesel's Secretive Texts* (Gainesville: University of Florida, 1994) 175–84.

[297] See Robert Detweiler, *Breaking the Fall: Religious Readings of Contemporary Fiction* (Louisville: Westminster/John Knox Press, 1989) 47–48; Robert Alter, *After the Tradition*, 151–60; Johan Baptist Metz, *Faith in History and Society* (New York: The Seabury Press, 1980) 109–10; Elie Wiesel, *Legends of Our Time* (New York: Shocken Books, 1982) 8.

[298] See Walter Brueggemann, "An Ending That Does Not End: The Book of Jeremiah," in *Postmodern Interpretations of the Bible*, ed. A.K.M. Adams (St. Louis: Chalice, 2001) 117; and Kathleen M. O'Connor, "Jeremiah and Formation of the Moral Character of the Community," paper delivered at the SBL, Toronto, 26 November 2002, 12.

[299] Irving Greenberg, "History, Holocaust, and Covenant," in Yaffa Eliach, ed., *Remembering for the Future* (Oxford: Pergamon Press, 1988) 2903–30.

[300] Ibid.

[301] Alan Berger, *Crisis and Covenant: The Holocaust in American Jewish Fiction* (Albany: State University of New York Press, 1985) 28; and Michael Berenbaum, "The Additional Covenant," in *Confronting the Holocaust: The Impact of Elie Wiesel*, ed. A. Rosenfeld and I. Greenberg (Bloomington: Indiana University Press, 1978) 168–85.

[302] This book continues to reflect aspects of the modern Jewish struggle for faith and identity more than forty years after its publication.

[303] Wiesel, *All Rivers Run to the Sea*, 183.

[304] Ibid., 158, 168.

[305] Ellen Fine, *Legacy of Night: The Literary Universe of Elie Wiesel* (Albany: State University of New York, 1982) 34.

[306] Lifton, *Home from the War* (New Nork: Simon & Schuster, 1976) 101.

[307] A primary component of much of Wiesel's work is that of Hasidic legend, and especially the teacher as derived from the Hasidic spiritual guide or kabalistic master of his childhood. Various forms of the teacher or guide appear throughout the corpus of his work. The collective task of these teachers is to help Wiesel's protagonists and the reader to choose life by exorcising the visions that have previously paralyzed survivor and reader alike.

[308] Elie Wiesel, *Dawn* (New York: Avon Books, 1961) 25.

[309] Wiesel, *Dawn*, xix.

[310] See Ted Estes, *Elie Wiesel* (New York: Frederick Ungar Publishing Co., Inc., 1980) 41–44; and Ted L. Estes, "Elie Wiesel and the Drama of Interrogation," *The Journal of Religion* 56/1 (January 1976): 21–22.

[311] Wiesel, *Dawn*, 126; Robert McAfee Brown, *Elie Wiesel: Messenger to All Humanity* (Notre Dame: Notre Dame University Press, 1983) 63–64.

[312] For Paul Ricoeur, a parable is a metaphor with interactive elements in permanent tension: the conventional way of being in the world versus the way of the kingdom. The interaction between the two viewpoints results in a redescription of the possibilities of human life.

[313] See Wiesel, *Dawn*, 41.

[314] Wiesel seems ambivalent on this issue himself. There are times when he seems to encourage the use of force, as when he called upon Clinton to intervene in Bosnia. Concerning *Dawn*, Wiesel has said, "If night is everywhere, what *can* we do? Maybe political action—call it war, call it executions. So I explored it until I found out within myself that it is not an answer. Killing is never an answer." See Wiesel quoted in Irving Abrahamson, ed., *Against Silence: The Voice and Vision of Elie Wiesel*, vol. 3 (New York: Holocaust Library, 1985) 228.

[315] Though Wiesel's *Dawn* is something of a "period" piece on the birth of Israel, the questions he raises in this first novel seem to have an abiding relevance for the Middle East.

[316] Elie Wiesel, *All Rivers Run to the Sea* (New York: Alfred A. Knopf, 1995) 319–25.

[317] Wiesel, *The Accident* (1962; repr., New York: Avon Books, 1970) 79.

[318] Ibid.

[319] Ibid., 77.

[320] Alan Berger, *Crisis and Covenant: The Holocaust in American Jewish Fiction* (Albany: State University of New York Press, 1985) 68.

[321] See Robert J. Lifton, *Death in Life* (New York: Random House, 1967) 480.

# Notes

[322] See especially Primo Levi, *Survival in Auschwitz: The Nazi Assault on Humanity* (New York: Giulio Einaudi, 1958; Simon and Schuster, 1993) 88–90. Levi writes that the old men of the camps used the word "musselmann" to describe an extreme form of numbness—the "weak, the inept, the doomed...." Levi describes them further as "the backbone of the camp, an anonymous mass, continually renewed and always identical, of non-men who march and labor in silence, the divine spark dead within them, already too empty to really suffer. One hesitates to call them living: one hesitates to call their death death, in the face of which they have no fear, as they are too tired to understand. [He] is an emaciated man, with head dropped and shoulders curved, on whose face and in whose eyes not a trace of a thought is to be seen."

[323] Elie Wiesel, *Night* (1960; repr., New York: Bantam Books, 1982) 107–109.

[324] Walter Brueggemann, *The Prophetic Imagination*, 2nd ed. (Minneapolis: Fortress Press, 2001) 46–51.

[325] Ibid.

[326] Ibid.

[327] Wiesel, *The Accident*, 22.

[328] Ibid., 73–80.

[329] In a poignant interview, Marion Wiesel describes Elie Wiesel's tortured existence in the early to mid-1960s. Wiesel would often frighten women with his emotional distance. He worked compulsively, and would sometimes go for days without sleeping or eating. See Samuel G. Freedman, "Bearing Witness: The Life and Work of Elie Wiesel," *New York Times Magazine*, 23 October 1983, 69.

[330] Freedman, "Bearing Witness," 30, 110.

[331] Ibid., 111–12.

[332] Ibid., 123.

[333] Ibid., 123–25.

[334] Ibid., 126.

[335] Ibid., 126–27.

[336] Lifton, *Home from the War* (New York: Simon & Schuster, 1973) 276.

[337] Wiesel, *The Accident*, 39.

[338] I will discuss *The Town Beyond the Wall* in Chapter 11.

[339] See Wiesel, *The Accident*, 123. The theme of suicide is a personal one for Wiesel. See Wiesel, *All Rivers Run to the Sea*, 156, 178.

[340] Wiesel, *All Rivers Run to the Sea*, 347.

[341] Ibid., 348–49.

[342] Elie Wiesel as quoted in an article by Joseph Wershba, "An Author Asks Why the World Let Hitler Do It," *The New York Post*, 2 October 1961.

[343] Ibid.

---

[344] Elie Wiesel, *The Town Beyond the Wall* (New York: Random House, Inc., 1962) 61.

[345] Ibid., 52.

[346] Abraham Heschel seemed to play a similar role in Wiesel's life in the early 1960s.

[347] Ibid., 115.

[348] Ibid., 127.

[349] Robert J. Lifton, *Death in Life* (New York: Random House, 1967) 539.

[350] Wiesel, *Town Beyond the Wall*, 172.

[351] Ibid., 149–64.

[352] Ibid., 162.

[353] Ibid., 118.

[354] See Walter Brueggemann, *The Prophetic Imagination*, 2nd ed. (Minneapolis: Fortress Press, 2001) 1–37.

[355] See Wiesel, *Town Beyond the Wall*, 173.

[356] Robert McAfee Brown, *Elie Wiesel: Messenger to All Humanity* (Notre Dame: Notre Dame University Press, 1983) 70. The theme of the unburied dead, exemplified in the grandmother's ashes, signifies the immensity of pain associated with the Holocaust and that without a proper burial or memorial there is no possibility of closure. See Wiesel, *The Accident*, 35, 127.

[357] Wiesel, *Town Beyond the Wall*, 178.

[358] See David Patterson, "Literary Response and Remembrance: A Bakhtinian Approach to the Holocaust Novel," in Yaffa Eliach, ed., *Remembering for the Future* (Oxford: Pergamon Press, 1988) 1518.

[359] Robert Alter, *After the Tradition: Essays on Jewish Writing* (New York: E. P. Dutton & Co., Inc., 1969) 155. See also the helpful discussion of the concept of the "double" in Wiesel's work in Ellen Fine, *Legacy of Night: The Literary Universe of Elie Wiesel* (Albany: State University of New York, 1982) 79–108.

[360] Sigmund Freud, "The Uncanny," in *Collected Papers*, vol. 4, ed. Ernest Jones (New York: Basic Books, 1959) 387; and Otto Rank, *Beyond Psychology* (New York: Dover Publications, 1941) 92–96.

[361] Fine, *Legacy of Night*, 84.

[362] Ibid., 77.

[363] Ellen Fine, *Legacy of Night: The Literary Universe of Elie Wiesel* (Albany: State University of New York, 1982) 58.

[364] Robert J. Lifton, *Death in Life* (New York: Random House, 1967) 539.

[365] James Fowler calls this new stage "Conjunctive" faith. See James Fowler, *Stages of Faith: The Psychology of Human Development and the Quest for Meaning* (San Francisco: Harper & Row, 1981) 197–98.

[366] Elie Wiesel, *All Rivers Run to the Sea* (New York: Alfred A. Knopf, 1995) 332.

[367] Elie Wiesel, *The Town Beyond the Wall* (New York: Schocken Books, 1964) 179.

[368] Wiesel does not give a date for his first meeting with Heschel, but places him in his memoir prior to his return to Sighet in 1964.

[369] Marilyn Henry, "Lehrhaus tribute to 'the quintessential Conservative Jew,'" *Masoret: The Magazine of The Jewish Theological Seminary of America* 2/2 (Winter 1993): 3.

[370] Susannah Heschel, "Heschel In Selma," *Hadassah* 66/10 (June 1985): 45–46. These two pages of the article were found in Wiesel's papers in the archives of Boston University. The article has a picture of Heschel walking with Martin Luther King Jr. during the Selma to Montgomery march. See box 5, folder 12.

[371] Abraham Joshua Heschel, *The Prophets: An Introduction* (New York: Harper & Row, 1962) 5.

[372] Susannah Heschel, "Introduction to the Perennial Classics Edition," in Abraham Joshua Heschel, *The Prophets: An Introduction* (New York: HarperCollins, 2001) xiii—xx.

[373] See Wiesel, *All Rivers Run to the Sea*, 353.

[374] Ibid., 378–80. Wiesel describes Lieberman as "my generation's greatest Talmudist." He also tells the story of how he met Lieberman and how Lieberman became his teacher.

[375] Wiesel, *All Rivers Run to the Sea*, 402.

[376] Ibid., 338.

[377] Elie Wiesel, *Legends of Our Time* (New York: Shocken Books, 1982), 112.

[378] Ibid., 112–13.

[379] Ibid., 111.

[380] Wiesel, *All Rivers Run to the Sea*, 357–59.

[381] Ibid., 360.

[382] Wiesel, *Legends of our Time*, 121.

[383] Wiesel, *All Rivers Run to the Sea*, 365.

[384] Elie Wiesel, *The Gates of the Forest* (New York: Shocken Books, 1966) 194–99.

[385] Jack Riemer, "Wiesel's World—the Horror and the Glory," *Hadassah Magazine* 52/5 (January 1970), found as an unnumbered, single page in the Wiesel Collection, box 82, folder 1970, Boston University.

[386] See especially Fowler, *Stages of Faith*, 184–98.

[387] Riemer, "Wiesel's World—the Horror and the Glory."

[388] Elie Wiesel, *All Rivers Run to the Sea* (New York: Alfred A. Knopf, 1995) 11–13.

[389] Ibid..

[390] Erik Erikson, *Gandhi's Truth: On the Origins of Militant Nonviolence* (New York: W. W. Norton & Company, Inc., 1969) 102, 129–32.

[391] Ibid., 132.

[392] Elie Wiesel, *The Jews of Silence: A Personal Report on Soviet Jewry* (New York: Holt, Rinehart and Winston, 1966) 7.

[393] Wiesel, *All Rivers Run to the Sea*, 365–66.

[394] Elie Wiesel, *The Jews of Silence* (New York: Holt, Rinehart and Winston, 1966) vii.

[395] Ibid., 3–9.

[396] Ibid., 22.

[397] Ibid., 23–30.

[398] Ibid., 27–29.

[399] Ibid., 27–29.

[400] Elie Wiesel, "A Visit to the Jews in the Soviet Union," *The California Jewish Voice*, 1 April 1966. See also Wiesel, *The Jews of Silence*, 99–100.

[401] Wiesel, *The Jews of Silence*, 58–66.

[402] Ibid., 84.

[403] Elie Wiesel, *A Jew Today* (New York: Vintage Books, 1978) 29–30.

[404] Wiesel, *The Jews of Silence*, 44–56.

[405] The term "covenant of friendship" (literally "covenant of brothers") comes from the biblical book of Amos where it appears to be a phrase from earlier times. See Amos 1:9.

[406] Ibid., 3–7.

[407] Wiesel, *All Rivers Run to the Sea*, 366.

[408] Elie Wiesel, "A Visit to the Jews of the Soviet Union."

[409] Wiesel, *All Rivers Run to the Sea*, 370–77; and Wiesel, "A Visit to the Jews in the Soviet Union."

[410] Wiesel, *All Rivers Run to the Sea*, 370.

[411] This was true first in the world Jewish community. By 1967, Wiesel was in contact with the Jewish community in South Africa and publishing materials for their readership. By 1969, he was invited to come to South Africa on a speaking tour. See the correspondence between Harry Hurwitz, editor of *The Jewish Herald* (Johannesburg, South Africa), and Elie Wiesel dated 3 April 1967, and between the South African Zionist Federation and Wiesel dated 8 October 1969. This correspondence, along with the correspondence with Soviet Jews, is located in the Wiesel Collection of the archives of the Boston University Library, box 34, folder South Africa.

[412] Wiesel, *All Rivers Run to the Sea*, 368.

[413] Paul Ricoeur sees demythologizing as a realm where the "hermeneutics of suspicion" controls the mode of consciousness. Yet a move to a post-critical realm with a restorative hermeneutic is also possible. See especially Paul Ricoeur, *The Symbolism of Evil* (Boston: Beacon Press, 1967) 350–52. This post-critical realm is the stage of Conjunctive faith (or Paradoxical-Consoladative faith). See James Fowler, *Stages of Faith: The Psychology of Human Development and the Quest for Meaning* (San Francisco: Harper & Row, 1981) 184–89.

[414] Robert Alter, *After the Tradition: Essays on Jewish Writing* (New York: E. P. Dutton & Co., Inc., 1969) 160.

[415] These terms come from the stage descriptions of James Fowler. See Fowler, *Stages of Faith*, 174–98; and Fowler and Robin Lovin, *Trajectories in Faith: Five Life Stories*(Nashville: Abingdon Press, 1980) 28–29.

[416] Jack Riemer, "Wiesel's World—the Horror and the Glory," *Hadassah Magazine* 52/5 (January 1970), found as an unnumbered, single page in the Wiesel Collection, box 82, folder 1970, Boston University.

[417] Elie Wiesel, "A Visit to the Jews in the Soviet Union," *The California Jewish Voice*, 1 April 1966.

[418] Wiesel writes in *Legends of Our Time* that he is not sure why he went back so quickly. "Perhaps because I needed to confirm, for myself, that what I had seen and heard the year before was not...a dream...." See Wiesel, *Legends of Our Time* (New York: Schocken Books, 1966) 144.

[419] Elie Wiesel, *All Rivers Run to the Sea* (New York: Alfred A. Knopf, 1995) 372–75.

[420] Elie Wiesel, interview by Frederick L. Downing, Boston University, 5 October 1995.

[421] Wiesel, *All Rivers Run to the Sea*, 273–75.

[422] Elie Wiesel, *Legends of Our Time* (New York: Shocken Books, 1982) vii-viii.

[423] Robert McAfee Brown, *Elie Wiesel: Messenger to All Humanity* (Notre Dame: Notre Dame University Press, 1983) 232.

[424] James W. Fowler, *Stages of Faith*, 187.

[425] James E. Young, *Writing and Rewriting the Holocaust: Narrative and the Consequences of Interpretation* (Bloomington: Indiana University Press, 1988) 95–107.

[426] Wiesel, *And the Sea Is Never Full* (New York: Alfred A. Knopf, 1999) 82.

[427] Elie Wiesel, *Messengers of God: Biblical Portraits and Legends* (New York: Random House, 1976) xi.

[428] James E. Young, *Writing and Rewriting the Holocaust*, 107. See also James E. Young, "The Prophet at the Y," *New York Times*, 20 October 1991.

[429] See the Talmud, Baba Bathra 14 b.

[430] Elie Wiesel, lecture, Schara Tzedek Synagogue, Vancouver BC, 6 May 1978; also published in Elie Wiesel, "Why Remember?" *Vancouver (B.C.) Jewish Western Bulletin*, 14 December 1978, and reprinted in Irving Abrahamson, ed., *Against Silence: The Voice and Vision of Elie Wiesel*, vol. 3 (New York: Holocaust Library, 1985) 47.

[431] Ibid., 108. Wiesel's concern with the Torah is tellling. In Hasidism there is no valid study outside of the Torah.

[432] Wiesel, *Messengers of God*, 5–7, 31.

[433] Ibid., 28–32.

[434] Ibid., 37–40.

[435] Ibid., 38–40.

[436] Ibid., 40–59.

[437] James E. Young, *Writing and Rewriting the Holocaust*, 107.

[438] Ibid.

[439] Wiesel, *Messengers of God*, 69–75.

[440] Ibid., 70–95.

[441] Ibid., 95–97.

[442] Ibid., 103–12.

[443] Ibid., 112–15.

[444] Ibid., 106–107.

[445] Ibid., 122–25.

[446] Ibid., 139–41.

[447] Ibid., 140.

[448] Ibid., 153–68.

[449] Ibid., 181–83.

[450] Ibid., 188–99.

[451] Ibid., 176–202.

[452] Wiesel, *All Rivers Run to the Sea*, 121.

[453] Wiesel, *Messengers of God*, 211–16.

[454] Ibid., 233–34.

[455] Ibid., 233–35.

[456] See W. Randolph Tate, *Biblical Interpretation: An Integrated Approach* (Peabody MA: Hendrickson Publishers, 1991) 146–47. Tate writes, "As we read a text we infer meaning, and that meaning is in some measure determined by our understanding of our world." Terry Eagleton states, "All literary works...are 'rewritten', if only subconsciously, by the societies which read them; indeed there is no reading of a work which is not also a 're-writing.'" See Terry Eagleton, *Literary Theory: An Introduction* (Minneapolis: University of Minnesota Press, 1983) 12.

# Notes

[457] On autobiographical theory, see especially James Olney, *Metaphors of the Self: The Meaning of Autobiography* (Princeton: Princeton University Press, 1972) 34. Olney writes that "the self expresses itself by the metaphors it creates and projects...but it did not exist as it now does and it now is before creating the metaphors."

[458] For an understanding of Ricoeur's view on the modern quest for meaning, see Paul Ricoeur, *The Symbolism of Evil* (Boston: Beacon Press, 1967) 351; and Paul Ricoeur, *Essays on Biblical Interpretation* (Philadelphia: Fortress Press, 1980) 23.

[459] Elie Wiesel, *All Rivers Run to the Sea* (New York: Alfred A. Knopf, 1995) 384–85. This speech was printed in a collection of Wiesel's essays. See Wiesel, *One Generation After* (New York: Random House, Inc., 1965, 1967, 1970) 213.

[460] Wiesel, *One Generation After*, 217.

[461] Wiesel, *All Rivers Run to the Sea*, 354.

[462] Wiesel, *One Generation After*, 222–23.

[463] Elie Wiesel in Harry James Cargas, ed., *Harry James Cargas in Conversation with Elie Wiesel* (New York: Paulist Press, 1976) 109.

[464] Elie Wiesel, television interview, *Book Beat*, 16 December 1978. An adaptation of this interview can be found in Irving Abrahamson, ed., *Against Silence: The Voice and Vision of Elie Wiesel*, vol. 3 (New York: Holocaust Library, 1985) 106–108.

[465] See Eugene Borowitz, *A New Jewish Theology in the Making* (Philadelphia: Westminster Press, 1968) 156. As a God-intoxicated Jewish child, Elie Wiesel was also immersed in the messianic traditions of Judaism, which emphasize not only a concern for salvation but also the completion of the created order and the redemption of the world. Wiesel seems to be deeply influenced by the tradition of *Tikkun*—the restoration of the world or the gathering of the sparks. According to the Kabala, there was a cosmic cataclysm at the beginning of the world. Messianic redemption means not only a concern with the self but with others as well. That is, one begins to serve God by serving the children of God. Also, in the texts of the prophets like Isaiah, Jeremiah, and Ezekiel, one reads that symbolic action among the prophets was an important function. Such an active demonstration was not a simple effort to reinforce what had been heard, or to create a visual aid. As Johanes Lindblom puts it, "such an action served not only to represent and make evident a particular fact, but also to make this fact a reality." See Lindblom, *Prophecy in Ancient Israel* (Philadelphia: Fortress Press, 1962) 172. See also Wiesel, *All Rivers Run to the Sea*, 354.

[466] Elie Wiesel quoted in Cargas, ed., *Harry James Cargas in Conversation with Elie Wiesel*, 112.

[467] Wiesel, *All Rivers Run to the Sea*, 167, 338. See also the picture of Elie and Marion in 1970 in Wiesel, *And the Sea Is Never Full* (New York: Alfred A. Knopf, 1999). Wiesel does not give a precise date for his meeting of Marion, only "in the middle of the 1960s."

[468] See Fern Narja Eckman, "Out of the Inferno...," *New York Post*, 10 December 1968.

[469] See Wiesel quoted in Cargas, ed., *Harry James Cargas in Conversation with Elie Wiesel*, 111.

[470] See Samuel G. Freedman, "Bearing Witness: The Life and Work of Elie Wiesel," *New York Times*, 23 October 1983; Wiesel, *And the Sea Is Never Full*, 43.

[471] See James Fowler, *Stages of Faith: The Psychology of Human Development and the Quest for Meaning* (San Francisco: Harper & Row, 1981).

[472] See Wiesel, *All Rivers Run to the Sea*, 416–17; and Samuel G. Freedman, "Bearing Witness," 69.

[473] Wiesel, *All Rivers Run to the Sea*, 338.

[474] See Wiesel's comments on how easy it is to make the sad little girl smile in Wiesel, *And the Sea Is Never Full*, 11. The implication is that he spends time with Jennifer, which means in part that Jennifer occupies a place in his thoughts.

[475] Samuel G. Freedman, "Bearing Witness," 69; Edward B. Fiske, "Elie Wiesel—The Jewish Superstar," *International Herald Tribune*, 2 February 1973; and Elie Wiesel in Cargas, ed.; *Harry James Cargas in Conversation with Elie Wiesel*, 111–12.

[476] James W. Fowler and Robin W. Lovin et al., *Trajectories in Faith: Five Life Stories* (Nashville: Abingdon Press, 1980) 30–31. See also Jim Fowler and Sam Keen, *Life Maps: Conversations on the Journey of Faith* (Waco TX: Word Books, Publishers, 1978) 88–90.

[477] See Elie Wiesel, *A Jew Today* (New York: Vintage Books, 1978) 35–37.

[478] Elie Wiesel quoted in Abrahamson, ed., *Against Silence*, 3:107.

[479] Wiesel, *A Jew Today*, 35–36. This episode of Wiesel's speaking out on behalf of an oppressed people beyond his own ethnic group is reminiscent of Martin Luther King Jr.'s speaking out on the Viet Nam War. Both situations involve a sensitive individual viewing the picture of a child in a time of war. See Frederick L. Downing, *To See the Promised Land: The Faith Pilgrimage of Martin Luther King, Jr.* (Macon GA: Mercer University Press, 1986) 266–67.

[480] Ibid., 35–37.

[481] The letter was originally published in *The Jewish Chronicle*, 30 March 1979. It later appeared in Elie Wiesel, *A Jew Today*, 121–29. See Also Bob Costas, "A Wound That Will Never Be Healed: An Interview with Elie Wiesel," in Harry James Cargas, ed., *Telling the Tale: A Tribute To Elie Wiesel* (St. Louis: Time

Being Books, 1993) 163; Wiesel in Abrahamson, ed., *Against Silence*, 3:107; and Harry James Cargas, ed., "Harry James Cargas Interviews Elie Wiesel," *U.S. Catholic/Jubilee* 28/5 (September 1971): 31.

[482] In the early interview with Cargas, Wiesel says, "Not being an Israeli I don't have, fortunately, the same problems that they have. I have many contacts with Arabs."

[483] Wiesel in Abrahamson, ed., *Against Silence*, 3:107.

[484] Wiesel, *A Jew Today*, 123–27.

[485] Ibid., 127–28. Wiesel has been criticized for not speaking out more on the Israeli/Palestinian issue, though it is clear that he has made statements in support of human rights for the Palestinians as in the open letter to the young student. In the second volume of his memoirs, Wiesel writes, "I can say in good faith that I have not remained indifferent to any cause involving the defense of human rights. But, you may ask, what have I done to alleviate the plight of the Palestinians? And here I must confess: I have not done enough." See Wiesel, *And the Sea Is Never Full*, 125. Wiesel's "overweening conscience" is still with him. Here he finds himself in a kind of double bind. Psychologically, the central theme of his life has become abandonment/solidarity. Early in life he came to experience the fear and reality of abandonment, the tragic adolescent fulfillment of which was the Holocaust. His moral journey, however, brought him to juxtapose human solidarity as an existential and spiritual response to the trauma. Wiesel's commitment to Israel is as a real flesh-and-blood "refuge" he needs after the loss of his family and his home in Sighet. It is a "place to be" that he protects adamantly for himself and other Jews. It is a unique form of particularism. Yet, his journey to the depth of his own religious tradition convinces him that he must protect the rights of all others, and that includes the Palestinians. Wiesel makes a telling comment in *The Jews of Silence* when he says, "For the Jews of Russia, Israel is not simply a geographical location but an abstract principle, a part of their own inner spiritual life." The same is obviously true for Wiesel. See Wiesel, *The Jews of Silence* (New York: Holt, Rinehart and Winston, 1966) 80. For a critique of Wiesel on this issue, see Mark Chmiel, *Elie Wiesel and the Politics of Moral Leadership* (Philadelphia: Temple University Press, 2001) 79–114; Marc Ellis, *Beyond Innocence and Redemption: Confronting the Holocaust and Israeli Power* (New York: Harper & Row, 1990) 110–12; and Arthur Hertzberg, "An Open Letter to Elie Wiesel," *New York Review of Books*, 18 August 1988.

[486] Elie Wiesel, *And the Sea Is Never Full*, 93; and Wiesel, *A Jew Today*, 62–63. For a record of part of Wiesel's visit to South Africa see Elaine Durback, "A Speaker for the Silenced," *Cape Times* (Capetown, South Africa), 2 August 1975.

[487] Wiesel, *A Jew Today*, 61–63.

[488] See Richard Arens, ed., *Genocide in Paraguay* (Philadelphia: Temple University, 1976). Wiesel's epilogue is titled "Now We Know," and also appears in Wiesel, *A Jew Today*; and in Abrahamson, ed., *Against Silence* 3:371–72. The essay in *A Jew Today* indicates that the essay was actually written in 1974, though the Arens book was published in 1976.

[489] Wiesel, *A Jew Today*, 38–39.

[490] Ibid., 39–40. The current situation of the Aché tribe is unclear. The brutality waged against the tribe continued into the 1980s. Though deforestation of the land continues as does displacement of the tribe, the population of the Aché is now approximately 1,500.

[491] Elie Wiesel, "'I Wrote This Play Out of Despair,'" *New York Times*, 16 March 1976. See also Elie Wiesel, *Zalmen, Or the Madness of God: A Play* (New York: Random House, 1974). The play first aired on radio in France and then played in the United States.

[492] See Nina McCain, "Elie Wiesel: Witness to Evil," *Boston Sunday Globe*, 3 October 1976, 1.

[493] Harry James Cargas, "Scholars Probe Works of Elie Wiesel at New York Conference," *St. Louis Jewish Light*, 13 October 1976, 3.

[494] See Elie Wiesel, "An open letter to President Giscard d'Estaing of France," *New York Times*, 20 January 1977.

[495] These lectures were published under the title *Dimensions of the Holocaust: Lectures at Northwestern University* (Evanston IL: Northwestern University Press, 1977).

[496] See Brigitte Witkowski, "Elie Wiesel: Storyteller," *Catholic New Times* (Toronto), 13 March 1977; and Shelley Abramson, "Why Elie Wiesel writes and talks, and why a new generation listens," *Oregonian Forum*, 11 March 1977.

[497] Dennis Diamond in a letter dated 14 November 1977, found in the Wiesel Collection, Boston University, box 34, folder South Africa.

[498] See Wiesel quoted by Leni Reiss, "Wiesel Casts Spell; Captivates Audience," *Phoenix Jewish News*, 30 December 1977, 5.

[499] See Elie Wiesel, *Four Hasidic Masters and Their Struggle Against Melancholy* (Notre Dame: University of Notre Dame Press, 1978). See also Jack Riemer, "Elie Wiesel at Notre Dame," *Jewish Advocate*, 24 August 1978. On the significance of this occasion, Riemer notes that the Catholic and Jewish worlds "had existed side by side and never touched in Eastern Europe [but] came together in Indiana. In Eastern Europe the priest was the enemy to the Jew, the Jew was the devil to the priest. Now in Indiana the priest was the student, the companion in search…[of] keys to his own spiritual situation."

[500] Lily Edelman, "Elie Wiesel: A Jew for All Seasons," *ADL Bulletin* (November 1978). See also Lily Edelman, ed., "Building a Moral Society: Aspects of Elie Wiesel's Work," *Face to Face: An Interreligious Bulletin* 6 (Spring 1979) 3.

[501] See Bob Latta, "'Voice of Protest' Needed to Stop Cambodian Massacre, Author Says," *Wichita Eagle* (Wichita KS), 19 May 1978.

[502] See Elie Wiesel, "Plea for the Boat People," in Abrahamson, ed., *Against Silence*, 3:158.

[503] This picture was found in Wiesel's files in the Wiesel Collection at Boston University, box 58, folder Cambodia.

[504] See Wiesel, *And the Sea Is Never Full*, 89–90. See also Henry Kamm, "Marchers with Food Get No Cambodian Response," *New York Times*, 7 February 1980.

[505] Wiesel, *And the Sea Is Never Full*, 90.

[506] Ibid., 91.

[507] David A. Wohl, "Students View 'The Day After,'" *Daily Free Press*, 21 November 1983.

[508] Transcript of ABC NEWS *Viewpoint*, "'The Day After'–Nuclear Dilemma," 20 November 1983, 2–6.

[509] Ibid., 7.

[510] Ibid., 12–14.

[511] See Wiesel, *And the Sea Is Never Full*, 91–94.

[512] See Rudy Abramson, "Reagan Trip to Include Death Camp: Emotional Appeal to Cancel Visit to Cemetery Rejected," *Los Angeles Times*, 20 April 1985, 1.

[513] Ibid., 23.

[514] Ibid.

[515] Elie Wiesel, "The Nobel Address," in Wiesel, *The Kingdom of Memory: Reminiscences* (New York: Summit Books, 1990) 231–33.

[516] Ibid., 234.

[517] Elie Wiesel, "On Global Education," Boston University manuscript, Wiesel Collection, box 1, folder 27, 18 January 1990, 1–3. See also Wiesel, *And the Sea Is Never Full*, 145.

[518] Wiesel, "On Global Education," 4–6.

[519] Elie Wiesel quoted in an AP story, "'Black Hole in History': 50 years after, Holocaust Museum dedicated," 23 April 1993.

[520] The term "overweening" comes from Erickson. See Erik Erickson, *Gandhi's Truth: On the Origins of Militant Nonviolence* (New York: W. W. Norton & Company, 1969) 117–18.

[521] See Erik Erickson, *Gandhi's Truth: On the Origins of Militant Nonviolence* (New York: W. W. Norton & Company, 1969) 117–18.

# Index